Marquart's Works

VOLUME IX

LUTHERANS

Edited by
Herman J. Otten

LUTHERAN NEWS, INC., New Haven, Missouri

Marquart's Works
Copyright (c) 2014 Lutheran News, Inc. All Rights Reserved.
No portion of this book may be reproduced in any form, except for quotations in reviews, articles, and speeches, without permission from the publisher.

Library of Congress Card
Lutheran News, Inc.
684 Luther Lane
New Haven, MO 63068
Published 2014
Printed in the United States of America
Lightning Source, Inc., La Vergne, TN
ISBN #978-0-9832409-5-2

TABLE OF CONTENTS

FOREWORD..i

PREFACE..iii

THEOLOGICAL LIBERALISM AT CONCORDIA SEMINARY -
A DECLARATION OF FACTS...1

SCHARLEMANN CASE SETTLED...12

QUO VADIS LUTHERAN WITNESS - MARQUART COMMENTS
ON *LUTHERAN WITNESS* AND NEW THEOLOGY
COMMISSION..18

GREAT EXPECTATIONS...27

MEDITATION ON A TOWER..30

CHRISTIAN GIVING..33

REFORMATION JUBILEE LECTURES... 40

THE MEANING OF THEOLOGICAL DISCUSSION IN LCUSA
....44

STILL ATTACKS DEITY OF CHRIST...52

THE INVITED AND UNINVITED GUEST..62

DATELINE ANAHEIM...64

CANDID OBSERVATIONS...72

*ANATOMY OF AN EXPLOSION - MISSOURI IN LUTHERAN
PERSPECTIVE*...76

A GENERALLY FAVORABLE REVIEW -
MARQUART'S *ANATOMY OF AN EXPLOSION* 86

INTEGRITY BAROMETER: FALLING..89

REACTIONS TO THE OFFICIAL RESULTS OF
INTER-LUTHERAN (LCUSA) THEOLOGICAL
DISCUSSIONS SINCE 1972..93

"NEW LUTHERAN CHURCH" WILL NOT BE LUTHERAN
SAYS LCMS PROFESSOR..98

THE EX-LUTHERAN MERGER...100

APOSTASY IN VALPARAISO'S CRESSET.....................................107

SANTA CLAUS THEOLOGY...112

LEVELS OF FELLOWSHIP...116

AVOIDANCE OF CONFESSIONAL CRISIS....................................119

"THE CHURCH AND HER FELLOWSHIP, MINISTRY, AND
GOVERNANCE" - FEMALE PASTORS SHOULD NOT BE
RECOGNIZED...121

LUTHERAN CONFESSIONAL REVIEW...125

ROBERT D. PREUS..127
DR. ROBERT DAVID PREUS AN APPRECIATION....................144
ROBERT D. PREUS: A PERSONAL TRIBUTE............................149
LHF BOARD NAMES MARQUART..152
A TRUE DOCTOR OF THEOLOGY..154
MARQUART OVERTURE SENT TO 2004 LCMS
    CONVENTION...156
QUESTIONS OF 'DUE PROCESS'...158
LAW/GOSPEL AND "CHURCH GROWTH" OR QUO VADIS
    (WHERE ARE YOU GOING), LUTHERAN MISSIOLOGY?.......159
THE CHURCH IN THE TWENTY-FIRST CENTURY:
    WILL THERE BE A LUTHERAN ONE?...................................170
SEMINARY HOSTS LUTHERAN/CATHOLIC DIALOGUE..........187
DOCTRINE AND OUTREACH...191
THE SHAPE AND FOUNDATION OF FAITH.............................192
A WORD OF ENCOURAGEMENT..206
PUTTING MISSOURI BACK ON TRACK....................................208
"BUREAUCRATITIS" BASHED...219
MARQUART DEFENDS THE RIGHTS OF LAYMEN..................224
OVERTURES FOR LCMS CONGREGATIONS TO ADOPT........227
A VERSION TO SANCTIFICATION?...230
PLACING HUMAN REGULATIONS ABOVE GOD'S WORD.......233
INDEX...235

FOREWORD

Dr. Marquart was a beloved Professor by all the students that sat in his classes. His ability to simplify great theological concepts made him a favorite Teacher for all the students who attended the Seminary. He not only instilled in us a love for Theology, but he also showed us how it was to be applied in a pastor's daily calling.

However, these writings are not just for pastors. Even dedicated laymen will be able to grasp and learn from this great Teacher of the Church. Whenever and wherever Dr. Marquart made a presentation, you would soon see that he was eagerly sought out, not just by pastors but also by laymen. They too recognized his genius in refuting those who denied the Word of God. He was as popular with laymen as he was with pastors. Here in these volumes you will once again be able to take your place and listen to this great Teacher, as he clearly enunciates various topics from a thoroughly Lutheran perspective. Since these multiple volumes consist of the various topics that Dr. Marquart addressed over his illustrious life, you will find it hard to put these volumes down.

Having Dr. Marquart's writings in book form will once again allow this fearless Champion of the Church to speak to the issues that continue to plague the Church from one generation to the next. False doctrine continues to be rehashed and sent out with new clothes. As the Proverb goes, "there is nothing new under the sun." Dr. Marquart had the remarkable ability to dissect what the issue was, and why it was, and still is, false doctrine. Confessional Lutherans from all over the world were always eager to attend Dr. Marquart's lectures. They recognized that he was a giant among men. Anyone concerned about the welfare of the Church will want to have these volumes on their bookshelf.

It appears that the Almighty Savior of the Church, in His infinite wisdom, chooses to send out only a few Teachers of the Church. One may make a very short list of these esteemed gifts from God. Luther, Chemnitz, Gerhard, Walther, Pieper, Preus, and Marquart. Their writings stand the test of time. These men did not write for some passing fad, that is here today and then blown away by tomorrow's changing wind vane. Any pastor or layman, who has a desire and love for the Truth, will not be disappointed with these volumes. Every congregation that has a love for the Lord and His saving Gospel, would do well to purchase the writings from these Teachers of the Church. God had His good reasons for raising these men up and sending them out, and it would be wise for pastors and laymen to read, mark, learn and inwardly digest the writings of these great defenders of the Gospel.

Rev. Herman Otten is to be commended for publishing the writings of Dr. Kurt Marquart. This may well be Rev. Otten's finest and most enduring contribution to the Church.

Rev. Ray R. Ohlendorf
Salem Lutheran Church
Taylorsville, NC
4th Sunday in Lent 2014

Acknowledgements

Well Herman,

As usual you find yourself doing what unsere beliebte Synode should have done long ago. The fact that CPH has not already published a book of Kurt's writings is an absolute travesty. It is an indictment of the politics before theology which has destroyed the orthodoxy of the LCMS. Our Savior Lutheran Church will stand by you in the worthy project. Back in the dark days when Bohlmann and his supporters were after Robert Preus we published a number of Kurt's magnificent essays on Robert's behalf. Modern Missouri has never produced another theologian comparable to him either in confessional fidelity or eloquence. We are proud and eager to take part in this belated effort. "Gottes Wort Und Luthers Lehr Vergehet Nun Und Nimmermehr."

Larry White, Pastor
Our Saviour Lutheran Church
Houston, Texas

Thanks to Luke Otten for arranging the publication of these volumes and to Naomi Finck, Natalie Hoerstkamp, for type-setting.

Thanks to Grace Otten for recognizing the importance of publishing *Marquart's Works* ever since they first began appearing in *Christian News* more than 50 years ago. Thanks to Scott Meyer, "America's confessional Lutheran" lay historian and President of the Concordia Historical Institute whose appreciation of Marquart's works and encouragement helped make the publication of these volumes possible.

PREFACE

Dr. C. F. W. Walther, first president of The Lutheran Church-Missouri Synod, has been rightly referred to as "The American Luther." As the editor of a Christian weekly for 51 years, the undersigned has reviewed thousands of books. During all these years he has published the writings of many theologians. The index at the back of Volume V of the *Christian News Encyclopedia* lists the names of hundreds of theologians whose writings have appeared in *Christian News*. Some, like Kurt Marquart, were also good friends. Yet, the editor knows of no theologian who deserves the title "The International Lutheran" more than Kurt Marquart. The editor's wife, Grace, is a graduate of Concordia College, St. Paul Minnesota and Valparaiso University. There she studied under some prominent theologians who later became professors at Concordia Seminary, St. Louis and Seminex. In 1963 Grace Otten and Kurt Marquart were *CN*'s reporters at the Fourth Assembly of the Lutheran World Federation in Helsinki, Finland. Following the LWF Assembly she and the editor's brother, Walter, who knew Marquart for 54 years, accompanied him on a twenty city lecture tour in the U.S. Grace shares the editor's evaluation of Kurt Marquart. She helped make it possible together with Luke Otten, Ruth Rethemeyer, Mary Beth Otten, Kristina Bailey and the Missourian Publishing Company, Washington, Missouri, to get *Marquart's Legacy* published in 2006 not long after his death. The 76 page *Marquart's Legacy* is available from *Christian News* for $5.00. It includes photos of Marquart and family and information about two professionally made videos showing Marquart in action.

Marquart's Legacy begins with a brief biography of Kurt Marquart. Then follows "Remembrances of a Former Seminary Roommate," the editor of *Christian News*. Next comes "The Lasting Legacy of Kurt Marquart" as expressed by many who knew him well.

The appendixes list the writings and reports of Kurt Marquart which have appeared in 44 volumes of *Christian News* (1962-2006), *A Christian Handbook on Vital Issues*, the five volumes of the *Christian News Encyclopedia, Luther Today, What Would He Do or Say?* and *Crisis in Christendom-Seminex Ablaze*. The lasting legacy of a great theologian and genius like Kurt Marquart can best be found in his works. *CN* suggested in 2006 that the Lutheran Church-Missouri Synod's Concordia Publishing House should publish *Marquart's Works*.

The questions at the end of each section are included to make *Marquart's Works* helpful for study. In an age when faith in historic Christianity is declining in all of the major denominations, *Marquart's Works* can be used to encourage and strengthen faithful Christians and begin a 21st Century Reformation and 21st Century *Formula of Concord* by the 500th anniversary of the Reformation in 2017.

Herman Otten
Reformation, 2014

iii

THEOLOGICAL LIBERALISM AT CONCORDIA SEMINARY – A DECLARATION OF FACTS

By the editor
Christian News, January 24, 1972

Editor's note: Dr. James C. Burkee in his award winning Power, Politics, and the Missouri Synod – A Conflict that Changed American Christianity, Fortress Press, 2011, Foreword by Martin E. Marty, wrote that "Herman Otten ushered in an ugly time at Concordia Seminary" (35). Otten and Marquart are supposed to have used underhanded and McCarthy methods. These documents show what kind of methods Marquart and Otten followed.

This document was submitted by the editor of *Christian News* to the Board of Control of Concordia Seminary, St. Louis, on December 4, 1958. We are now publishing it to show that the Board of Control, which in the past has insisted that no false doctrine was being taught or tolerated at Concordia Seminary, was given evidence showing that false doctrine was being taught and tolerated at Concordia Seminary. This document is in the Concordia Seminary versus Otten case arranged by Kurt Marquart.

APPENDIX C
A Declaration of Facts
Below is a chronological summary, in academic years, as concise as possible, of the major events which finally culminated in the disciplinary action against me. This is by no means a complete picture, but is meerly the visible part of an iceberg. I could not possibly relate all the hundreds of other contacts and events, many of them also important, which belong in the picture. The materials here gathered, however, represent facts which I personally witnessed or for which I have available the testimony of witnesses and/or written documentation.

1952 – 1953
During this period, while I was acquiring the rudiments of theological learning, I became aware, in a general way, to the fact that a "new spirit" was manifesting itself on the campus. This was conceded both by those who favored it and by those who opposed it. I was not at all alarmed, since I considered the "new spirit" a healthy corrective for the dead orthodoxy and scholastic dogmatism which I had come to associate with our Synod's past, and which I regarded as a danger to vital Christian faith.

1953 – 1954
During this year I realized that not only abuses of orthodoxy but orthodoxy itself was under attack. The doctrine of inspiration was the subject of vigorous discussion. At last some students formally petitioned the faculty for clarification on the doctrine of inspiration. Many, though by

no means all, of those who signed the petition could not accept the doctrine of inspiration set forth in the *Brief Statement*.

The faculty responded by conducting an evening of lectures and discussions on the problem. Unfortunately, however, many of those who objected to the *Brief Statement* doctrine of inspiration felt that they could reconcile their views with the faculty presentation, and so the debate continued.

Shortly before the conclusion of the academic year, two students who were regarded as the theological leaders on campus, attempted to persuade me of the reasonableness of their theological position. They denied the traditional doctrine of inspiration and inerrancy of Scripture, and the historicity of the Genesis creation account. While I had always known that some students held this position, I was now told that they had faculty support.

1954 – 1955
The Schoedel Case

During the early Fall of this year Mr. Kurt Marquart, a first-year man, and I had had lengthy discussions with Mr. William Schoedel, a fourth-year man. Mr. Schoedel tried to convince us that Scripture was not inerrant, nor verbally inspired, that Genesis 1-3 must be taken symbolically, and that theistic evolution was a perfectly acceptable position. When, a few months later, we heard that Mr. Schoedel was to be appointed as teacher in our Synodical school in Milwaukee, we were rather distressed. At first we went to Mr. Schoedel in order to establish whether he still held the views expressed previously. He replied affirmatively. We thereupon told him of our distress over the fact that he was to receive a position in which he could propagate his views, which we considered wrong and dangerous. We proposed, therefore, that either he or we should bring Mr. Schoedel's opinions to the attention of the Dean of Students. Mr. Schoedel asked us to do this, and we did.

A few days later the Dean summoned Mr. Marquart and me, and informed us that Mr. Schoedel was orthodox and that we had misunderstood him. Astonished and incredulous, we requested a joint meeting with the Dean and Mr. Schoedel. This meeting was held in the Dean's office. At first Mr. Schoedel expressed himself at length in terms of pious generalities which did not meet the issues we had raised. He spoke eloquently of the Christocentricity of Scripture and the Genesis account, of the truth of the creation, of the profound meaning of the Fall, and of the unquestionable authority of "Word of God". It finally became necessary to get to the real issues by means of specific questions. Mr. Marquart asked Mr. Schoedel two questions: One) "Do you accept Adam and Eve as real historical persons?" And 2) "Do you accept the doctrine of the plenary inspiration of Holy Scripture, as it has been taught traditionally in the Christian Church?" Both questions were answered negatively, though amid repeated protestations of loyalty to the Word of God, etc. There was nothing more to discuss and the Dean dismissed Mr. Marquart and me.

A week or so later we were shocked to hear that Mr. Schoedel was teaching in Milwaukee. By means of a letter (Exhibit A.) we respectfully asked the Dean for clarification of the situation. The Dean insisted that the whole thing had been a misunderstanding, a case of "talking past one another." But since we had put the matter in writing, the Dean said, he had to pursue it officially. A special committee was appointed, consisting of Drs. Spitz and Merkens, to look into the matter. The matter remained pending for several months, and no committee meetings were held. At last the Dean informed us that no meeting would be necessary, since the doctrine of the Word was being discussed with Mr. Schoedel by the local authorities in Milwaukee.

In spite of all this, Mr. Schoedel became a member of the Valparaiso University faculty.

The Lapp Case

At the very end of the academic year an incident occurred which is fully described in Exhibit B. Due to the late timing, the administration told us, nothing could be done. Exhibit B includes a request for clarification of the status of the *Brief Statement*.

1955 – 1956

Although I vicared during this year, I am prepared to support every statement in this section by documentary evidence or the testimony of eyewitnesses.

The Dorn – Marquart Letter

In desperation over the theological turmoil on campus Messrs. Paul Dorn and Kurt Marquart at length decided to appeal formally to the faculty for theological clarification. This was done under date of April 30, 1956 (Exhibit C) (Ed. Published in January 10, in 1972 *CN*).

One rather inconclusive exploratory meeting was held on the basis of this letter. Present were the Systematics Department, the Administration, faculty advisors, student leaders, *Seminarian* and staff members, and representatives of various theological points of view. No conclusions of any sort were reached.

Shortly thereafter the Dean of Students requested Mr. Marquart to draw up a series of theses on the basis of which a discussion might be held. (These "doctrinal points" are appended to Exhibit C.) That discussion, again held in the presence of the Systematics Department, never got beyond the third point of the first section. Mr. William Jacobson and others publicly argued for the permissibility of a "mytho – poetic" view of Genesis. Again no conclusions were reached, but no further meetings were held.

To this day the following theological questions of the Dorn – Marquart letter have received no clarification:

"Are Orthodox teachers and confessional documents still expected to set forth the pure Word of God itself, though in extra-biblical terms, or are they expected meerly to approach the Word of God? Are Orthodox theological formulations to be regarded as correct restatements of divine

3

truth itself, or are they merely historically – conditioned approximations, "in, with, and under" which the real truth is to be sought?

As regards publica doctrina, does the Missouri Synod still teach, permit and tolerate only one publica doctrina? Above all, does a *Brief Statement* still represent the official position of the Missouri Synod, to the exclusion of all antithesis? Is it proper and permissible to regard the *Brief Statement* as abrogated (i. e. as official position) and all those points which are not explicitly reiterated in the Common Confession? Is the *Brief Statement*'s doctrine binding in conscience upon every public teacher of Synod, also with regard to Holy Scripture, the Trinity, Election and Conversion, Creation, Church, Ministry and Ordination, Open Questions, or is it possible for a non-unionistic Synod to have an official position which is binding upon no one in particular, but only on 'Synod in general?' Is it proper and permissible to regard only those points of doctrine as binding which are explicitly taught in the Lutheran Symbols, or is the acceptance of all scriptural doctrines, including all those listed in the *Brief Statement*, still required for church – fellowship in and with the Missouri Synod?

It has been repeatedly asserted, for instance by Dr. Repp, at a meeting with various representatives of your board on February 13, 1958 that the faculties " Mutual Responsibility, etc." (Exhibit D) deals with the issues raised. But "Mutual Responsibility" says nothing about the *Brief Statement*, the inerrancy of Scripture in all matters of which it treats, and the historicity of Genesis, all major issues of concern, formally brought to the faculty's attention. The issues remain unresolved!

The *Seminarian*

Furthermore, the Dorn – Marquart letter contained specific complaints against the students' theological journal, the *Seminarian* (Exhibit C, pp. 7-9). This matter was completely excluded from the discussions with the Systematics Department.

The Jacobson Case

The January, 1956 *Seminarian* contained an objectionable article, "Luther and Orthodoxy" by William Jacobson (See Exhibit C, p. 7). Also, Mr. Jacobson openly maintained the "Mytho-poetic" view of Genesis. Yet he was allowed to graduate. Two months later, he joined the Unitarian church.

Exhibit A
Concordia Seminary
March 8, 1955
Dear Dean Wuerffel,

First of all, please do not misunderstand the purpose of this letter. It was simply an expedient chosen out of consideration for your busy schedule. Also such matters can be stated more concisely on paper than an oral conversation.

At first we intended to serve discreet silence about the case of Mr.

Schoedel. Soon, however, it became apparent that the "other side" is not only publicizing the case, but was presenting it in such a light as made us look like uncharitable, "super-Orthodox," inquisitorial busy-bodies, intent on collecting all motes from our brothers' eyes. These uncharitable sentiments were spread in the name of "charity," the kind of charity, however, which presumes to be a substitute for truth, and which Luther called "accursed charity."

Because we and others felt, and still feel, that our action in the Schoedel case was our duty before God, we naturally could not remain silent but began to defend our position against those who think that the whole matter was but a minor, and duly exaggerated "misunderstanding" which could be satisfactorily resolved by proper application of psychoanalysis to our "desire for attention," "destructive, complex," "narrowmindedness," or whatever psychological aberration is said to motivate us.

Moreover, the implied principle that underlies most of such criticisms of their actions is that age and learning are adequate criteria of truth. Yet a Sunday school child who knows Jesus as his Savior is a greater theologian than the greatest scholar with all his degrees who lacks such faith!

We readily admit, of course, that in Old Testament scholarship we are worse than amateurs compared to Mr. Schoedel. We also concede that Mr. Schoedel might have, and probably did operate on the basis of different "primary assumptions." But we fail to see how these admissions could disqualify us linguistically, so as to disable us to understand clear statements in simple English, which any layman and child can comprehend, such as: "I deny the actual, literal historicity of the Adam and Eve story, which narrative is a Babylonian myth;" Or: "I deny the historicity of the giving of the Law at Mount Sinai. The Mosaic Code development from the Hammurabian Code;" Or: "I deny the doctrine of the plenary inspiration of the Holy Scriptures, as it has been taught traditionally and the Christian Church."

You can imagine our disturbance when Mr. Schoedel's position was not only defended by some, but the rumor was being spread that "the Dean said Schoedel had a valid approach," and this was glowingly taken to mean that you endorsed this position! Of course we could not believe that this was your intention, and we promptly pointed out the difference between a "valid approach" and "valid conclusion."

It remains true, however, that this whole matter is shrouded in uncertainties and ambiguities, aggravated by malicious gossip and strange rumors. It is for this reason that we herewith respectfully and humbly request such clarification and advice on these issues, as you may deem appropriate to give us at your convenience.

Respectfully submitted,

Herman Otten

Kurt Marquart

/S/

Exhibit B

Concordia Seminary
June 2, 1955

Dear Dean Wuerffel:

After our discussion with Paul Lapp yesterday afternoon (about which he has, no doubt already informed you) he proposed to make an appointment with you to attempt to compose our differences, or rather to discover whether they exist. But since you are probably even busier than usual these last few days, we thought it best to prepare and present this statement in the eventuality that an appointment cannot be obtained. Here then is our side of the story, and we will be happy to correct any errors or inaccuracies, should such be pointed out to us.

Several days ago Robert Elosser mentioned to Herman Otten a conversation between him (Elosser) and Paul Lapp, at which the latter had supposedly made statements to the effect that the inspiration of St. Paul was not basically different from that which pious Christians of today experience, and that if we had other reliable documents of the New Testament era, these would be accepted in the same way as the New Testament. It was Bob's distinct impression that Paul Lapp's statements cannot be squared with the *Brief Statement*. This placed us in a very unpleasant position. What to do?

In view of the friendly way in which we parted with you at our last meeting, and in view of the lateness of the year, we can assure you that we were certainly not very eager to precipitate any difficulties. Accordingly Herman went to Dr. Spitz and asked him what ought to be done. His advice was to take it up at once. Anticipating the possibility, Herman asked Dr. Spitz what to do if Paul Lapp refused to answer on the grounds that it was none of our business. "Take it up with the Dean immediately," was the reply.

It was then decided that Herman should see Paul alone. As it happened however, Paul was out of town, and Herman could not reach him for a day or two. Then (Tuesday, May 31) Paul Dorn and I (K. M.), walking past Dorm J, decided to check if Paul Lapp had returned. We found him in his room, and stated that we would like to discuss something with him that was of great concern to us. We made an appointment for the next day, without further specifying our purpose. Yesterday Paul Dorn and I met with Paul Lapp for two hours. This is what happened.

I opened the conversation by saying that because people are frequently misquoted and/or their statements taken out of context, we felt constrained, especially in view of unwholesome tendencies in our Synod, to discuss with him a quotation attributed to him. I then mentioned the quotation regarding the inspiration of St. Paul, and, upon his insistence, also the source. To this he replied that he would not give us an answer, because, in view of recent history, he thought that this would be disruptive of the "unity on this campus," and that a simple answer might be used by us to cause "division and offenses." Unless he could first assure himself that we were not causing such "divisions and offenses," he would not give us an answer, in fact his conscience would prevent him from doing so. I said that we would be happy to discuss any point of our conduct, but reminded him that we had come with the request for an answer and instead he evaded the issue by asking us all sorts of questions.

Asked for an explanation of his earlier remarks about "McCarthyism," Paul Lapp said he didn't like the fact that we "accused some brothers to the faculty." Thinking that he was referring to the case of Mr. Schoedel, I explained that our action had not been taken behind his back, nor was it decided upon hastily. I explained that McCarthyism consisted in the use of false or exaggerated accusations and of inadequate evidence, and that it was precisely because we wanted to avoid McCarthyism that we came to see him.

Thereupon he told us this: "The Dean told me that you and Herman Otten told him that you had wanted to discuss my *Seminarian*-article with me, and that I had refused to do so." (This must be a misunderstanding. I do not recall either Herman or myself ever telling you anything of the kind. True, Herman had tried to reach Paul Lapp several times, but the latter had not been in his room. Actually, neither a discussion, nor a request for one had taken place between Herman and Paul Lapp. And as for myself, I didn't even know Paul till a few days ago. What we might have said is this: both Fred Dodge and Horst Hoyer had discussed Paul's article with him. One of them (I think Fred) had told us that Paul refused to commit himself definitely on specific issues, contending that his article was not "intended to present a whole message," and that no implication should be attributed to it, since it was "addressed to the existential moment," whatever that means.)

Herb Schmidt, Paul Lapp's roommate now joined the conversation and these are, in essence, the main points made on both sides:

1) There ought to be considerable liberty for diversity of theological opinions in Synod.

2) It is presumptuous for us to believe that we could determine the official and binding position of our Synod in a specific instance.

3) The *Brief Statement* is not binding; only the Confessions are.

4) We ought not to feel that we have the right to impose "our" "frame of reference" on others.

5) The doctrine of the inerrancy of Holy Scripture is not as important as we claim it is.

6) Much more important than any specific point of doctrine and the "interaction among brethren," " the spirit of forgiveness," "mutual trust and acceptance."

7) We stated that we did not per se question Paul Lapp's position, but asked him for clarification of a specific point. In such specific matters general character-references avail nothing.

Time and time again we appealed to Paul Lapp to give us an answer, only to be told that since our whole "frame of reference" was different, he could not do so until more basic issues had been discussed. But these issues could not be discussed at this time, since it would take too long! And even if specific answers would be given, we had no right to take any action thereupon until we had become thoroughly acquainted, and had gotten into the habit of "brotherly interaction." More homilies on love followed. We suggested that we approach those more basic matters via the specific issues at hand. No, first a foundation had to be laid! It was no use discussing Verbal Inspiration till we had gone into the historical background, MODERN CRITICAL STUDIES, etc., etc. we replied that this was not necessary for a simple statement of one's stand on Scripture, but that these sources were obviously necessary to prove Paul Lapp's position. We suggested that he first state this position and then proceed to defend it. No! Our "frameworks" differ too much! The very idea of "a true visible Church" is unacceptable! So is the "invisible Church!" Doctrinal certainty, in the sense of specific points, is pride and presumption, since we are also in theology "simul justus et peccator!" We wonder just how "different" a "frame of reference" may be and still be acceptable in our synod!

On "brotherly trust" approximately the following dialogue ensued:

They: "Your whole approach is wrong! You must trust the brother. Instead you come to judge!"

We: "Not to judge, but to ask for information."

They: "Suppose we don't agree, what will you do then?"

We: "We will try to discover whether or not it is merely a matter of semantics."

We: "We have no choice but to bring it before the authorities."

They: "This is not brotherly. You have not come to share mutual insights but already consider the possibility of accusing me."

We: "This possibility is always real, no matter with whom we are dealing. If my closest friend were to disagree with Synod's positions, I would be in duty bound to bring this to the attention of the authorities. In fact if I myself disagreed with the *Brief Statement*, I would have to leave."

They: "Do you accept me as a brother?"

We: "I did till I was made aware of the quotation attributed to you."

They: "But now you don't?"

We. "I can neither deny it nor unconditionally affirm it. I am 'agnostic' in the matter, and my decision can obviously be contingent only upon your answer. It is entirely up to you. So will you answer the question now?"

They: "You cannot be 'agnostic'; you must accept me as a brother."

We: "Even if I had evidence to the contrary?"

They: "In spite of evidence. You must consider everyone a brother till he has been formally excommunicated."

We: "In that case no one can ever be excommunicated, since you cannot excommunicate a brother."

They: "Non sequitur."

We: "Sequitur!"...

We: "Do you believe in doctrinal discipline?"

8

They: "Yes, but not as it has been handled sometimes."

We: "What do you expect us to do? What 'approach' or 'method' must we follow with you to get you to answer our question and stop acting like a Sphynx?"

They: "We are much more concerned with more basic things; our witnessing to each other, the unity on this campus, etc. My reply would confuse matters."

We: "Your refusal to reply is much more confusing!"

They: "With your frame of reference you would be inclined to misinterpret my reply."

We: "That's why we are here. We want YOUR own interpretation, not ours!"

No results! Seeing the futility of further efforts we got up to go. Paul Lapp then suggested an appointment with you, to which we agreed.

While still refusing to either affirm or deny the quotation attributed to him, Paul Lapp ended the conversation by saying that the conversation in question had taken place under irregular circumstances, at 1 a.m., that Bob Elosser and he, Paul Lapp, had joked about our "heresy-hunting" (Paul Lapp saying, "They'd consider me a heretic too"), that Bob Elosser very likely told us about this matter with a "tongue-in-cheek" attitude merely to "goad" us on to further "heresy-hunting," and that Bob had told him, i.e. Paul Lapp, that he could probably overthrow our positon with one blow!

For the moment this disturbed us greatly, for if true, this would mean that in practically all of his dealings with us – among which had been several very interesting, inspiring, serious, edifying discussions – Bob had been committing the worst of hypocrisy. Accordingly we went to see Bob. He told us that in so serious a matter as sacred theology he wouldn't think of having a tongue-in-cheek attitude—except perhaps to the extent in which he sees the flagrant inconsistency of Missouri's self-righteous fanfare about the *Brief Statement* on the one hand, and open disavowals on this campus on the other. He said he could have no possible motives for "goading" anyone on to any sort of trouble. In fact, Bob said, he feels as a guest on this campus, and intends to maintain a proper neutral position. He did say that if Paul Lapp's statement could be harmonized even with the Common Confession, not to mention the *Brief Statement*, this would require a skilled word-juggler. Bob told us that although he had warned Paul Lapp that he would quote his statement to us — to which Paul had not objected – yet after he (Bob) had done so, he felt constrained to inform Paul of his action. THEREFORE LAST SUNDAY MORNING BOB TOLD PAUL LAPP THAT HE HAD QUOTED HIM TO US, and that "if he really accepted the doctrine of the *Brief Statement* he had nothing to fear." Thus Paul Lapp had known since Sunday what was to come! Yesterday morning, before our talk with Paul Lapp, some prominent fourth-year men were heard clamoring about "the investigation committee being 'out to get' Paul Lapp and others!" Now who is impugning whose motives? Who is practicing McCarthyism? What happened to "brotherly interaction", "Trust", "Unity on the campus" and other pious slogans? Or is our side the only one that is bound to these macarisms?

Dean Wuerffel, let us assure you, we don't enjoy this! If we were not convinced that the welfare of the Church is at stake, we would have remained silent. This is an ugly and deplorable matter. But what to do? We realize that we are not authorized to check the doctrinal reliability of graduates. This is the faculty's duty and privilege. But, as Luther said, in an emergency rules do not hold. When it burns everyone rushes to quench the fire. When a bank is being robbed and the authorized officials, i.e., policemen are not present, it is the duty of citizens to summon them. It will not do merely to deploy the nastiness of the whole affair.

Furthermore, we did not "hunt" for this case. We were confronted by a fact. Our only choice was between doing our duty and not doing it. Our duty, when confronted with a quotation by a brother indicating the possibility of doctrinal aberrations, is clearly not to denounce him to the authorities, but to ascertain the sense and intention of the quote in question. But when this rather simple and reasonable request is refused by the brother, then, obviously, the matter cannot be ignored, but must be pursued further. It is in this spirit that we respectfully submit this matter to you. Please remember that we ARE NOT ACCUSING PAUL LAPP OF ANY FALSE DOCTRINE. We are merely asking that he commit himself since neutrality in this matter is unthinkable. Nor, it seems to us, can some general pledge to the Confessions or some other general statement be considered an adequate answer to a specific objection. We should like to know of brother Lapp (1) if he made the statements attributed to him, or others to that effect, and (2) if so, how and if they are to be brought into harmony with the doctrine that Scriptures "contain no errors or contradictions, but that they are in all their parts and words the infallible truth, also in those parts which treat of historical geographical, and other secular matters, and that it is taught by direct statements of the Scriptures." (*Brief Statement*, #1.) If it is argued that such statements are not explicitly found in the Confessions, and that they are on that account not binding, we earnestly request an explanation as to what is meant by the statement that the *Brief Statement* IS THE official position of our Synod over against other Lutherans.

Very sincerely yours,

Kurt Marquart

I have read this report, found it to be accurate, concur in its views, and likewise join in its requests.

Paul Dorn

Note

In order to avoid the impression of underhanded tactics, and in order to afford brother Lapp an opportunity to take exception to possible inaccuracies or bias contained in this report, a copy of it is herewith simultaneously presented to him.

1. When was the Board of Control of Concordia Seminary given evidence that false doctrine was being taught and tolerated at the seminary? ____

2. When did Herman Otten become aware that a "new spirit" was manifesting itself at the St. Louis seminary? ____
3. Many students who petitioned the faculty could not accept ____.
4. What did William Schoedel believe about inspiration and Genesis? ____
5. Schoedel became a member of the ____ faculty.
6. William Jacobsen argued for ____.
7. The Dorn-Marquart letter asked if the *Brief Statement* still ____.
8. "Mutual Responsibility" said nothing about ____.
9. William Jacobsen joined the ____ Church two months after graduation.
10. A Sunday school child who knows Jesus as his Savior is a greater theologian than ____.
11. "McCarthyism" consisted in the use of ____.
12. Who was Paul Lapp's roommate?____
13. When a bank is being robbed and no policemen are present it is the duty of a citizen to ____ them.
14. Did Marquart act in an uncharitable manner? ____

SCHARLEMANN CASE SETTLED

From "What Is Troubling the Lutherans? Part III The Right,
The Lutheran Church-Missouri Synod, News and Views, June 1961

Finally on August 22 Behnken sent a letter to every pastor and teacher of the Missouri Synod explaining that the matter with Scharlemann had been settled. In the light of the above facts, the President of a large church body could hardly dare to hope that this constituency would accept this letter as a "settlement" of the case. We shall let just a few "Missouri" men speak for themselves.

A pastor from Texas wrote on August 30, 1960:

My dear and Right Reverend Doctor:

Your eagerly awaited letter of August 22, regarding the controversy surrounding Dr. Scharlemann, proved to be, I must say, a most painful bit of reading. In essence it means that Dr. Scharlemann has now been persuaded that his denial of Inerrancy was not really a denial of Inerrancy!

After the assurance given us by you at the Texas District Convention, I was confident that you would really settle the matter. But if you really hope that your current letter will "put an end to the disturbance and to the many attacks," then I am afraid that I for one must disappoint you. Quite on the contrary, your efforts at restoring peace to our synod can result only in an intensification of the war. Allow me to make it quite clear that I must respectfully but categorically decline your letter as a settlement. Better no settlement at all than a "settlement" which is pure illusion. And while my respect for your person and office prevents me from employing rather more emphatic language, I cannot, by remaining silent, acquiesce in the intolerable situation created by your letter.

Before briefly stating my concerns, let me say two things. In the first place, insistence upon the necessity of a retraction on Dr. Scharlemann's part is not simply a matter of Shylockian pound of flesh. I think you realize that. What is at stake is nothing less than the doctrinal — and that means *spiritual!* — integrity of our Synod. Dr. Scharlemann's attack upon the very foundation of Synod's doctrinal position is so flagrant and obvious, that if it is tolerated (i.e. if no retraction is demanded) then absolutely *anything* may from now on be taught in Synod — and will be, you may be sure! This means tempting God to send us a terrible famine of the Word, against which a hundred Evangelism Departments would be powerless; for of what use are all the clichés about "spreading the Word" when no one knows any longer what the Word is?

Secondly, opposition to Dr. Scharlemann's position does not mean lack of appreciation and sympathy for some of his basic concerns. If, with the *Brief Statement*, I must reject his doctrine as blasphemous, I am fully aware that the blasphemy is not intentional! Wasn't it to a very well-meaning St. Peter, touchingly concerned about the safety of Our Lord's

Person, that He said: "Get thee behind Me. Satan"? Dr. Scharlemann has grappled with some very real problems, and apparently has agonized in pastoral concern over the intellectual-spiritual difficulties of our studying youth. All this is admirable. But the pity of it is that Dr. Scharlemann's solutions, while eliminating certain problems with one stroke — too easily, in fact — eliminate the Formal Principle of Sacred Theology. Therein lies the tragedy: Troubled by genuine concerns, Dr. Scharlemann simply cuts the Gordian knot and removes not the misapplications of the principle, but the principle itself!

Now to the particulars.

I shall not weary you with a recitation of the voluminous evidence, with which, I must assume, you are familiar. Let me say merely that I am prepared to prove, anywhere and at any time, the following propositions:

I. Dr. Scharlemann has denied the Scriptural *doctrine* (not just the word) of Inerrancy, and has adopted the anti-Scriptural historical-critical approach.

II. Denial of the Inerrancy automatically involves denial of the Scriptural concept of Inspiration.

III. Even more seriously, Dr. Scharlemann advocates the neo-modernistic Brunner-Baillie notions of Revelation, which not only eliminate entirely the historic Christian doctrine of Inspiration, but in principle dissolve all fixed, objective, dogmatic truth in the corrosive, nihilistic acids of Existentialism. This is the entire thrust of the Scharlemann essays.

Now, either these three propositions are wrong, and I am slandering Dr. Scharlemann. In that case I expect to be corrected by you and to be pressed for a retraction. Or else they are correct. But then the issue goes far deeper than the use or non-use of a word, and Dr. Scharlemann owes Synod a rather comprehensive retraction. *Tertium non datur.* Which, then, shall it be?

Your letter urges three points in favor of Dr. Scharlemann: (1) He is now willing to *use* (how?) the *word* "inerrancy". (2) He says he has always accepted Verbal Inspiration. (3) He says he has always accepted the doctrinal content of the *Brief Statement.*

I must confess that the relevance, not to mention the cogency, of these points escapes me entirely. It is incomprehensible to me how you can write as if the basic issue were the use or non-use of a word ("inerrancy")! In the first place, liberals, when pressed, have always been willing to use words like "inerrant" and "infallible", in fact *any* traditional term. Secondly, Dr. Scharlemann has denied the *fact* of inerrancy. Thirdly, you yourself — in an official and therefore lawfully published Presidential letter— have acknowledged that it is Dr. Scharlemann's approach or position, not his use of words, that is untenable. Fourthly, the entire thrust of the Scharlemann position is directed against the orthodox doctrine of

Scripture, in the interests of the dissolutionistic Brunner-Baillie theory of Revelation! Hence, what *words* Dr. Scharlemann may or may not find it useful to employ, has absolutely nothing to do with the case. *Real* issues must not be swept under purely *verbal* rugs!

As for your other two points, are they not self-defeating? If Dr. Scharlemann has *always* believed Verbal Inspiration and the *Brief Statement*, then this was also true when he was publicizing his denials, in which case, however, these assurances are worse than meaningless. Or was Dr. Scharlemann also confessing the *Brief Statement* when he wrote:

> In this paper I propose to defend the paradox that the Book of God's truth contains errors . ... I entertain the hope that this sentence (*Brief Statement*'s definition of Inerrancy. K.M.) could not, in the wording quoted, pass this faculty today, or, if it did, would receive some very careful and limiting definitions. For as the statement reads, it is a pure rationalization, built on the assumption that our Scriptures are, like the *Book of Mormon*, a gift that fell straight from heaven . . . I have quoted this particular sentence from the *Brief Statement* because it rather accurately describes what actually passes for inerrancy in our circles, etc.

I remember quite vividly a series of meetings between students and faculty in 1957, when Dr. Scharlemann, defending some students who denied the Inerrancy, insisted that no one could be bound to the doctrinal content of the *Brief Statement*! And at San Francisco Dr. Scharlemann argued desperately against the *Brief Statement*'s binding force. Aren't these rather odd endeavors for one who has "always believed and accepted the doctrinal content of the *Brief Statement*"? Had Dr. Scharlemann really believed the doctrinal content of the *Brief Statement* to be divine, Scriptural truth, he would have insisted that not only he but anyone else is bound to teach accordingly.

Permit me to comment on some other items in your letter. You say — and apparently this is supposed to have some sort of mitigating effect — that Dr. Scharlemann's essays were "of an exploratory nature only and were not to be construed as the last word on the subject." In the first place, I do not find the concept of "exploratory heresy" a very comforting one. Is a man free nowadays to attack any doctrine, so long as his attack is merely "exploratory"? What has happened to our concepts of *confession?* Can a man confess the Holy Trinity while experimenting, say, with "exploratory" Arianism? In the history of the Church error has often clothed itself in the "humble" garb of "tentativeness". In the second place, the pitifully skeptical basis of contemporary "theology," to which Dr. Scharlemann has *surrendered at a* rather decisive level, is such that from these premises no "last word" *on anything* can ever be spoken. This sort of "theology" is forever groping about in the twilight for an ever receding horizon of "truth," which by definition remains unattainable! On this basis, when will Dr. Scharlemman find the "last word"? When outside observers shall have ceased disagreeing about the sacred mysteries of our holy Faith? When committees of experts shall have succeeded in combining truth and error, Scripture and Rationalism, Christ and Belial, into one uniform, homogenized mishmash?

There was a time when our Synod did not consider Dr. Scharlemann's position even debatable! Of course, that was in the dark ages of Confession, before the discovery of the magical *perpetuum mobile* of Discussion! In 1891 a Dr. Ruperti had left a Pastoral Conference in Europe on the grounds that the set of theses proposed for consideration was not debatable in the Lutheran Church. And the theses were practically identical with Dr. Scharlemann's position! *Lehre Und Wehre* commended Dr. Ruperti, and praised him especially for realizing that such theses are not even debatable among Lutherans. *Lehre und Wehre,* July 1891, pp. 13 ff. Cf. September, 1855, pp. 275 ff. and December 1891, pp. 23 ff. Dr. Scharlemann's "discoveries" are not exactly news to our Synod!

You say that the case of Dr. Scharlemann was handled "not in a legalistic but in a truly evangelical manner." Because nothing decisive has been done? Because Dr. Scharlemann is still with us? Because he has been "helped" to see that a denial of Inerrancy is not a denial of Inerrancy? No, my dear and reverend Doctor! When error is covered up and the truth compromised, then that is not only unevangelical but anti-evangelical, Gal. 1:7-9! With this sort of "evangelical" discipline even Arius could have been "saved for the Church." Synod must not surrender to the sentimental-liberal thesis that "legalistic" means "firm", and "evangelical" something like "spineless" or "milquetoastish." I am sorry if this seems distasteful, but it is time that certain things be said rather frankly in Synod.

In this connection, I must advert to an oddity. Please recall a certain disciplinary case at the Seminary, with which you are very familiar: A student had stepped on certain influential toes, and has been kept, to this day, out of the Sacred Ministry. His eligibility will not even be considered until he shall have acknowledged the alleged sinfulness of his action, for which allegation, however, there is not a shred of Scripture proof. Now, the poor student must recant, but not Dr. Scharlemann. The former "violated love," i.e. annoyed Seminary officials with awkward revelations. The latter taught false doctrine. The "sin" of the former is forbidden neither in Scripture, nor in the Symbols, nor in the *Brief Statement*; it was simply invented at the Seminary for the occasion. The sin of the latter is clearly repudiated in Scripture, the Symbols and the *Brief Statement*. Nevertheless, the former must "repent" "retract", etc., while the latter goes scot-free, upon some easy and meaningless "explanations." The former is out of the Ministry, while the latter remains to teach future ministers! Why this difference? Why, are anti-liberals persecuted (in the name of an Orwellian "love"), while pro-liberals are coddled? Why is the camel swallowed, and the gnat strained out?

Whoever is responsible for this revolting disparity in discipline, should ponder rather seriously the 82nd Psalm: "... How long will ye judge unjustly, and accept the persons of the wicked? Selah. Defend the poor and fatherless: do justice to the afflicted and needy . . ." Does prestige or truth determine the course of events in Synod? And the disparity to which I alluded is too glaring to *be* dismissed lightly. After all, it involved the same disciplining agencies!

Your letter refers to various "attacks" which you deplore. Whatever I have seen in print and in "open letters" seemed perfectly justified. We should be grateful that we have a few watchmen on the walls of Zion who refuse to be lulled to sleep and to become dumb dogs! Who else tells us what goes on in Synod today? Certainly not our official organs. *C.T.M.* has become "polite," "sophisticated, and irrelevant, while the *Lutheran Witness* assumes more and more of the character of a "promotional" glamorizer of the Organization, solemnly chronicling handshakes and dentifrice-grins.

Incidentally, was our Texas District resolution, which accused Dr. Scharlemann of attacking the Inerrancy, one of those deplorable "attacks"? You certainly did not even hint at such an idea at that time, and you spoke at length and repeatedly on the subject of that resolution!

Permit me, then, to plead most earnestly — not as a matter of favor, but as a matter of right, divine and human, as well as by virtue of your own promises to our Distinct Convention — that you secure either Dr. Scharlemann's immediate suspension from office or a clear-cut retraction of his errors. And in conclusion allow me to repeat my previous pleas for decisive action in other critical matters! The open modernism of Pelikan and Marty, the heretical utterances of *Cresset* and *Seminarian,* the open revolt of the English District, *Una Sancta* Romanism, Synodical affiliation with the National Council of Churches, the Thiele-immortality matter, and so forth. These open sores on our Synodical body cannot be tolerated much longer. We cannot develop two or three different religions in Synod. There must come the time of separation, and soon. Do not force us, who treasure Synod's Confessional heritage, into the unnatural position of rebels against our own Synod! We detest the role, but we shall not hesitate to play it, when conscience and integrity demand this!

With cordial greetings, and a heavy heart, and in the firm hope of divine assistance for you and our other responsible leaders, I remain,

Respectfully yours,
Kurt Marquart.

cc.: The Rev. Albert Jesse, President, Texas District

P. S.: I can see no reason to treat this letter as confidential.

Ed. Dr. Martin Scharlemann later changed his position. In 1973 he signed "Crossroads" a document which affirmed the inerrancy of the Bible. He became supporter of *Christian News* and helped *CN* with a revision of An American Translation of the Bible.

1. Dr. Scharlemann in essence was persuaded that his denial of inerrancy was really not ____.
2. What is at stake is the ____ of our Synod.

3. Marquart was prepared to prove ____.
4. Liberals have always been willing to use words like ____.
5. In 1957 Scharlemann defended some students who ____.
6. When error is covered up and the truth compromised then ____.
7. The "sin" of the student kept out of that Sacred Ministry was ____.
8. The *Lutheran Witness* assumes more and more ____.
9. What open sores on the synodical body could no longer be tolerated? ____

10. Dr. Martin Scharlemann in 1973 signed ____ and became a supporter of ____.

QUO VADIS LUTHERAN WITNESS
MARQUART COMMENTS ON LUTHERAN WITNESS AND NEW THEOLOGY COMMISSION
Christian News, June 3, 1963

Friendly observers who may have dismissed the alarming *Lutheran Witness* editorial "Turning Point" (August 21, 1962) as a regrettable but isolated blunder, will have to revise their estimates upon reading the April 30, 1963, issue. Here the "new direction" is so brazenly explicit, that an effort of the will is required to remember that one is reading the Missouri Synod's official organ, and not merely something published by that self-appointed new intellectual elite, whose claim to scholarly standing appears to consist primarily in the cultivation of an abstruse and evasive vocabulary, and in endless rehearsals of a limited range of fashionable "theology's" more popular clichés—which once indeed were new but have since, alas, grown as tiresome as wilted salad!

I. "Synodogram"

It is good to see here references to the great theological issues of our time. And it is very much to be hoped that the laity will take a genuine interest in these matters. Unfortunately, however, *Witness* readers are not likely to be encouraged in this direction by this particular "Synodogram". Despite the employment of admirable techniques of mass communication, the real issues are beclouded rather than elucidated.

In the first place, the tone is altogether more reassuring than the circumstances would warrant. The life-and-death struggle of Christian theology within the Missouri Synod is presented as a sort of interesting intellectual adventure, which will require enormous efforts on the part of the experts, but which will inevitably produce a solution the rightness of which is a foregone conclusion. The Synodical President, Dr. Harms, is quoted as saying: "...I know what the final outcome will be. Our studies will make it clear that the Word of God with all its doctrines is our sure and immovable constant." In other words: Don't worry, all is well, there will always be a Missouri, and Big Brother will take care of you!

It is difficult to be patient in the presence of this chronic official complacency, which is forever begging the question and assuming what remains to be proved.

When the familiar pattern of over-protective paternalism begins to appear in Church or State, the rank-and-file have every reason to fear that what claims to be an exhilarating draught of the elixir of truth, may in fact turn out to be a paralyzing dose of the anesthetic of propaganda!

Candor

In the second place, judged by the canon of candor, the article leaves much to be desired. It stubbornly maintains the absurd but convenient official delusion that the present controversy within the Missouri Synod is not a deep cleavage over dogmatic fundamentals, but only a misunderstanding, on the surface level of language, "formulation," etc. If the Commission on Theology and Church Relations proceeds from this assumption, then it cannot hope to serve as an instrument of reform, but is doomed to the role of a discussion club. If it is a foregone conclusion that all parties concerned are to retain membership in Synod, and must therefore be accepted as orthodox theologians laden with valuable "insights," then all that is needed is a Scholarly Society for the Advancement of Verbosity, which could from time to time illustrate and confirm the unchallengeable working axiom of "doctrinal unity" by issuing reassuring dialectical formulations "in which both we and they are right" (Luther). And so Nero would fiddle merrily, while Rome continues to burn! May one hope that the Commission includes men who can and will prevent such a travesty?

This whole business of changing "formulations" while retaining the "substance" is highly suspect from beginning to end. It is the standard excuse for even the most extreme heresies. Thus a writer who questions the personal pre-existence of Christ, and therefore His real Divinity, also asserts that he is preserving the "religious intention," that is, the substance of the Nicene Creed, while changing only certain antiquated "thought forms," etc.! (Joseph Sittler, "A Christology of Function," *The Lutheran Quarterly*, May, 1954).

Once an orthodox formulation of doctrine has been agreed upon by the Church, there is no need to keep on changing it. Certain aspects will indeed have to be defined more precisely, in response to new heresies, but this does not invalidate the previous formulation. New formulations build on the foundation of their predecessors; they do not hang in air. The natural tendency will be to move from vaguer and more general formulations to more exact, precise, and specific ones. When this direction is reversed —and the modern clamor forever newer (but not binding!) "formulations" favors not stricter, more precise, more exclusive language, but on the contrary, looser, vaguer, more inclusive terms!—the suspicion is unavoidable that it is in fact from substantive doctrinal positions of the past, and not merely from words and terms, that men seek to be emancipated! Or why should one oppose traditional formulations, if one does not oppose their traditional content? Is that not senseless logomachy? What we need is a few clear, incisive Scriptural definitions, "so that pure doctrine can be recognized and distinguished from adulterated doctrine and so that the way may not be felt free and open to restless, contentious individuals, who do not want to be bound to any certain formula of pure doctrine, to start scandalous controversies at will and to introduce and defend monstrous errors, the only possible consequence of which is that finally correct doctrine will be entirely obscured and lost and nothing beyond uncertain opinions and dubious, disputable imaginations and views will be transmitted to subsequent generations" (Preface, *Book of Concord*).

Substance Not Language
The fact of the matter is that Neo-Orthodoxy is asserting its right to

exist in the Missouri Synod. And this tissue of "monstrous errors," which reduces all theology to "nothing beyond uncertain opinions, etc." is locked in mortal combat with the substance, not merely the language, of Missouri's previous, orthodox doctrinal position. Any formulation, which would by-pass and thus conceal this conflict, would be not merely worthless, but positively pernicious. And formulations which would really be "relevant," i.e. such as would unequivocally reject the modern errors, would be bitterly opposed by those who now agitate against the allegedly "inadequate," "irrelevant," etc., formulations of the recent past! All plans, on the part of orthodox Missourians, which would fail to take into account these elementary realities, are doomed to utter failure.

In the third place, it is startling to find Missouri's official organ explicitly treating theology as a science. One asks in amazement: Have these theological journalists never read the first volume of Pieper's *Dogmatics*? Have they not understood and remembered what they read?

"If the term 'science' denotes a certain knowledge, in opposition to mere views, hypotheses, etc., theology is the perfect science, the only reliable science on earth. All other sciences are based on human observations and human deductions, and in the nature of the case—*errare humanum est*— the information offered by philosophy, astronomy, medical science, etc., is more or less unreliable. But the Christian theologian gets his information from the Bible, which is God's Word, the depository of God's own observation, opinion, and doctrine. Such a science cannot contain any error—*errare in Deum non cadit*—and cannot give any unreliable information" (Pieper, *Christian Dogmatics*, Vol. I, pp. 107-108).

It is clear that Pieper here uses the term "science" in its medieval sense of certain knowledge, rather than in the modern sense of systematized empirical observations. It is also clear that it is in this latter sense, in which Pieper refused to apply the term to theology, that the *Lutheran Witness* now uses the word "science." To admit the validity of the critical approach in theology is to change the role of Scripture from absolute authority, rule, and norm, to a mere corpus of raw-materials, which scientific "theology" then studies critically, in the same way as all other sciences process their "data." This scientific "theology" cannot possibly be *doctrina divina*, divine teaching, resting on divine authority, but it is *doctrina humana*, human teaching, theory, opinion, observation, conclusion, etc. Would any perceptive student of the subject honestly deny that this is the natural and obvious sense and meaning of the "Synodogram," particularly when read in conjunction with the other two items, yet to be treated?

We sincerely hope that the "Synodogram" does not at this point represent the position of the CTCR, which many sanguine observers, including the present writer, regard as Missouri's last hope. If the Commission were to accept the neological concept of theology as a science, it could spare itself all further efforts; for this fundamental concession would amount, in principle, to a capitulation to the proton pseudos of the modern apostasy. Further discussions, no matter how competent technically, would then be mere palaver, from which one might expect a brilliant post mortem at best, but never a diagnosis leading to a cure!

"Theology or Doctrine"

The ominous sentence "Misunderstanding arises when people simply equate theology with doctrine," cannot be allowed to pass unchallenged. What does it mean? Does it mean that there are people who wish to make doctrines out of some purely exegetical or historical points (say, whether the expression "brothers of the Lord" is to be taken in its strictest sense, or in a wider sense; or whether Leo X was really forced by medical considerations to abandon the custom of the annual kissing of the Pope's big toe)? It must of course be admitted that while for an orthodox theologian some exegetical questions (e.g. whether the Old Testament contains direct, predictive prophecies regarding a personal Messiah; or whether Christ actually said the things attributed to Him in St. John's Gospel) are indeed settled by the authority of Christ and His infallible Scripture, and are therefore matters of doctrine. Neo-Orthodox writers, also those within the Missouri Synod, have no such inhibitions. Is the warning against "equating" theology with doctrine designed to accommodate these gentlemen? One can hardly suppose otherwise.

In the last few years we have again and again witnessed the official method of conjuring away all doctrinal conflict: The points in controversy are simply declared to be matters of "theology," interpretation, etc., but not of "doctrine". This system conveniently disposes of the very possibility of real doctrinal controversy. The underlying myth of "doctrinal unity" is simply taken as a dogma, as a rule of the game, so to speak, which no good sportsman would have the bad manners to question. Whenever disagreements do arise, they are then automatically assumed to be non-doctrinal! In this scheme of things "doctrine" becomes a shadowy concept, a vague slogan, a commodious verbal parenthesis, within which the most heterogeneous positions can be safely and neatly contained, managed, "united," and accounted for! The resultant much-advertised "doctrinal unity" is a threadbare fiction. Doctrinal conflicts cannot be made to disappear simply by ordering them into some mythical "non-doctrinal" limbo! What disappears is not the conflicts, but the honesty, clarity, vision, truth, faith, courage, integrity, etc., which are necessary to face and resolve them!

Was Dr. Pieper spreading "misunderstanding" when he wrote, as if to refute this very sentence of the "Synododgram":

"Objective theology (*theologia positiva*) is, as our old Lutheran dogmaticians say, nothing else than Scripture itself arranged according to doctrines...It follows that (Christian) theology is not made up of the variable notions and opinions of men, but is the immutable divine truth or God's own doctrine (*doctrina divina*)-...The moderns are determined to establish their anthropocentric theology in the Church— not content with defending it (claiming, e.g., that they are teaching "the old truth" in "a new way"), they launch vicious attacks against those who insist on taking the Christian doctrine from Scripture, on

21

teaching the *doctrina divina*;..Theology is commonly divided into dogmatic, historical, exegetical, and practical theology. And it is the dogma, that is, the doctrine of Scripture, which stamps these various branches of theology as theological disciplines and unifies them...it is evident that the dogma is the unifying core of the various theological disciplines. The dogma, the Scriptural doctrine, is the essential element in every discipline, which integrates all branches of sacred theology ...in spite of the demand for an "undogmatic" Christianity, we declare: "Only dogmatics is edifying," namely, dogmatics as *doctrina divina* revealed in Scripture, the only doctrine which may be taught in Christ's Church. In the Christian Church, doctrine is the all-important thing...The theologian who no longer believes that "supernatural truths" are imparted through Scripture, through the doctrine of Scripture, but denounces that as conducive to "intellectualism," has lost sight of the obligations of his sacred office" (*Christian Dogmatics*, Vol. I, pp. 52-102).

True and False Humility

This takes us, in the fourth place, to that unfortunate quotation attributed to Dr. Bouman. The present writer, who as a St. Louis Seminary student had learned to love and respect Prof. Bouman as a pillar of Scriptural, Confessional theology in the midst of "change and decay," read this statement with profound sadness, for under the circumstances it sounds like a weary disengagement, indeed a concession of defeat presented to an arrogant and triumphant neology! If the controversy in the Missouri Synod were concerned with relatively minor matters, or if it were a question of adiaphora or of ethical problems like dancing, usury, life-insurance, etc., one could understand and approve the tone of humility. Even then, however, a Biblical theologian, when stating the principle, would surely want to claim something more than mere fumbling attempts at orthodoxy. ("Our spiritual fathers wanted to be loyal to the Word of God and the Lutheran Confessions." Weren't they? "They tried to formulate doctrine, etc. We too want to be loyal to Scripture and the symbols..." Aren't "we"? Are Lutheran pastors and professors expected to be orthodox, or is it sufficient that they merely try to be? How our Confessional forefathers, like Luther, Walther, Pieper, detested the mock humility of skepticism!)

As things are, however, the controversy is not about trivia, but about the very foundations of the Faith. Whether Scripture is the inerrant Word, truth, and revelation of the living God, and whether the harbingers of the Neo-Orthodox antithesis are to be permitted to continue their propaganda within the Missouri Synod, are questions which Confessional theologians should be able to answer forthrightly and without any false modesty or reticence. There is a "humility" which is really a sophisticated form of pride. Mariolatry has ever and anon disguised itself as humility: "We are too sinful to approach God directly; let His Mother present our petitions!" True humility means obedience to God and His Word. A "humility" which encourages doctrinal uncertainty, particularly with respect to such crucial issues as those raised by Neo-Orthodoxy, is of that false kind of which Peter became guilty (St. John 13:8), against which also the Apostle St. Paul warns (Col.2:18), and from which the papists argue that it is presumption to be certain of grace, that one must approach God through the Saints, etc. It is to be feared that Dr. Bouman has, despite the best intentions, given aid and comfort to the neologists, who suffer from a sad inversion with regard to pride and humility: Where they ought to be "proud," that is, firm, certain, adamant, and unyielding, namely in the defense of God's honor, Word, truth, and Church ("I have more understanding than all my teachers: for thy testimonies are my meditation, I understand more than the ancients," Ps. 119:99, 100), there they are "humble," that is, uncertain, confused, compromising. But where they really ought to be humble, namely when it comes to man's honor, learning, scholarship, wisdom, etc., they are proud!

And a theologian is "responsible" not when he is willing to practice as much "humility" (tolerance?) as is necessary to keep synodical apple-carts from coming unglued, but when he is inflexible in his demand that all other interests be subjected to the cause of faithful confession (not merely discussion!) in word and deed, of the full divine doctrine revealed in Scripture.

II. "Critics Under God"

We need not linger long with this piece. It is a guarded but unmistakable effort to secure popular acceptance for the critical approach in theology. "It is unfortunate that scholarly study of the origin and text of the Bible is called Biblical criticism." Indeed! Lest some Knight of Charity should rush in and gallantly suggest that perhaps only textual ("lower") criticism is meant, it should be said at once that the article contains no such limitation. On the contrary, what is advocated is the critical approach in general, including, believe it or not, "form criticism," which is definitely of the "higher," if not the "highest" (Bultmann!) variety! It is all stated very innocently, to be sure, and there is no reference to that naughty and perhaps upsetting concept of form criticism: "myth". But the direction and intention of the article are brazenly clear. With the substance of this whole matter we have recently had occasion to deal extensively ("The Crisis in Christendom," March-June, and September issues of *The Australian Theological Review*, reprinted, we understand, in a recent issue of *The Faithful Word*). Suffice it to say here that orthodox theologians will continue to call a spade a spade, and to reject the critical approach in theology for what it is: an insolent assertion of human rebellion against the divine authority of Scripture. And are we really, seriously expected to abandon our historic Scriptural understanding of the nature of Theology merely because *Webster's New Collegiate Dictionary*, reflecting heretical and apostate usage, asserts that theology "also includes the 'critical, historical, and psychological study of religion and religious ideas'" ("Synodogram," second paragraph)?

III. "Theology—A Disturbing Science"

This is easily the *piece de resistance*. The outlook which this article conveys is that familiar, fashionable one. All the usual clichés ("Platonic and Aristotelian thought-forms"), the false definitions of theology, dogma, and doctrine, and the skeptical Barth-Brunner notions about personal, as opposed to propositional truth, are present and accounted for. The only new thing in all this is that such positions are now actually advocated in the official organ of the Missouri Synod. Having dealt with these issues in "The Crisis in Christendom," we shall restrict ourselves to but a few observations.

Divine Rule or "Plastic Ruler"?

Regarding Barth, whose skeptical theology is quite evident even from the few quotations adduced in the article, the writer, who signs himself "O.S." (and who, incidentally, speaks of the "overwhelming wholesomeness" of the Barth volume cited), comments: "One hesitates to measure a giant with a plastic ruler." One should! Indeed, in theology one should not only hesitate, but utterly refrain from measuring anything with a "plastic ruler". The real tragedy lies in the fact that the Missouri Synod's official organ is open nowadays to writers who admittedly have only a "plastic (!) ruler" to which to measure things, while its columns are evidently closed to those who would measure the current aberrations according to "the comprehensive summary, rule, and norm according to which all doctrines should be judged and the errors which intruded should be explained and decided in a Christian way" (*Formula of Concord, Epitome. Introduction*). Of course, if one wishes to be a "scientific" theologian, then one must be satisfied with plastic rulers, for in that case one has renounced the very idea of an absolute divine rule and standard!*

All this abject, wide-eyed Lilliputian awe and wonder in the presence of the neological "giants" and their popularizers, particularly when contrasted with the accompanying superciliousness toward traditional, orthodox theology, suggests the type of "intellectualism" which is commonly characterized by the prefix "pseudo". As everyone knows, sophomoric "non-conformity" is in reality a hyper-conformist affectation. If we are going to be bold, independent, courageous, etc., thinkers, then we should practice these virtues also on the sacred cows of the heretical "theology" which happens to be the fashion, and not only on the poor, backward, old orthodox Fathers, who happen to be out of fashion! Is it terribly "courageous" and "responsible" to subject orthodoxy to endless critical indignities, but then to whine about Charity whenever others refuse to stultify their critical faculties in deference to Barth, Brunner, Aulen, Tillich, and, yes, Pelikan, Marty, Scharlemann, and even—dare we say it—synodical concocters of reassuring fairy-tales? Is it allowed to attack the inerrancy of Scripture, but forbidden to question the inerrancy of theologians, committees, and officials who are attempting to force the Synod into a latitudinarian straitjacket?

Change on Inerrancy

And since when does the *Lutheran Witness* applaud modernistic journals (*Presbyterian Outlook*), particularly when the latter blatantly attack the infallibility of the Bible? Do not such shocking manifestations impart a ring of cynicism to the everlastingly repeated assurances that the Synod has not changed, that its' doctrinal position remains the same, etc.? Well it is changing! In 1891 a Dr. Ruperti had left his pastoral conference in Europe on the grounds that the theses proposed for consideration (Kier's rejection of the orthodox doctrine of inspiration and inerrancy, in language very similar to Dr. M. Scharlemann's!) were not debatable in the Lutheran church. Dr. Pieper, writing in *Lehre und Wehre*, strongly commended Dr. Ruperti's stand, particularly his realization that such positions are not debatable (*nicht discutierbar*) among Lutherans (July, 1891, pp.13 ff.)! And now the official organ of a Synod which claims not to have changed, referring to a modernistic article with the suggestive title, "Do We Need an Infallible Bible?" not only exhorts its readers to favor "having such questions discussed," but even asserts that "the substance of the argument" (i.e. of the modernistic article) "certainly has worth in itself!" If this is not a "change," nothing is! Will that sort of thing be retracted? Do responsible officials actually read and think about such articles? Or will we be expected to pacify ourselves with the "insight" that the whole thing is not at all a matter of doctrine, but purely one of "theology," and that while the doctrine remains the same, we must tolerate this sort of subversive propaganda because, after all, theology is "a disturbing science"? (The more disturbing the more scientific?)And will this evasion be considered "courageous, responsible churchmanship"? Appeasement, latitudinarianism—and let us face it, this is what is meant —are cowardly, irresponsible, and dishonest. It is ludicrous to portray them in heroic roles. Genuine theological courage and responsibility speak a different language. And if that is ever put into practice, it will be found infinitely more "disturbing" than those sophisticated tickling-systems with which neology now satisfies "itching ears" (2 Tim. 4:3)!

Hard Line vs. Soft Line

The situation as portrayed by the three items reviewed is grave indeed. The disease has advanced so far that it appears to have destroyed the patient's awareness of it! Much will depend on how the new Commission on Theology and Church Relations conceives of "courageous, responsible churchmanship". It would appear that the Commission has essentially two alternatives: It must decide to pursue either a "hard line" or else a "soft line" policy toward the growing Missouri liberalism. The "hard line" would mean that neology is recognized for what it is, and that formulations are developed which can and will be used to bring about organizational separation between the orthodox and the neologists. This is Missouri's only hope, though that course of action becomes daily more difficult. The "soft line" would mean endless talk and no action, much barking, but no bite! It would mean recognizing the neologists' right to synodical membership. And this is the essence of Church-destroying unionism, latitudinarianism, indifferentism! (It is ironic that the major American Protestant denominations were delivered into the hands of the Modernists not by officials and leaders who were personally Modernists, but by such as were personally "conservative," but, for lack of vision and/or courage, followed the path of least resistance, i.e. latitudinarianism church politics and it is not for nought that mankind has generally treated overt enemies more leniently than collaborators!) Nor can the choice between these two courses of action be postponed much longer. Latitudinarianism is of such a nature that an abstention means the same as a vote for it! A thorough, sober, responsible approach can never mean postponement of the cure —no matter how ideal in theory—until after the patient's demise! Confessional Christians throughout the world are praying ardently that the Missouri Synod may yet be spared that dreadful fate, toward which at the moment she is moving so inexorably! May God guide the important Commission on Theology! Its task is difficult enough now; but before long it may be impossible! "Arise, O Lord; let not man prevail" (Ps. 9:19)!

—K. Marquart

1. The real issues were _____ by the *Lutheran Witness*.
2. The "life-and-death struggle" in the LCMS was presented as _____.
3. The Commission on Theology and Church Relations cannot hope to serve as an instrument of reform if _____.
4. Once an orthodox formula has been agreed upon then there is no need _____.
5. What we need is a few clear _____.
6. Neo-Orthodoxy is exerting its right to _____ in the Missouri Synod.
7. If "science" denotes certain knowledge, ___ is the only perfect science on earth.
8. True humility means _____.
9. When is a theologian responsible? _____
10. The *Lutheran Witness* advocated _____.
11. The Missouri Synod is now open to those who only have a ___ ruler to measure things.
12. It is allowed to question the ___ of Scripture but not the ___ of theologians.
13. The "soft line" means endless _____ and no _____.

* *Editor's Note: "Text and Authority: Theological and Hermeneutical Reflections on a Plastic Text", an essay Concordia Seminary, St. Louis Professor Jeffrey Kloha presented in November, 2013 in Oberursel, Germany, and "Responses from Rev. Jack Cascione, Dr. John Warwick Montgomery, and Rev. Brandt Klawitter", are in a 42 page pamphlet published by Christian News. Cascione, Montgomery, and Klawitter maintain that Kloha's position is contrary to Scripture and the Lutheran Confessions. The faculty of the St. Louis seminary, its Board of Regents, Presidium, and Council of Presidents of the Lutheran Church-Missouri Synod found Kloha's essay acceptable.*

GREAT EXPECTATIONS

Christian News, August 26, 1963

It is safe to predict that certain publications, which need not be named right away, will regard the Helsinki Assembly of the Lutheran World Federation as a welcome excuse for redoubling their missionary zeal in behalf of that body. We may brace ourselves for impassioned pleas, particularly on two themes: (1) The LWF has changed; and (2) We must join in order to "witness."

Has the LWF Changed?

The writer left Helsinki prior to the final sessions, and therefore cannot report on the fate of the proposed constitutional amendments. The most significant of these were the inclusion in the "doctrinal basis" of the words, "confess the Apostles', Nicene, and Athanasian Creeds," and the substitution of the word "further" for "bear" in the phrase "bear joint witness".

Both of these changes are purely verbal. The former will change or reduce LWF membership as little as the latter will change or reduce LWF functions. The reality behind the re-decorated verbal facade will remain exactly the same. This was made very clear to the present writer in one of the official discussion groups. "What is the practical meaning of the statement that the LWF 'confesses', say, the Athanasian Creed?" we asked. "Does this mean that a follower of Bultmann, who regards the substance of the Athanasian Creed as just so much mythology, will no longer be permitted, say, to represent the LWF in anyway?" The chairman, in reply, gave as his opinion that if Bultmann cared to come, and if his church would send him, he would be welcome! And in any case, wouldn't it be interesting to have him?

But what sort of "confessing" is this, which allows mythological "Interpretation"? A Hindu could "confess" the Creed that way too! The fact is that despite all the talk about a common "confession" (understood purely formally), the LWF is a welter of theological camps without real inner unity.

The second change ("bear" to "further") seems calculated to meet the objection that the LWF functions directly as a church. But changing one word won't meet the objection! Helsinki, in fact, beside consolidating and centralizing its administrative structure, also considerably strengthened and confirmed the churchly character of the LWF. "The Nature of the Lutheran World Federation," an official pamphlet issued by the Theological Commission, clearly and repeatedly concedes the "churchly character" of the functions of the LWF. Prof. W. Clifford Nelson's lecture, "The One Church and the Lutheran Churches" takes for granted the essential one-ness of the member churches and urges ever greater outward manifestation of this unity. The Assembly itself was to resolve that the Executive Committee ask such member churches as are not in fellowship with others, to state their reasons. Originally, the proposal had included an affirmative side, to ask who was in fellowship with whom. But the negative version was recommended because, as it was explained, church-fellowship between all Lutheran churches was to be taken for granted as self-evident, only the exception to be noted!

At this point one ought to marinate again a rather persistent "red herring": In answer to the charge that the LWF acts as church, it is argued passionately that the LWF is not, administratively a "super-church", but a federation! That is tediously irrelevant. Take for example a statement so typical of the argument in the "Nature" pamphlet: "The LWF cannot force its member churches to do anything." Very well, but could one not say the same thing about the Missouri Synod? Could one not argue: "Missouri is not a super-church, which can force its member congregations to do anything. It is only advisory, discharging only such tasks as are assigned to it by the congregations. Therefore it is a federation of congregations, a synod, not a church!" (Or The U.S.A. is not a country or nation, because it is a federation of states!)

Since when is churchliness measured in terms of the ability to coerce? For Anglicans the concept "Church" may mean a certain administrative structure. Lutherans should be free of this superstition. Churchly functions imply churchly nature, whatever the external arrangement. And the LWF is bound to become more not less churchly in its functions!

"Witness"

Let us this time not belabor the obvious by arguing that to join a syncretistic ecclesiastical body is to cancel, by virtue of the very act and fact, whatever verbal "witness" one may later imagine oneself to be giving. Illegitimate foundations simply cannot support anything legitimate.

Let us, however, raise another issue: It will presumably be publications like *The Cresset* and *The American Lutheran* which will pontificate most about "witnessing", (If *The Lutheran Witness* should schizophrenically join the chorus, we might simply ask: "Sayest thou this of thyself, or..?") The question which these journals ought to be asked is this: "What have you contributed toward a positive witness for Scripture and Confession?" It is ironic that the "witness" of the very journals which are habitually the loudest in demanding "witness," has been, on the whole, false witness, that is, compromise with liberalism!

If Missouri's "witness" depends on these gentry then that which they would no doubt be pleased to call "dialogue" with the LWF would, upon close inspection, turn out to be the usual monotonous monologue of the established, respectable Discussion-game, which knows no divine truths or doctrines, but only questions, problems, concerns, emphases, insights; interpretations, etc.

From this, good Lord, deliver us!

K.E.M.

1. Is the LWF open to theologians like Bultmann? ____
2. The LWF is a welter of ____ without any ____.

3. Is the LWF not a church because it calls itself a federation? ____
4. The "witness" of The American Lutheran and *Cresset* has on the whole been ____.

MEDITATION ON A TOWER

The Lutheran News, June 13, 1966

Some recent issues of LUTHERAN NEWS and a Luther Tower publicity packet arrived here just in time to combine with the star of the Gospel for Exaudi (John 15:26-16:4) into one brilliant conjunction of meaning.

So Concordia Seminary finally celebrated its architectural coronation! And on the very day in May when the Red Slave Empire observes its annual ghoulish war-dances! It was Luther, thundering against the modern Pope and Turk: "The Word shall stand despite all foes!"

Or was he? Symbolically, yes. But what of the reality? Does Concordia Seminary still have a right to have a Luther Tower — or even only a Walther Arch? Does it still teach the theology for which it was built and dedicated?

Alas, another spirit now seems to dominate those beautiful buildings! Almost every week new and ever more shocking evidence appears that God's Word is now hated and despised where once it reigned supreme! Through a thousand cracks the New Theology is oozing in—or out?! Exploratory essays, secret essays, ambiguous "formulations," endless explanations, evasions, excuses, procedures, prevarications! And while the theological obscenities go unrebuked year after year, swift denunciations and defamations follow any Confessional protest, John 16:2!

Thank God, the pious mask is at last being torn off all this hypocrisy. While the new Luther Tower stands helplessly enveloped in nebulous theology and unctuous rhetoric about "the Word," the "Gospel," and soon, an increasing number of men whose lives are commemorated there are beginning to wake up to the frightful reality. A pastoral conference resolving to tell all to their people, because they can see that the errors are not being corrected; a professor, like Jeremiah of old, giving an "Honest Answer" with all the fiery eloquence of an outraged conscience; a rising school of intelligent young theologians refusing to hold on, superstitiously, to the tails of all the important liberal sacred cows: all these are signs that the hour of decision is coming. At last silence will be impossible, even in high places.

Dishonesty of Pretending

Cannot the Silent Service see the dishonesty of pretending that no one is teaching false doctrine, when the very C.T.M. lends itself to such obvious attacks on Scripture as Dr. A.C. Piepkorn's "What Does 'Inerrancy' Mean?" (September, 1965)?

The arguments of that article have been sufficiently answered by Dr. Montgomery and others. I will add only two footnotes. First, Dr. Piepkorn has embedded in his article, toward the end, a conscientious scruple which, if taken seriously, would bring down his whole essay like a house of cards. He cautions against violating, for fear of "being classified as obscurantists . . . our Lord's words, 'Whosoever is ashamed of Me and of My words in this adulterous and sinful generation, of him will the Son of Man be ashamed when He comes in the glory of His Father with the holy angels' (Matthew 8:38)." Dr. Piepkorn does something very remarkable here, which no opponent of Inerrancy in our circles has as yet done: he introduces a Scriptural, a prior argument, a genuine theological leaven, which if allowed to leaven the whole lump, would destroy the entire objection to Inerrancy! The rest of the article, to be sure, is the usual approach, trying to resolve the Inerrancy issue on the basis of a posteriori human observation, impression, research, etc. Yet if we are truly not ashamed of such words of the Son of Man as John 3:12 and John 10:35, then we must accept the Scripture as inerrant on its own testimony and authority, before and without any scholarly inquiries into alleged errors and contradictions. Secondly, Dr. Piepkorn's forte is of course the Lutheran Confessions, it is therefore particularly disappointing that he does not do justice to them. While admitting that "Lutheran clergymen and professors affirm... everything that the Lutheran symbols say about the Sacred Scriptures," Dr. Piepkorn plays irrelevantly with the word "vocable," and stages an elaborate safari into The Oxford English Dictionary, but studiously avoids telling us specifically what the Symbols do in fact say about the Sacred Scriptures. He says merely that "the freedom of the Sacred Scriptures from error is largely an un-articulated assumption of undefined scope"!

Special Pleading

Now that is special pleading with a vengeance! With Dr. Piepkorn's well-known penchant for almost pedantically meticulous citations of the ipsissima verba, particularly of the Symbolical Books, he had no right to omit to tell us, for example, that Luther's *Large Catechism* says with all due articulation: "God's Word can neither lie nor deceive" ("Gottes Wort kann nicht feilen," "nec potest errare nec fallere," Baptism, 57)!

And there, in the Latin, we have even the very "vocable" which, together with the negative prefix "in" (see Oxford Dictionary) gives us our word "inerrant"!

Now suppose that the Catechism had said: "God's Word can both lie and deceive." Undoubtedly this quotation would then be cast in our teeth with maddening regularity in English, German, and Latin, at every mention of Inerrancy! But since it says the opposite, it must be muted into "a largely unarticulated assumption"! This is tendentious "Haggadah," not an objective exposition of the Lutheran Confessions.

Some of Dr. Piepkorn's colleagues, working in the very shadow of the Luther Tower, have published even more blatant attacks upon the Bible and the Reformation. And then there are the River Forest essays.

And the official fury? It spends itself largely in a cowardly castigation of those who refuse to be dumb dogs or to cry "Peace, peace," when there is no peace.

Is Missouri imitating the suicide of the Anglican Church?

Malcolm Muggeridge, in his "The Dying Cult of the Church of England" hits pretty close to home when he writes of "Honorable and Right Honorable Members ardent for the Thirty-Nine Articles embodying (as the Royal Warrant puts it) 'the true Doctrine of the Church of England agreeable to God's Word,' about which they know nothing, and care less, and which few of the bishops and clergy on whose behalf they are legislating any longer even pretend to believe, though all have solemnly assented to them to become ordained.

"A ribald scene indeed. Who would ever suppose that a secular enterprise so conducted could possibly thrive or, for that matter, be permissible? Current professional and even business standards would preclude acceptance of a salaried post on the strength of a consciously fraudulent declaration" (THE BULLETIN, Sydney, Feb. 19, 1966, p . 32).

When WILL You Speak Up

To overlook and ignore all this, to excuse, cover up, and protect this shamelessly massive assault upon the very foundations of the Church, and then to name the tower of the very institution which prides itself on its confusion of tongues, after the great Reformer, is surely to invoke upon oneself the terrible woe spoken against those who "build the tombs of the prophets and adorn the monuments of the righteous" (Matthew 23:29)!

Pastors, professors, officials — you who still have a conscience — when will you speak up? How long can you keep silent—and still save your souls? Cut through the slimy cobweb of lies! Take a stand, and be interiorly free again! Imitate Our Savior in rejecting "influence" purchased at the price of even one moments' adoration of Satan, Mat. 4:9ff!

Perhaps you will lose an official position. But think of your joy on the Day of Judgement, when you will be excused from the "special ceremony for dignitaries from the Greater Jerusalem area?"!

1. Does Concordia Seminary still have a right to have a ____ Tower or ____ arch?
2. Another spirit seems to dominate ____.
3. What follows any Confessional protest? ____
4. Dr. A.C. Piepkorn attacked ___ in the September 1965 CTM.
5. Piepkorn does not do justice to ____.
6. Luther's *Large Catechism* says "God's Word can ____."

CHRISTIAN GIVING

Christian News, January 29, 1968

Not just any kind of giving, even if the amount is large, is pleasing to God. In God's Word He tells us what is pleasing to Him. And it is the duty of the Church to instruct us in that Word, as it applies to all areas of Christian life. And giving is no exception. See also Appendix A: "Should the Church Mention Money?"

I. Why?

Why give? What is the right reason and motive? That is the basic issue.

Answer:

1. Gratitude:

It is evil to give to God's Church merely because men expect it of us, in other words for the sake of men, to satisfy them, "so they won't bother us." It is better to give out of duty to God. But giving is still not pleasing to God if viewed as a grim and glum duty. What pleases Him is if we gladly offer of our possessions OUT OF GRATITUDE AND LOVE FOR GOD! He is pleased when we serve Him with our money BECAUSE we know that He is everything and we are nothing; BECAUSE He created us, gave us life and blesses, and provides for us; BECAUSE He came to earth after we had rejected Him, and gave Himself as a ransom for our sin; and BECAUSE His Spirit through Word and sacrament freely works and sustains in us faith in the Redemption of Christ, through Whom we have pardon, peace, joy, life, truth, and every blessing, and God Himself, for time and for eternity. Here are a thousand good reasons for sacrificing to Him of our possessions.

2. God's Needs:

God as He is in Himself, of course, has no needs, much less does He need anything here on His created earth, Psalm 50:12. But God has made the needs of men — and especially of His children — His own needs, and desires that we should serve Him by serving them, St. Matthew 25:35-45. WHAT SWEET AND THRILLING PRIVILEGES AND WHAT AWFUL RESPONSIBILITIES LIE HIDDEN IN THAT MYSTERIOUS SENTENCE: "Ye have done it unto Me!"

The greatest need of humanity is not physical — though this too must not be forgotten — but spiritual. Men need above all the holy Gospel in Word and Sacrament, so that their immortal souls may be regenerated and kept alive for Eternity. The Church has the God-given task to spread and administer the God-given Gospel, and she has the God-given right to receive financial support for her institutions, which cost money! 1 Cor. 9:14, Gal. 6:6,7.

The Church could and should be doing a hundred times more than she is, but there is not sufficient man-power, nor sufficient money! Unless Christians are generous for Christ, the Church must beg and plead to just barely meet minimum needs. But what must unbelievers and scoffers think of the Christians and their Church when they see her begging and pleading for a pittance, while sky rocketing billions are lavished on luxuries and entertainments? If necessary, the Church will beg and plead — for she must care more for the honor of Christ than for her own dignity — but let us see that it becomes unnecessary!

II. What?

What, then, is Christian giving, and how should it be regarded?

Answer:

1. Worship

The only correct view of giving is that our offerings are part of our worship, our service to God.

God saved us by His Gospel, not simply that we might sit and wait for eternity, but that we might be "an holy priesthood, to offer up spiritual sacrifices," 1 Peter 2:5. The whole life of Christians, as priests of God, is a "living sacrifice," Romans 12:1. And since much of our life has to do with money, it must be included in our life of sacrifice. To be sure, it is a small part of our worship, compared to such other spiritual sacrifices as faith itself, patience and forgiveness toward others for Christ's sake, the incense of public and private devotion to God, and so on. But just because money is small and mean compared to the really great things in the Christian life, let no one imagine that money doesn't matter:

He that is faithful in that which is least is faithful also in much; and he that is unjust in the least, is unjust also in much, and if therefore ye have not been faithful in the unrighteous mammon, who will commit to your trust the true riches? Says our Lord, St. Luke 16:10-11.

Since giving is part of our worship, this fact receives recognition at the Liturgy: Our gifts are brought to the Altar, and there sacrificed to God, in love and gratitude, together with all that we are and have:

"Receive, O God, our bodies and souls, our hearts and minds, our talents and powers, together with the offerings we bring before Thee, for Thou hast purchased us to be Thine own." (General Prayer)

Our money is merely a small and humble token, which represents our whole being, at the Altar. And is it not fitting that the symbols of our sell-sacrifice should be brought to that place from where we receive all the unspeakable gifts of God, His Word, His Absolution, His Benediction, and Himself, in His body and blood? Since "without faith it is impossible to please Him," (Hebrews (11:6) even large amounts given without faith, are offensive to God. But the smallest mite, given by a child of God, is hallowed by the sacrifice of Christ, and therefore precious, dear and pleasing in His sight! Only let it be offered in faith, as worship!

2. Christian giving is therefore NOT:

"Paying Dues":
As if the Church of God were a club, where a fee entitles us to membership or rights! To a man who thought he could purchase spiritual rights from God and His Church, St. Peter declared, in the Name of God: "Thy money perish with thee... Repent" (Acts 8:21 ff.)

Membership in the Church costs nothing and it costs everything: Nothing, because the humblest beggar is welcome to all the riches of Christ's grace, without payment or charge, Isaiah 55:1 ff.; and everything, because the whole life of Christians becomes a living sacrifice. To withhold anything is to "step outside one's Baptism," to deny Christ as Lord. And no man can have Christ for a Savior if he refuses to have Him for his Lord! Whoever does not wish to belong to Him entirely, cannot belong to Him at all, for "ye cannot serve God and mammon," St. Matthew 6:24.

"Meeting a Budget":
Meeting the budget should be the result, not the purpose of our giving. The budget is a bare minimum. Our gift should reflect our love for Christ, not our calculation of church-expenditure. And though we know that a portion of our gift will be used for the most menial church-maintenance items, such as painting or plumbing, we dare not look even upon this portion as a cold cash transaction, a mere payment of bills, for even the most menial things are sacred in Christ! Zion it is said: "Thy servants take pleasure in her stones, and favor the dust thereof," Psalm 102:14. And shall we not cherish those dear "stones" within which the life-giving Word and Sacraments are celebrated?

"Envelope-filling":
To throw some left-overs into an envelope, just because it needs to be used somehow, is certainly a grievous insult to God. He does not want careless and thoughtless service, mere habit. Much less does He want leftovers. The first and choicest portion belongs to Him. Perhaps it is significant that of Cain we read merely that he "brought of the fruit of the ground an offering unto the Lord." But of Abel we read that be brought of the "firstlings of his flock," Gen. 4.

Our sealed Pledge card is to be an aid to us in approaching the whole matter thoughtfully and with care, and not leaving it to chance or easy habit.

III. How Much?

In the Old Testament, the faithful were commanded by God to give the tithe (10 per cent) of their net income to the Church. Compare Malachi 3:8-12, and note especially the promise of blessing for compliance, and the threat of the divine curse for non-compliance.

In the New Testament we are not bound by the ceremonial law. But shall we, who have the greater gifts from God, serve Him less zealously than His Old Testament people? The tithe is a good starting point. And many Christians tithe, and find joy and blessing in the practice, even material blessing. But we must remember that material gain must never be a purpose in our giving — else it is mockery — though it may please God to give it to us as a result.

In determining how much we shall allot to God through His Church, we must not think of our "fair share," because that is a form of merely "meeting the budget." In our giving we must forget about others, how much they are or should be doing. We must not think, for example, that if the budget is $100, and there are 100 members, our "fair share" is $1. If I am a poor widow, living with others, without any income, even $1 is too much. But if I am a prosperous farmer or businessman and earn thousands per year, even $100 is too little under some circumstances. It all depends. We shall not make any laws for one another.

Whatever our situation, St. Paul writes: "Upon the first day of the week let every one of you lay by him in store, as God has prospered him," I Cor. 16:1. In other words, we are to give in proportion to our income. In every case it should be a sacrifice; and giving away what we don't need anyway is not a sacrifice.

This is where the Pledge card comes in. It is to help us to make our giving orderly, and thoughtful, rather than haphazard. At the beginning of the year, estimate the income for that year, then prayerfully and conscientiously decide what proportion of that is going directly to God through His Church. Then record the figure on the card, put it in the envelope, seal it, and bring it to church, so that it may remain at the Altar through the year. No one else will ever look at it. It is between you and God. At the end of the year, it is returned, and you can compare your promise with your performance. And if anyone does not wish to use the cards, that is his privilege, but it doesn't excuse him from Christian giving, along with the rest of us.

The Pledge Card is not a trick to get more money, but an aid to a responsible, serious outlook on giving ...

As regards the principle of pledging, consider... God's people in the Old Testament made vows to Him: and those vows were acceptable to Him.

Vows in general: Ps. 66:13 - "I will pay Thee my vows."; Ps. 50:14 - "Offer unto God thanksgiving and pay thy vows unto the most High." and others.

Specific vows: Numbers 6:2 ff.: The Nazirites; Gen. 28:20 ff: Jacob vows tenth part of his goods; I Sam. 1:11: Hannah vows to give her son to God; Ps. 132:1 ff: David vows to recover the Ark of Covenant; Numbers 21:2,3: Israel's vow to God, His acceptance;

It is true, that vows made to the Lord are not trifling matters, and that every effort should be made on our part to pay them — see Eccles. 5:4,5; Numbers 30:2,3; Job 22:27.

It is also true that we should not vow in uncertain or foolish things where we have no promise of God's support — e.g. Jepthah, Judges 11:30; Herod and John the Baptist.

But giving to the Lord is not without clear commands and promises to God; moreover, it is an indication of our love for God and our faith and trust in Him.

We do not hesitate to make solemn promises to the Lord in other matters of faith and conduct — though we know that we are altogether insufficient of ourselves to keep these promises: e.g., in Baptism, at Confirmation; at Confession and the Lord's Supper, etc.

Ought we not, then, to emulate Jacob and boldly and trustingly make our vows to Him, looking to Him in faith to provide us with the ability and the wherewithal to fulfill them?

May Our Gracious Savior direct our hearts and minds to serve Him well in this matter as in all others, may He daily bless us, and daily cleanse us from sin. And "to him that knoweth to do good and doeth it not, to him it is sin," James 4:17. Amen.

CONCLUSION:

Appendix A

"Should the Church Mention Money?"
Yes, because God's Word does!

Some people are (rightly) so disgusted with financial racketeering in the name of religion, that they are (wrongly) annoyed and suspicious at any mention of money in the Church. Now, it is true that in our age of specialization even the matter of church-contributions has become a profitable business! There are large commercial organizations — strictly profit-making business corporations mind you — which exist for the sole purpose of organizing church-contributions! But they are not the real evil. The real evil is the spiritual bankruptcy and the lack of character and sell-respect shown by those churches which allow holy things to be made a matter of business. They might as well employ professional (non-Christian) organizations to organize church-attendance, or perhaps even develop charity and patience among the members! The whole thing is an insult to the Church, an abandonment of her sacred rights, prerogatives, and duties, to the world. Imagine St. Paul asking non-Christian outsiders, pagans, Jews, or heretics, to come into his churches, for a fee of course, to organize "Christian giving"!

The "fund-raising" organizations have developed "techniques" which, they claim, can be equally effective in all churches AND SYNAGOGUES! In other words, there is nothing Christian about these "techniques." They are simply psychological devices (not to say tricks) to get more money out of people, on the same general basis as we are daily (and successfully) exhorted to buy this or that soap, cigarette, or toilet paper! The principled

Christian cannot but regard the whole enterprise as a rather cynical affair, calculated not to make people better Christians (where? in synagogues?) but, as the appeals put it quite openly, to "double or treble the budget!" And how foolish to think that something is good merely because it is successful! The principle, not the amount, matters!

Churches can — and do — practice financial racketeering even without employing outside agencies, simply by copying their methods. A publication in an American Lutheran Synod complains: "Men in the field complain that they cannot do the Lord's work locally because so much work, mostly that of raising money, has to be done for Synod. Some pastors and parish finance committees go so far as to say, 'We have become revenue collectors for Synod!'" Some "stewardship" literature leaves the horrible impression that "spiritual life" is being measured directly by the budget, and worse, that what worries the writers is not the low state of "spiritual life" itself, but the low state of finances, and that the improvement of the former is desired not for its own sake, but as a means for raising the latter!

Does this mean that the Church of Christ should not mention money? Quite on the contrary! The more men abuse money, the more she must teach them the right use of it. When the Pope teaches falsely concerning the Sacraments, for example, no one expects the Church to keep silent about Sacraments, but on the contrary, to teach the more vigorously about them, the more they are perverted by others. The same applies to Christian giving.

But when the Church of Christ says earnest things about money, she does so because she loves men and their souls, not because she covets their money. She must teach men the way of Christ, also in this matter. And she does it in the spirit of St. Paul, who said: "Not because I desire a gift: but I desire fruit that may abound to your account," Phil. 4:17.

May God preserve us all from greed! And may He be our Treasure!

Lay not for yourselves treasures upon Earth, where moth and rust doth corrupt, and where thieves break through and steal; but lay up for yourselves treasures in Heaven, where neither moth nor rust doth corrupt and where thieves do not break through nor steal; for where your treasure is, there will your heart be also! St. Matthew 6:19 ff.

1. What pleases God is if we offer our possession out of ____.
2. God has made the needs of men ____.
3. "Ye have done it unto ____.
4. The greatest need of humans is not ____ but ____.
5. Our offerings are part of our ____.
6. The whole of life of Christians, as priests of God, is ____.
7. Even the smallest mite, given by a child of God, is ____.
8. Membership in the Church costs ____ and it costs ____.
9. Meeting a budget should not be the ____ of our giving.
10. Our sealed pledge card should be ____.

11. The tithe is a good ____.
12. We are to give in ____ to or income.
13. The Pledge card is an aid ____.
14. Giving to the Lord is an indication of ____.
15. Should the Church mention money? ____
16. Should the Church use non-Christian outsiders to organize "Christian giving?" ____
17. Is something good merely because it is successful? ____

REFORMATION JUBILEE LECTURES
Review Article
By the Editor

Christian News, April 8, 1968

The Winter and Spring issues of *The Lutheran Synod Quarterly* contain the four Luther lectures which were delivered at Bethany Lutheran College, Mankato, Minnesota, on October 30 and 31, 1967. This presentation was a part of the Evangelical Lutheran Synod's observance of the 450th anniversary of the Reformation. The lecturer was Pastor Kurt Marquart of Toowoomba, Queensland, Australia. These lectures were designed for and delivered to pastors and lay people.

The first two lectures, entitled *The Word As Truth*, are presented in the Winter *Quarterly*. In them Pastor Marquart examines the matter of Revelation, Inspiration, Inerrancy, Hermeneutics.

According to Marquart, "Where people pay attention to substance rather than mere words, it will be readily admitted that inerrancy is not only implied but actually taught by the Lutheran Confessions. Consider the clear statements in the *Large Catechism*, Baptism, par. 57: 'Verbum Dei nec potest errare nec fallere' (God's Word can neither err nor deceive). Can anyone honestly interpret this as anything other than inerrancy? This little clause was far more relevant to Dr. A. C. Piepkorn's ostensible topic, 'What Does "Inerrancy" Mean?' (*Concordia Theological Monthly*, September, 1965) than wandering stars and other exotica he dug up. Yet it is not even mentioned!

"One of the strange, irrational factors haunting modern Lutheran discussions of inerrancy is an obsessive fear of being identified with 'Fundamentalism' and its alleged distortions. Why isn't there an even greater fear of being identified with liberalism and its apostasies? Attempts to 'avoid both extremes' usually result in a pietistically sugar-coated liberalism" (5).

Commenting on Jaroslav Pelikan's *Luther the Expositor*, a companion volume to the Concordia-Fortress American Edition of *Luther's Works*, Marquart notes that "Although the book SEEMS to be well documented, it is disproportionately short on facts and long on interpretation. Haziness results from an impressionistic treatment of evidence." Marquart quotes from a review by Dr. H. Hamann, Sr.: "As regards his general appraisal of Luther's theology. Dr. Pelikan is, to say it roundly, too greatly influenced by certain modern Luther scholars to be entirely reliable. For he has adopted the literary vice of some Luther Forscher who manage to walk, with eyes tightly closed, past dozens and hundreds of the clearest possible pronouncements of Luther in order to pitch and pounce upon some doubtful passage, on the strength of which they attempt to foist upon the Reformer teachings quite different from, and perhaps utterly opposed to, those which he actually professed and defended" (14).

It is regrettable that both seminaries of The Lutheran Church-Missouri Synod had to have Pelikan, an evolutionist, rather than an orthodox Lutheran theologian as one of their main speakers when they celebrated the 450th anniversary of the Reformation last October.

Marquart observes that "History shows that churches which have opened the doors to a figurative interpretation of Genesis, have lost their doctrinal substance. I know of not a single exception. Even authoritarian Rome has tasted the hermeneutical-dogmatic destruction that follows leaving 'the doctrine of Evolution an open question,' as Pius XII put it in *Humani Generis* of Oct. 12, 1950. This may baffle the historian, or strike him as purely co-incidental, but the theologians must see the necessary connections between the Genesis issue and the rest of Christian theology" (48). The Australian theologian points out that "When the origin and unity of the human race and the origin of original sin are shrouded in mythological fog, the clear contours of the Cross and the Resurrection soon disappear too. What meaning can the Atonement have if man, instead of having fallen from a state of original perfection, has actually been evolving toward such a state from animal origins? Christ the Redeemer becomes Christ the Example (as in de Chardin's 'Omega Point'), and the Gospel becomes Law! Those who mumble piously about seeing 'Law and Gospel' in Genesis, ought to bear this in mind." (50). Marquart claims that "Biblical theology, on the contrary, cannot surrender the facticity of Genesis without thereby committing suicide" (51).

He continues:

"All the issues raised by modern theology converge so massively on the Genesis question, that this matter, far from being a minor exegetical point, has in fact become the decisive battle ground of modern Lutheranism. It is a crisis pregnant with dogmatic, hermeneutical, ecclesiastical, and historical consequences of great magnitude. Such a decision cannot be made lightly. It will determine whether the Church of the Reformation can survive in our century, or whether it will repeat the other historic churches' tragic history of doctrinal dissolution. Compromise and accommodation are impossible. Either Christ must win, or Darwin, either the theology of creation or the mythology of evolution, either Biblical authority or scientistic 'naturalism,' either Christianity or atheism! Kyrie eleison!" (53).

Marquart concludes his first essay titled "Truth and/or Consequences": "Christ and His Scriptures or atheism: that is the real, honest choice. The seamless robe of Biblical Christianity will be either treasured or gambled away whole. But it cannot permanently be divided!" (58).

Our Roman Catholic readers should pay careful attention to what Marquart says in his second lecture on "The Church of The Augsburg Confession As The True Ecumenical Movement." The lecturer notes: "What must be seen clearly is that the biblical-evangelical strain which so impresses Lutherans, is only one element in Rome's theological revolution. The real direction of Vatican II was not towards this, but as the phrase *apertura a sinistra* implies, towards the latitudinarian type of 'Theology' represented by the World Council of Churches. And this is not really a theology, but a whole museum of theologies. Now, if you want a museum you will have to take one or two 'Lutheran' displays into the bargain. But they are as harmless as museum tigers!

"That this was the real direction of the Vatican Council is clear not only from the subsequent chaos, but from expressions at the Council itself. Thus a Mexican bishop described Freemasonry as 'an organization whose origins, as we know from history, are completely Christian, which still remains partially Christian, and is now renewing its Christian character,' and then suggested 'a reappraisal of the penalties decreed by the Church'.

"Rome's dogmatic confusion is particularly acute in Europe. In Holland, for example, leading Roman theologians have not only attacked transubstantiation, but, as the new *Dutch Catechism* shows, have begun a 'reinterpretation' of fundamentals like the Virgin Birth. The shift of emphasis from the facts of the Gospel to their 'meanings' is ominous. Indeed, it has been quipped that 'in Holland everything changes—except bread and wine'!"

"Where it will all end, no one can foresee. It behooves us to celebrate neither Rome's imagined acceptance of the Reformation, nor her present doctrinal chaos, which can only mean a frightful acceleration of Christendom's general plunge into dissolution" (69-70).

Marquart concludes his second lecture: "Whether the Vatican can absorb the World Council of Churches and transform itself in the process from 'the ghost of the Roman Empire sitting crowned upon the grave thereof (Hobbes) to a more modern ghost of a commonwealth of churches with the Pope as its figurehead, remains to be seen. But all signs seem to point in that direction. While naive and not so naive Lutherans look about them and cry incredulously, 'Where, where is this dreadful Super-Church?' they are at that very moment building it, and being built into it, through all those innocent looking federations now so popular! Whether it is LWF or LCUSA, NCC the illicit and unecumenical premise is everywhere the same: that Christian unity can come by way of **'Organizational Recognition Or Fractional Obedience To The One Lord'** (Franzmann)!

"And when the Behemoth Church shall at last stand before us complete, as a theologically ever looser but organizationally ever more centralized federal structure in which everyone may believe and teach; as he pleases — except for the heresy of 'separatism' – will that be the one united Church of Christ? No, it will be the great Counter-Church, of Babylon, of Rev. 17!" (102-103).

"Lutherans should be the last to be deceived by this fraud. For it was Luther who saw the issue so clearly: 'The holy Church of Christ speaks thus: I BELIEVE one holy Christian Church; the mad church of the Pope speaks thus: I SEE one holy Christian Church.'

"In these last days of sore distress, when the Word of God is crowded out of the Holy Place more and more by secular abominations of desolation, the Church of the Augsburg Confession has a unique opportunity to teach men to talk by faith and not by sight, to seek Christ's Church by

42

her pure Marks, and not to be misled by masks. When men find the Shepherd — by His pure Voice (St. John 10)—they have also found the Sheepfold. But if they look merely for sheep, they may follow a wolf unawares into the valley of the shadow of death. To proclaim Christ's Life-giving Voice, to be a humble but incorruptible stewardess of His mysteries, this is the massively ecumenical task of the Church of the Augsburg Confession. In fulfilling it faithfully she is in fact the true Ecumenical Movement of our time. This is her grace and her glory — but also her judgment!" (102-104).

We urge our readers to write to Bethany Seminary, Mankato, Minnesota, for all four of these *Reformation Jubilee Lectures*. We know of no published lectures, sermons, or essays delivered in connection with the 450th anniversary of the Reformation which can equal these lectures.

1. Where people pay attention to substance rather than mere words, it will be readily admitted that ____.

2. What did Marquart say about Piepkorn's "What Does 'Inerrancy' Mean"? ____

3. Attempts to avoid the "extremes" of Fundamentalism and Liberalism generally result in a ____.

4. Marquart said that Pelikan's *Luther the Expositor* is ____.

5. Marquart showed that history has shown that churches which have opened the door to a figurative interpretation of Genesis have lost ____.

6. "Biblical theology" cannot surrender the facticity of Genesis without ____.

7. What has become the decisive battle ground of modern Lutheranism? ____

8. The real direction of Vatican II was toward ____.

9. It behooves us to celebrate neither Rome's imagined ____ nor her ____.

10. Lutherans should be the last to be deceived by ____.

11. The holy Church of Christ says ___ one holy Christian Church, the mad church of the Pope says ___.

12. When men find the Shepherd by His clear voice they have also found the ____.

13. What is the massive ecumenical task of the true Ecumenical Movement of our time? ____

THE MEANING OF THEOLOGICAL DISCUSSION IN LCUSA

Christian News, October 28, 1968

(Hon. Pres. F. W. Noack and Pastor K. Marquart, Toowoomba, Australia)

When the Detroit Convention (1965) of The Lutheran Church-Missouri Synod decided reluctantly to join with the American Lutheran Church (ALC) and the Lutheran Church in America (LCA) in forming the Lutheran Council in the U.S.A. (LCUSA), the main argument for the venture was that this was a wonderful opportunity for theological discussion among the churches involved, and that it could lead to Dr. C.F.W. Walther's dream of one orthodox Evangelical Lutheran Church in North America.

The official report on LCUSA, prepared by Drs. Martin H. Franzmann and Alfred O. Fuerbringer, and published in the CTM [1] prior to the 1965 Convention, was jubilant in its optimism:

One thing is very clear: theology, the study and discussion of the Gospel in all its fullness and all its meaning for the life of the church, will be in the center of things. The proposed constitution lists among the "Purposes and Objectives" of the organization:

    a) To further the witness, the work, and the interests of the participating bodies.

    b) To seek to achieve theological consensus (that is, a full agreement and a common will and purpose concerning the Gospel) in a systematic and continuing way on the basis of the Scriptures and the witness of the Lutheran Confessions.

And the constitution expressly states (Art. R, Sec. 3) that "all the participating bodies shall take part in the Division of Theological Studies," whereas each participating body may or may not participate in any of the other activities of the council.

This gives us a wonderful opportunity....The new emphasis on theology in the proposed council looks like an answer to our prayers...We shall be heard by them in a way that we have not been heard before and shall be able to share with fellow Lutherans those theological gifts which God has given us.

The time has now come to begin a preliminary assessment of these expectations in the light of LCUSA's actual performance to date.

From September 10 to September 23, 1967 four conferences were held in various parts of the United States under the sponsoring of LCUSA's Division of Theological Studies. The theme was "Christology," and a total of about 120 people participated in the discussion of ten essays, prepared by theologians of the three main member churches. Among the essayists were the well known Drs. Martin Heinecken (Philadelphia, LCA), Herbert J. A. Bouman (St. Louis, Missouri Synod), and Alvin N. Rogness (St.

Paul, ALC).

We have not seen any of these essays. Apparently they were not mass-distributed. What did receive wide circulation, however, and that free of charge, was a 36-pp. summarizing booklet, entitled *Who Can This Be?... Studies in Christology*, and published as "a guide to study and discussion" by the Division of Theological Studies of LCUSA. (Reproduced in August 26, 1968 *Christian News*, ed.)

One gains the impression that the essays behind the booklet represented a fairly wide range of theological positions, which have not been reconciled, and probably were not intended to be reconciled, in the study guide. The doctrinal substance of the latter therefore resembles the camel, of which a wag remarked that it is the animal that looks as if it has been put together by a committee.

No one who is at all acquainted with the work of Prof. Bouman can doubt that at least his essay, "The Significance of the Dogma Concerning Christ as Defined by the Council of Chalcedon," represented orthodox Christology. Indeed, a few statements of an orthodox background have survived into the final study document. The strongest examples are probably these, from p. 28:

> The Redeemer redeemed, not only in the sense that he was divine and his work was then infinite, or in the sense that he was human and his work was therefore meritorious, but primarily because these two possibilities were united in one person...

> We, of course, believe that the crucified and risen Christ is eternally present everywhere.

Yet not even these statements are unambiguous, particularly in the strange light of this, on p. 30: "Christ—in the sum totality of his being—has risen. Even as the death of Christ upon the cross was total, so was the resurrection. Even now the two natures cannot be separated." This seems to suggest not the truth that by virtue of the Personal Union, Mary was the Mother of God, that God died on the Cross, etc., but the idea that Christ's "divine nature" itself and as such could and did die and rise again!

It is noticeable that the booklet avoids, except by way of quotation from traditional creedal material, the direct assertion that Christ is God. Instead, we have the ambiguous formula "God in Christ."

The title of Dr. Heinecken's essay, "In Defense of Chalcedon," sounds good, but its Barth oriented modern champion is not likely to have led the ancient Council to anything but a Pyrrhic victory. Although the Chalcedonian definition receives some compliments in the summarizing treatise, and is even printed in full, a line of criticism recurs which in principle reduces the classical Christology to irrelevant verbiage. The point of the criticism is that traditional Christology was based on ancient Greek philosophy and therefore requires some sort of modern Umdeutung. Thus, the "orientation" of the Chalcedonian creed is said to be "ontological rather than functional, and the whole is explicated in concepts borrowed from the world of Greek metaphysical thought" (p.15).

This talk about "ontological" vs. "functional" approaches strongly suggests the position taken by Dr. Joseph Sittler (LCA) in his 1954 *Lutheran Quarterly* article, "A Christology of Function."Sittler argued there that the traditional two-nature doctrine was based on the ancient Greek metaphysics of substances and needed to lie restated in "functional" terms. For example, Christ's "pre-existence" might be taken to mean that the knowledge of the man Jesus existed in God's mind from all eternity, but that Jesus did not exist as a person before His human birth! In other words, Christ's "divinity" is but a Ritschlian Werturteil ("value judgment"), applied to Jesus "honoris causa," as Dr. F. Pieper used to remark.

Taken as a whole, the LCUSA study booklet lends itself much more easily to an interpretation along Sittler's lines, than, say, Bouman's. Indeed, the Preface, written by the Executive Secretary and the Assistant Executive Secretary of the Division of Theological Studies, apologizes for the few traces of traditional Christology evident in the booklet:

> It has been hoped that the presentations and discussions would develop a particularly sharp accent on the humanity of Christ and its relationship to the new humanism which is blossoming in contemporary society. However, these program hopes were not entirely realized. The primary focus of attention still fell on the divinity of Christ rather than on his humanity (p. 6).

If the following statements are not meant to lead in Sittler's direction, then what do they mean?

> In ancient times it was also possible to have a rather clear and precise concept of what divinity meant. Today this has been shaken, shaken perhaps primarily by the theologians ...rather than conclude that Jesus was divine because he conformed to a preconceived notion of divinity, we must follow precisely the opposite tack, recognizing that it is he who actually serves as our definition of God. If this is true, then the need for clarification between humanity and divinity certainly has not been diminished. But at the same time the possibility of the sharp polarity that was characteristic of more scholastic eras in the Christian church can no longer he maintained (p. 11).

The Jews understood Christ much better, when they stoned Him for claiming that "God was his Father, making himself equal with God" (Jn. 5:18) and for "being a man" yet making Himself "God" (Jn. 10:33). Certainly the expression "equal with God" implies a "preconceived notion of divinity." To say that Jesus "actually serves vague rhetoric not to be taken literally, or else it expresses "Christian atheism," the idea that no personal God exists, but that the "divinity" of Christ is simply His perfect humanity!

Indeed, something like this is suggested by the following statements, which can be harmonized with orthodox Christology, if at all, then only by being regarded as some sort of poetic paradoxes devoid of logical substance:

> George S. Hendry affirms that Jesus' divinity is to be found in his compassion, not in his genealogy... i.e. when he is a most compassion-

ate man he is also simultaneously most clearly divine...

If we conclude from this that Chalcedon had the effect of driving a wedge between the two natures of Christ so that the humanity of Christ was effectively, though not intentionally, destroyed, then it was an unfortunate bequest to the Christian Church, and we are now paying for it dearly. However, these chapters have affirmed that this was not the intention of Chalcedon (p. 25).

The patronizing talk about "what the Chalcedonian formula was attempting to say" (p. 12) is not reassuring. Sittler, in the article referred to above, also claimed that he was preserving the "intention" of the Council of Nicaea!

Often unorthodox views are not directly stated, but implied in the form of questions:

Does it mean that our Lord was truly a child of his times and that his utterances can only be understood in terms of the thought forms, the prevailing hopes, the fears of the first century? Does it mean that the worshipping groups of which Jesus was apart significantly colored his hopes and expectations for mankind? (p. 10)

Does the affirmation that Christ was divine necessarily imply that he was omniscient? (p. 12)

To what extent must we say that all creedal language is finally figurative language? (p. 12)

The suggestions for further reading also are heavily weighted toward the left. Names like Richardson, de Chardin, Bonhoeffer, Barth, Aulen, Barclay, Prenter, Routley, even van Buren, appear as authorities. The most conservative authors cited are probably Schlink and Kinder. But really penetrating orthodox Christological studies, like Olav Valen-Sendstad's *The Word That Can Never Die* (Concordia, 1966) are not even referred to.

The Office of Christ fares even worse than His Person in the LCUSA publication. Recall the joy of Drs. Franzmann and Fuerbringer that "the study and discussion of the Gospel in all its fullness and all its meaning for the life of the church, will be in the center of things." Then note this denaturing of the Gospel:

Man recognizes himself to be or not to be in the "in group" with all the joys and fears that recognition is capable of engendering. This may be simply another way of stating that life is more than food and clothing, more than things possessed. Man is exposed both to mechanistic and personalistic influences, and it is something of a gamble as to which will ultimately triumph, if either. Sociologists hope that the personalistic influences of life are on the ascendancy (p. 19).

There is a common striving for human health and wholeness which pervades all branches of knowledge. Is the biblical concept of salvation related to the objective of man's health-oriented quest? If it is, anthropological pessimism very well may be theologically heretical, culturally disastrous, and productive of misery in human life (p. 21).

Thought concerning Christ's work as reconciler is often cast in the context of some kind of appeasement, as though it were placating a Father's wrath. Alongside that view, possibly even against it must be set the thought that reconciliation may more properly fall in the context of revelation. Whether we have technically and accurately understood such terms as ransom, propitiation, expiation, blood of Christ, sacrifice, etc., insofar as they refer to Christ, is not here called into question. No doubt each term focuses upon a meaningful facet of Christ's redeeming work.

What is at least being suggested in this chapter is that these terms may actually reflect some misunderstanding of the nature of God, focusing too much upon his being a petty and wrathful deity whose offended disposition toward man somehow has to be appeased and hence transformed...

Erik Routley points out:
Reconciliation in the unique New Testament sense is not the bringing together of two parties who have fallen out, offence on the one side provoking anger on the other, retaliation of the second part being resented by the first. It is the restoration of a relation between two parties which one party broke by assuming in the other party a **hostility that was never there.**

When Christ came to reveal the Father, it was not to provide a picture that reflected some change in God, but to reconcile man to God on the basis of what God always had been...So the reconciliation was effected by demonstrating before men in specific acts the true character of God (pp.29-30).

If this is not an attack, a la Aulen, whose *Christus Victor* is suggested for further reading, on the *satisfactio vicaria*, then this whole passage is simply meaningless. Are the expulsion from Paradise, and the Flood simply mistaken myths which assume "a hostility that was never there?" Is St. Paul in Romans "focusing too much upon...a petty and wrathful deity . . .?"

Wingren's critique of Barth's position is to the point:

If Barth is permitted to construct his whole system in peace, remove the objective existence of evil, the natural knowledge of God, the rule of law in the world, place the revelation of God through the incarnation in the center, define the gospel as a word about God's disclosure of himself; if he can do all this, then within this framework he can use the whole vocabulary of the New Testament. He can speak of our sin and guilt, our hostility to God, our demonic character. Everything is there, but it is within the frame of reference of our ignorance, and it is a reality only on the basis of our ontological mistake which makes the nonexistent evil into something that exists. Barth has the ability to a very large degree of being able to employ the language of scripture in a system that is totally foreign to the Bible. [2]

It is not surprising that even the revolutionary Umdeutung of the Gospel gets its due near the end of the LCUSA booklet:

> Historically, Lutheran churches have aligned themselves more with the preservation of the status quo rather than with the forces which have sought liberation from dominating governmental structures. If existing structures seem to protect and strengthen the already rich, while the victims of poverty find their miserable lot intensified, how might a revolutionary gospel about a revolutionary Christ speak to the question of social and political change? (p. 35)

We shall not here speculate about the real intentions behind the treatise we have been reviewing. But about its church political effect there can be very little doubt. The Preface, while stressing the wonderful unity allegedly demonstrated by the discussions, makes the point that the various chapters of the booklet "will allow men to take a variety of positions and hopefully contribute to an openness of faith and thought that will strengthen the churches" (p. 7). There it is: a "variety of positions" on Christology is to be regarded as permissible within the Lutheran churches of America! Without interfering with their supposed "unity", the intention of Missouri's theologians no doubt was to make an orthodox theological contribution. The result, in the hands of LCUSA's Division of Theological Studies, has become a propaganda piece in favor of "openness of faith and thought"! The "dialogue" is adroitly turned into a monologue-with-echo! In future orthodox theologians like Prof. Bouman will have to ask themselves in all seriousness whether their contributions, in this setting, can really serve their intended purpose of edifying Christ's sheep, or whether they do not rather supply Sittlerian wolves with free sheepskins for easier access to the sheepfold!

But if the one argument in favor of LCUSA, theological discussion, has in fact turned into an argument against it, should not the whole arrangement be thoroughly reviewed by the Missouri Synod?

One thing should be very clear, and that is that in principle LCUSA is exactly the same thing as LWF. Both are federations of autonomous churches without complete altar and pulpit fellowship. Except for the insertion of "Unaltered" before "Augsburg Confession," the Preamble of LCUSA's constitution repeats word for word the confessional paragraph of the LWF's constitution.

Neither LCUSA nor LWF carries on theological discussion on the basis of a free conference type of arrangement insisted on by Dr. C.F.W. Walther.

Regarding LCUSA, Franzmann-Fuerbringer quotes Rogness:

> For the churches to be allied...with one another in the task of examination, definition, reproof, correction, and communication would be splendid strategy for this hour. To know whom we have believed, to rest securely in the Word alone, to understand and appreciate the treasure God has given us historically as Lutherans, to communicate

in the form of sound and relevant words, and to do this as pledged brothers and not as uneasy strangers, this . . . is to meet the need of this heterodox hour. [3]

And the LWF's Department of Theology Report to the 1963 Helsinki Assembly stated:

> Therefore one of the basic principles of the theological work of the LWF is that it is carried out in the fellowship of the Church...Listening to each other in fellowship makes possible a sharing in the common spiritual gifts of the Church. [4]

Before the Missouri Synod agreed to participate in LCUSA, misgivings had to be allayed. "This does not mean," Drs. Franzmann and Fuerbringer assured the Synod in their CTM report, "that all the participating bodies unite to do religious teaching or carry on campus ministries together (which would amount to pulpit and altar fellowship)." Yet precisely this is now being done.

A crucial clause in the constitution of LCUSA is Article V g (Functions): "To perform specific services on behalf of one or more of the participating bodies upon purchase of service basis." This is a masterstroke of ecclesiastical diplomacy, inasmuch as the term *cooperatio in sacris*, which Missouri's rank and file would have opposed, is not used, while the thing itself is unobtrusively accommodated!

The late Dr. Behnken, whose support at Detroit had probably won passage for the dubious LCUSA resolution, later regretted this involvement. He told us (Noack) personally, shortly before he died, that had he known the real direction of LCUSA's development, he would never have supported participation in this agency, to this connection it is interesting to ponder the editorial comment about Dr. Behnken which the July 22, 1968 *Christian News* quotes from the May, 1968 *Cresset*, edited by Dr. O. P. Kretzmann, one of the leaders of Missouri's increasingly nervous liberals:

> He and we differed deeply and irreconcilably on many questions which, for both of us, went to the heart of our understanding of the nature of the Church and its proper role in the revolutionary world of the mid-twentieth century. Differing as we did, both of us felt compelled to neutralize, as far as possible, the influence of the other. Neither of us fully succeeded, and the Church remains torn between two opinions.

There are signs that the next Missouri Synod Convention, to be held in Denver next year, may end the rudderless drifting toward the ALC and the LWF, and may demand a serious theological examination of these issues. If that happens, it is to be hoped that LCUSA's organic connection with the LWF issue will not be overlooked, and that this apertura a sinistra, draining away the life-blood of Missouri's orthodoxy, will be healed through a proper application of the Divine Physician's Law and Gospel.

Footnotes

1 Martto H. Franzmann and Alfred O. Fuerbringer, "The Lutheran Council in the

United States of America" CTM. (April, 1964), pp. 219-227.
2 Gustaf Wingren, *Theology in Conflict* (Philadelphia: Muhlenberg, 1958), p. 125.
3 Quoted in Franzmann and Fuerbringer, op. cit., p. 223.
4 Department of Theology, LWF, Report 1957-1963 (Helsinki Assembly Document No. 7), p. 6

1. Who prepared the official report on LCUSA? ____
2. The camel looks like an animal that had been formed by a ____.
3. LCUSA's Who Can This Be avoided the direct assertion that Christ is ____.
4. What did Joseph Sittler (LCA) argue in his "A Christology of Function?" ____
5. The Jews stoned Christ because ____.
6. The suggestion for further reading in the LCUSA document are heavily weighted ____.
7. Whose names appear among the authorities of the left? ____
8. What did Olav Valen-Sendstad write? ____
9. Wingren said that Barth had the ability to employ the language of Scripture in a system that is ____.
10. A "variety of position" on Christology is to be regarded as ____.
11. In principle LCUSA is exactly the same thing as ____.
12. Dr. Behnken later regretted his initial support of ____.
13. Dr. O.P. Kretzmann is one of Missouri's ____.
14. What was draining away the life-blood of Missouri's orthodoxy? ____

STILL ATTACKS DEITY OF CHRIST

Christian News, February 24, 1969

Congratulations
Christian News, December 23, 1968

The Rev. Herman Otten
Editor, *Christian News*
Praeceptor of Missouri Synod
Box 168, New Haven
Missouri 63068

Dear Praeceptor:

Congratulations! *Christian News* scores again!

This time you got President Harms (in his *November Memo*), Vice-President Nickel, and the whole Commission on Theology to jump through your hoop. I refer to front page story in the *Lutheran Witness Reporter* (Dec. 1) on "Concern Voiced on Christology Booklet." In this *report*, Dr. Theodore Nickel is portrayed and quoted as taking up cudgels against the LCUSA booklet: *Who Can This Be?* The CTCR of Missouri Synod "in a formal resolution has expressed its concern about the content of this booklet and has voiced objection to the method of procedure and distribution of the 'study guide.'" As usual, the objection is to method rather than substance; they do not take doctrinal issue, only procedural issue. But, as you know, it was the doctrinal issue which *Christian News* first raised which moved the official body to raise the objection and slap LCUSA on the knuckles.

Nowhere in the *Reporter* story are you given credit for raising the issue and developing it into controversial status in the Missouri Synod. That surely is a deliberate oversight; and you deserve better. You should be given full credit for it. In fact, the *Lutheran Witness Reporter* may be charged properly with suppression of news, since any cub *reporter* sniffing out the trail to origins —asking the elementary journalistic questions; who? what? where? when? why? how?—would find that trail leading directly to New Haven. But such suppression has not altered cases. You are, and remain, the Praeceptor of the Missouri Synod, an honorary (and real) title I bestowed upon you in a previous review of *Christian News*. Don't lose heart over the fact that the Missouri Synod itself refuses to confer the honor upon you; it's the effect that counts, not the name.

There have been intimations several times in recent issues that *Christian News* might fold because of lack of financial support. Many of your detractors have regarded that as good news. I do not; although we could not be more diametrically opposed on most issues. For you help keep issues open and public, rather than under the table. Besides, who wants to be captive to a kept press? Yours is open in its bias, the kind of partisan paper we need for open discussion. I only wish you were on another

52

side, or not so vindictive (the issues are open enough, without seeking to chop off heads, which does limit open discussion and mutual regard). But be that as it may, your supporters should keep you financially afloat. What sense does it make to forsake a winner? And you have now extended your winning streak into and through 1968. If you were a pitcher, you would be earning $100,000 a year for so consistently fanning out the other side.

I haven't read *Who Can This Be?* Now I must; since surely you must be wrong about it. If you are willing, I may even submit a review of it to your paper for your readership, for the sake of ensuing discussion. You see how your vendettas lead one to read what one might neglect?! (Note the inter-bang-?)
Wayne Saffen
The Lutheran Church at the University of Chicago.

Ed. *Who Can This Be?* by a division of the Lutheran Council in the U.S.A. was reproduced in the August 26, 1968 *Christian News*. The May 13, July 22, July 29, August 20, October 14, and October 28 issues of *Christian News* published articles stating that the LCUSA document questions the deity of Christ and denies Christ's vicarious satisfaction. LCUSA officials have still not repudiated the false doctrine contained in *Who Can This Be?* Dr. Oliver Harms, president of The Lutheran Church-Missouri Synod, has refused to say that the document contains false doctrine. We will publish a review of this document by anyone who wants to defend the LCUSA document and show where our evaluation of the document is in error. The November 4 *Christian News* reported that the Missouri Synod's CTCR had taken issue with *Who Can This Be?*

Naturally we regret our financial condition. A number of our LCMS readers, who originally helped us by subscribing for others, have left the Missouri Synod because of LCUSA and the theological liberalism tolerated within the Missouri Synod. Some who have left the LCMS feel they can no longer support us. We are still far short of the 25,000 paid subscribers we need to continue publishing.

x x x

The Editor
Christian News
New Haven, Mo., U.S.A.

Sir,

Permit me to reply to Pastor W. Saffen's defense (*CN*, Jan. 27) of the LCUSA booklet *Who Can This Be?* (herein under designated "the *Report*"). I am not concerned here to defend every single statement made by everyone in the "entourage" of *Christian News*. I wish merely to demonstrate the validity of the judgment on the *Report* contained in the article by Hon. Pres. F.W. Noack and myself (cited as "our article") — I challenge Pastor Saffen to refute — in clear, well-reasoned prose, not in columns and columns of whimsical verbiage — the following contentions:

1. The *Report* is primarily not a theological but a church-political instrument, explicitly designed to legitimize "a variety of positions" and an "openness of faith and thought" on Christology (*Report*, p. 7). This was the main point of our article, and Pastor Saffen has simply side-stepped it with his maneuver of separating "the theological question from the political question."

2. It is fair, indeed necessary, to assume that the *Report* addressed itself not to some hypothetical Christological discussion on the moon, but to the concrete situation in terrestrial, specifically American, Lutheranism.

Since LCUSA represents the whole spectrum from right to left, i.e. from Missouri to the Lutheran Church in America, the presumption is and must be that the whole range of this spectrum is to be covered by the proposed "variety of positions" and "openness of faith and thought".

Sittler

3. This means that the *Report* intends to make room also for Christologies like Joseph Sittler's, whose "A Christology of Function" (*Lutheran Quarterly*, May, 1954) questions even the personal pre-existence of Christ, thereby sacrificing the Nicene Christology to neo-Arian speculations. In view of Sittler's prominence not only in the LCA but in "Ecumenical" circles generally, one would have to be a pretty far-gone ostrich to imagine that the desired "variety" and "openness" were meant to exclude rather than include Sittler's neo-Arianism. The LCUSA editors cannot be so innocent as never to have heard of Sittler! Indeed, the *Report*'s "functional-ontological" argument resembles nothing so much as a thumb-nail sketch of Sittler's 1954 article.

Read that article. Then reread the *Report*. You will have to agree with our judgment (Oct. 28, 1968): "Taken as a whole, the LCUSA study booklet lends itself much more easily to an interpretation along Sittler's lines, than, say, Bouman's".

Pastor Saffen may chew on this sentence from every angle, but he will find himself unable to gnaw any holes into it!

We gladly admit that, say, Prof. Bouman's contribution must have been orthodox to begin with, but contend that in the finished product it amounts to little more than sheep's clothing for neo-Arian Wolves. Or, to vary the figure, the few orthodox remnants do not form the document's main thrust, but rather survive the editorial treatment only as scanty. vestigial, somewhat vermiform verbal appendices here and there! And we have the surgeons' apologies for even these sad remains (p. 6).

4. Even if all this were not the intention of the *Report*, it is certainly its necessary church-political effect. And by the way, even granting the best of intentions, one gets so weary of the angelic innocence of churchmen whose intentions are uniformly lofty, pure, and holy, but whose schemes are almost invariably bad, and result in further doctrinal sellouts and disasters! Perhaps we need a more wicked lot of church politicians, who would be more realistic, and a bit better able to foresee and control the effects of their stated policies and intentions!

5. Lest Pastor Saffen be tempted to shrug the whole thing off pleasantly as a draw, with something to be said for both sides, let us be quite clear about the nature of the argument: If it is our case that the *Report* seeks to create tolerance for a broad range of views, including neo-Arianism, then a little dose of apparent orthodoxy here and there constitutes no effective objection at all (after all, even the wildest modernist in the LCA would have to be prepared to tolerate the convictions of 99 per cent of the Missouri Synod's membership for a while!); but on the other hand, one single clear instance of pro-Arian latitude is fatal to Pastor Saffen's whole defense of the thing!

And such instances abound, as our article has shown. Pastor Saffen himself simply does not know what to do, for example, with the Hendry quote, and merely hopes lamely that "the *Report* does not deny in this statement what it consistently supports throughout, the creedal commitment."

I would not call patronizing talk about "what the Chalcedonian formula was attempting to say" (p. 12), or a hedging compliment to "the intention of Chalcedon" (p. 25) a "creedal commitment," much less a consistent one! Such is the "creedal commitment" of the *Report*, that on p. 11 we even read this: "Their formula, known as the Chalcedonian Creed, may leave a great deal to be desired." And even Sittler claims that his denial of Christ's pre-existence is within the "intention" of Nicaea! Then too, the "philosophic and semantic freight" of the Chalcedonian Decree, about which the *Report* has such grave reservations (p. 28), is just the kind of thing Sittler was trying to scrape off the ancient Christology in his 1954 article!

The Hendry quote on the other hand is clear, explicit, and uncomplicated by reservations, qualification, and limitations! Nor is it an isolated item: practically the whole bibliography leads in this Arian direction! (See Olav Valen-Sendstad's *The Word That Can Never Die* for some plain talk about various modern Christologies).

In defense of the *Report*'s mini-atonement doctrine even Pastor Saffen finds it difficult to say anything at all, though he tries. It would have been more candid simply to admit that the Routley quote (p. 29) is horrid, that Aulen's views are apostolic, that the "petty and wrathful deity" statement is a revolting caricature of Biblical truth, and that "man's health-oriented quest" (p. 21) and the Hope of Sociologists "that personalistic influences of life are on the ascendancy" (p. 19) are not Gospel, but, in their context, ghastly secular imitations of it!

More Sittler

6. Pastor Saffen's warm advocacy of the *Report*'s orthodoxy would be much more convincing, at least subjectively if not objectively, had not his Lutheran Campus Parish in Chicago recently announced an Ecumenical happening involving not only Joseph Sittler (yes, the very same one!), but even the Unitarians. Or shall we now be told that anno Domini 1969 the Unitarians too pledge allegiance to "the intention of Chalcedon"? Please, do explain. Pastor Saffen!

7. In conclusion, a few comments on specific points in Pastor Saffen's letter, which imply factual, logical, or theological fallacies:

(a) "How to reconcile the two views of atonement (1) that God was in Christ reconciling the world to Himself and (2) a vicarious satisfaction to God. Both are clearly taught in Scripture."

It is good that Pastor Saffen holds that Scripture clearly teaches the vicarious satisfaction. But Barth and Aulen clearly reject this doctrine, and they are clearly the god-parents of the *Report* on this point!

Actually there is no conflict at all between (1) and (2): God reconciled the world to Himself by assuming Himself the burden of His own Justice God is "Himself the victim and Himself the Priest ," and of course Himself the Recipient of the Sacrifice.

It is clear that God's love is prior to the atonement, and is not simply, as it were, a grudging effect of it: "For God so loved the world, that He gave His only-begotten Son..."

Lenten preachers must beware of giving the impression that while the Son loves us, the Father hates us, and only grudgingly consents to our acquittal, because the Son as it were forces Him to keep to the terms of the bargain, so that God, having received His Shylockian pound of flesh, cannot now exact punishment twice, much as He would like to!

Such homiletical fantasies are unbiblical and offensive. They bring orthodoxy into ill repute and invite the ridicule of the moderns.

The *Report* seems to me to reject not merely this sort of exaggeration and caricature of orthodoxy, but elements of the New Testament itself. It says:

"Whether we have technically and accurately understood such terms as ransom, propitiation, expiation, blood of Christ, sacrifice, etc., insofar as they refer to Christ, is not here called into question. No doubt each term focuses upon a meaningful facet of Christ's redeeming work. What is at least being suggested in this chapter is that these terms may actually reflect some misunderstanding of the nature of God, focusing too much upon his being a petty and wrathful deity whose offended disposition toward man somehow has to be appeased and hence transformed" (p. 29).

Now, either this is barbarically inexact English, or it criticizes the New Testament itself, for the terms which "may actually reflect some misunderstanding, etc." are all found in the New Testament! And the expression, "focusing too much upon his being a petty and wrathful deity" implies the absurdity that in some unspecified, moderate measure one ought to "focus upon his being a petty and wrathful deity"!

The possibility of criticizing the New Testament itself is, incidentally, guaranteed on p. 10: "The chapters of this handbook reflect the conviction that biblical criticism is here to stay." And "biblical criticism" as generally practiced and understood today is not merely textual criticism, but implies the interpreter's right to reconstruct, modify, and correct Biblical substance.

Heard of Romans I, Anybody?

(b) "It is interesting to note that both Ralph Lohrengel and Noack-Marquart assert the Jewish people's ability to know the true God without Jesus, (albeit the Old Testament Jews)... 'Noack-Marquart pull off a fast shell-game'. The document says, as they quote: 'In ancient times it was also possible to have a rather clear and precise concept of what divinity meant. Today this has been shaken . . . rather than conclude that Jesus was divine because he conformed to a preconceived notion of divinity, we must follow precisely the opposite tack, recognizing that it is he who actually serves as our "recognition of God". Now, follow the argument: "THEN people had preconceived notions of divinity to which Jesus was supposed to have conformed; TODAY people have no such preconceptions of divinity, so we must discover who God is in Jesus, who is the express image of the Father . . . But where's the argument? The document says that THEN people had preconceived notions of divinity and Noack-Marquart cite Scriptures to prove that they did. How does that disprove the document, when the problem the document comes as is that TODAY God has gone out of human consciousness ..."

Why is it interesting that we assert the Old Testament Jews' ability to know the true God without Jesus? Whom, pray tell, did Adam, Abraham, Moses, Elijah, etc. know if not the true God? Was it perhaps the Demiurge? And while they had prophecies, they certainly had no clear, complete picture of Jesus. Incidentally, Pastor Saffen's theological accomplices almost invariably deny all direct Old Testament prophecies about Jesus!

As to the "fast shell-game," Pastor Saffen here has completely misunderstood and bagatellised the *Report*. He writes as if the *Report* regarded the loss of a clear concept of God as some sort of regrettable defect, some deterioration since Biblical times. But it does nothing of the kind. It is not expressing regret that the Stalins, Ayers, Bertrand Russells, and Julian Huxley's of our time no longer find the concept of God meaningful, and therefore have to be approached apologetically through the historical figure Jesus of Nazareth.

Rather, the *Report* regards the current situation as a great advance. The old concept of God has been shaken not by rationalists, but "shaken perhaps primarily by the theologians" (p. 11), as the *Report* says in a crucial clause, omitted for some reason by Pastor Saffen in his use of this section! Clearly, the *Report* wouldn't dream of establishing what "the theologians" have shaken—the whole development is plainly meant to be approved.

The real conflict is not between THEN and NOW, but between faith, then and now, and unbelief, then and now. A Biblical, Christian theologian will then as now as a matter of course take for granted any "preconceived notions of divinity" assumed by Holy Scripture.

To say that Jesus "actually serves as our definition of God" (p. 11) is pure nonsense. Taken seriously this would have to mean: God is a being of human shape and size which originated in Palestine under Caesar Augustus, long after the universe had then formed!

On the contrary, Christ said: "Ye believe in God — believe also in Me!" To say to someone who already has a clear notion of God as a personal, intelligent, powerful, holy, etc.. Being Who created the universe, "this God has revealed Himself in Christ," makes very good sense. But to say "Jesus is God" to a person who has no idea of what is meant by the term "God" is meaningless. One might as well say, "Jesus is X", or, if Jesus is "the definition of God," one is left with the tautology, "Jesus is Jesus." Please consult Romans 1:19,20; 2:14-15!

Barbers, Freud and the Formula of Concord

(c) "but it is a fact that what people in barber shops are arguing about today is not over the three persons in one Godhead, as they did at the height of the Christological controversy in the days of St. Gregory of Nyssa."

I doubt that any serious Christology can or should pay much attention to what a pagan population chatters about in modern barber-shops! I do not know about barber-shops that specialize in that St. Gregory of Nyssa look. But in the ones I know the talk is not about any sort of Christology, whether "functional" or "ontological," but about the weather, motor and horse races, cricket (in the continental United States and its possessions read: baseball), hear, and an occasional bit of fornication. Not very promising Christological material, this. Alas, it's a different class of people that goes to barber-shops nowadays!

But does Pastor Saffen really imagine that the current "functional" gobbledygook gets through to modern people! I would wager that even the clientele of St. Gregory of Nyssa's Own Beauty Salon in Chicago would comprehend the basics of traditional Christology, but that even they would be baffled by "relevant" jargon like "the transcendence of God is. In fact, God's otherness-than-man in his being totally for us" (p. 25)!

(d) "If Freud is right about man's nature being id, ego, and super-ego, then Jesus had all three ...Whatever social, psychological, and human sciences reveal about the nature of man, it is what Jesus is like, excepting for sin."

But Freud's scheme is no more "scientific" than Plato's myth about the horses and the charioteer! Besides, the social, etc., "sciences" (the word is used by a kind of courtesy) can only deal with human nature as it is now, i.e. sinful. Their findings cannot therefore be automatically transferred to the sinless God-Man! It is difficult, for instance, to conceive of Freud's amoral "id" as part of human nature PER SE, as distinct from fallen, sinful human nature.

Human nature and psychology are baffling enough and are certainly more mysterious than the typical liberal, scientistic, optimistic approach admits. But the unique psychology of Christ, true God and true Man in one Person, is an inviolable shrine of mystery quite inaccessible to human speculation. The *Report*, in seeming to trample about heedlessly in these sacred precincts, lacks proper gravity and Christian reverence. It is not fitting for the creature to psychoanalyze his Creator and Redeemer!

(e) "As God he was omniscient; but as man he was not." This is heretical. It contradicts the communication of attributes confessed so clearly in Article VIII of the Formula of Concord.

(f) "The LCUSA account goes too far when it says that 'Likely Jesus was unaware of the resurrection which lay beyond the criminal's death.' But even so, like the rest of us, Jesus had to BELIEVE that God would raise him from the dead. He would not get up by himself if the Spirit of God did not raise him."

But if, as Pastor Saffen argues, Christ is "like us in every way excepting for sin," if omniscience would have made of him "a god pretending to be a man," then why object to the *Report*'s statement that "Likely Jesus was unaware of the resurrection?" After all, we have no such awareness, and Christ as man cannot have anything we don't have! Pastor Saffen seems to forget that Christ was and is not merely a sinless man, like Adam, but the unique God-Man!

As for the resurrection, Christ Himself says: "I lay down My life, that I might take it again. No man taketh it from me, but I lay it down of Myself. I have power to lay it down, and I have power to take it again" (St. John 10:17.18).

(g) "Noack-Marquart have trouble with this statement at the point where the idea is proposed that Christ's 'divine nature itself and as such could and did die and rise again.' As Lutherans, they shouldn't have such troubles. The Creeds all say that Jesus Christ, the God-man, the whole person, died and rose again... And the Lutheran Confessions say: 'The Son of God is truly crucified for us —that is, this person who is God, for that is what he is — this person, I say, is crucified according to the humanity.'"

Pastor Saffen seems not to have noticed the phrase "according to the humanity" in the quotation from the Confessions. The whole person suffered and died, but through and according to the human nature! What we objected to was the impossible notion that "the divine nature itself and as such" died and rose. Please check *Formula of Concord*, S. D., VIII, 20:

"On account of this personal union... it is not only the bare human nature...that has suffered for the sin of the world, but the Son of God himself has truly suffered (although according to the assumed human nature), and in the words of our plain Christian Creed, has truly died, ALTHOUGH THE DIVINE NATURE CAN NEITHER SUFFER NOR DIE" (Tappert, ed., *Book of Concord*, p. 595).

Does Pastor Saffen imagine that Christ's eternal divine nature disappeared between His death and resurrection? God was born of the Virgin

Mary, suffered, died, rose, and ascended; these are all true statements, but only by virtue of the Personal Union, and in this special sense. They cannot be changed into statements about Christ's divine nature itself and AS SUCH (again check Article VIII of the Formula).

(h) "'There is no point at which an unbeliever is forced by the evidence to confess: 'This is the Son of God.' That surely is the record of the Gospels themselves. Is *CN* using a different Bible?'"

I use the one with St. Matthew 27:54 in it: "Now when the centurion, and they that were with him, watching Jesus, saw the earthquake, and those things that were done, they feared greatly, saying. Truly this was the Son of God."

Conclusion

Summa summarum, the LCUSA *Report* makes room for "Lutheran" neo-Arianism. When I showed this *Report* to a competent, well-read university-trained theologian at our recent Albury Synod of the Lutheran Church of Australia, his reaction was: "This is terrible — it's the most blasphemous nonsense I've seen for some time!"

Well, I fear that this labor of love may not be taken as such. I have said some things sharply. The purpose was to jar Pastor Saffen's conscience into some slight doublings of his loose, happy-go-lucky dogmatism. He has some noble impulses. I do not expect an instant conversion. But I hope that as St. Augustine gradually thought his way through, and out of, the pretentious imposture of Manicheism, so Pastor Saffen will ultimately see the unresolved and unresolvable contradiction between Christian faith and modern, neo-pagan secular mythology—with all its works and all its pomp!

K. Marquart

Toowoomba, Queensland, Australia

Editor's note: The January 13, 1969 *Christian News* published this item:

"Wayne Saffen: A Gentleman

"The Christmas issue of *Christian News* contained a letter from the Rev. Wayne Saffen, Missouri Synod Lutheran campus pastor at the University of Chicago. Pastor Saffen, as he himself states, does not see eye to eye with the editor on most issues, but he has an openness and honesty that are becoming rarer in our day among liberals. He has written this periodical both to confirm news stories and sometimes to suggest corrections. His witty style of writing makes him a welcome contributor and we assure all those who are like him that they also may state their opinions on these pages."

The January 2, 1968 *Christian News* published "LCUSA's 'Who Can This Be?' An Answer to Certain Allegations in *Christian News*" an article of some 5,000 words by Wayne Saffen. "Wayne Saffen: Enter Confusion" appeared in the February 10, 1969 *Christian News*, "Missouri Marauder"

60

by Wayne Saffen in the June 7, 1969 *Christian News*, and "Lutheran Church-Preus-Otten Synod" by Saffen in the July 28, 1969 *Christian News* had its leading intellectual, Kurt Marquart, respond to him. He was one of the first in the LCMS to promote Dietrich Bonhoeffer. He founded the Bonhoeffer House at the University of Chicago. He wrote in the February 1968 *Lutheran Campus Pastor* "Critique:"

"We repeat, it is an impressive record. Concerns which had been generated when the editor (of *Christian News*) was still a student have almost all been validated by convention resolution: affirming a six-day creation, a historical Jonah, an inerrant Scripture, Adam and Eve as real historic persons, etc. Missouri Synod in convention assembled has vindicated almost every doctrinal stand of Herman Otten as its official position. Now, that has to be impressive. How can the synod, then, still withhold recognition of his ordination when it was carried out in strict accordance with the directions of C.F.W. Walther?

1. LCUSA's Who Can This Be designed not to be a ____ but a ____.
2. The LCUSA intends to make room for ____.
3. Joseph Sittler questioned the ____ of Christ.
4. Herbert Bouman's contribution amounts to little more than ____.
5. Practically the entire bibliography leads in the ____ direction.
6. Olav Valen-Sendstad's The Word That Can Never Die has some plain talk on ____.
7. It would have been more candid to admit that Aulen's views are ____.
8. Saffen's Lutheran Campus Parish in Chicago announced ____.
9. God is Himself the ____ and Himself the ____.
10. "Biblical criticism" as generally understood and practiced today is ____.
11. Saffen's theological accomplices almost invariably deny ____.
12. It is not fitting for the creature to psychoanalyze his ____.
13. To say "As God he was omniscient but as man he was not" is ____.
14. What Bible is *CN* using? ____
15. Summa summarum, the LCUSA Report makes room for ____.
16. Marquart hoped that Saffen will see ____.

THE INVITED AND UNINVITED GUEST

Christian News, February 24, 1969

Since the issue of Dr. Harms' and Dr. Bouman's visit to Australia has arisen in your pages, I have felt somewhat awkward about it. I fear that some circles may put two and two together about like this: Marquart sometimes writes for *Christian News*, and Marquart is in Australia: ergo, the information about the Harms-Bouman visit came from him.

I herewith wish to state categorically that this was not the case. In fact, I haven't the faintest idea about who supplied *Christian News* with this material.

As a member of our Commission on Theology and Inter-Church Relations, I am not of course at liberty to divulge information not intended for publication by the Commission. While I have never made a secret of the fact that I strongly object, on Biblical and Confessional grounds, to the Missouri Synod's present disastrous policy towards the ALC in particular and the Ecumenical Movement in general, I fully respect Dr. Harms' and Dr. Bouman's right to have private discussions with our Commission, and to have this privacy respected by our side. But of course there is nothing particularly confidential about the basic facts of Dr. Harms' invitation and visit. On the contrary, these should be a matter of public record in America and here.

One aspect in particular concerns me. One of your Australian correspondents quoted anonymously in your February 3 "Focus on Denver," makes the point that the Lutheran Church of Australia could not very well, on its own initiative, invite only Dr. Harms of Missouri, and not also Dr. Schiotz of the ALC. That is fair enough as far as it goes, but I must stress that the same applies to the Presidents of the Wisconsin Synod and the Evangelical Lutheran Synod. I and others would have voiced strenuous objections to any preferential singling out of Missouri over Wisconsin or the ELS. If their presidents had just happened to be passing through this country to or from New Guinea, or the South Pole for that matter, they would have been equally welcome to present greetings and to meet with our Commission on Theology. The record must be absolutely clear on this point.

Our Australian *Document of Union* states:
"We acknowledge ourselves to be in church fellowship with all Lutheran Churches which subscribe to the LUTHERAN CONFESSIONS in their constitutions and adhere to them in their public teaching and practice" (Par. 9).

The Australian Church now faces the problem of deciding just to which overseas churches this applies, and to which not. In view of the confused situation, globally, this will take time, as our recent Albury Synod pointed out. Meanwhile, I suppose, while the discussion goes on, individual judgments will differ somewhat. My own conscientious conviction is that I cannot accept any member church of the LWF or the WCC (or LCUSA for that matter) as meeting the standards of the above-mentioned par. 9. This means that I am in conscience bound to reject fellowship with the ALC and with Missouri, unless the latter returns to her former, orthodox position (by rejecting ALC fellowship and LCUSA, and taking a serious stand against its rampant internal liberalism). On the other hand I am convinced in my own conscience that the Wisconsin Synod and the ELS are the kind of confessionally faithful churches that are described in Par. 9. No power on earth can therefore force me to deny to these churches, and any other orthodox churches, congregations, or individuals in the whole wide world, the hand of full Christian fellowship.

I must stress again that these are strictly my own convictions and bind only me. I have here publicly expressed them in order to avoid giving offense to true brothers in the Faith anywhere. But only the Lutheran Church of Australia itself can decide what its own corporate attitude will ultimately be.

In conclusion, I hope that the relatively minor issue of the invitation to Dr. Harms will not be allowed to becloud the important matters facing your Synod at Denver. Wherever possible, I prefer to explain discrepancies on the theory of a misunderstanding rather than that of deliberate misrepresentation. Dr. Harms can rightly claim to have been invited, and your *reporter*, whoever he was, can rightly claim that the initiative for this invitation did not originate with the Lutheran Church of Australia, but arose out of the coincidence of our Albury Synod with Dr. Harms' engagement in New Guinea. Surely both sides can agree to something like this without further rancor!

K. Marquart
51 Fourth Ave.
Toowoomba, Queensland
Australia

Question
Marquart said he was conscience bound to reject fellowship with the ALC and the Missouri Synod unless the later returns to her ____.

DATELINE ANAHEIM

K.E. Marquart, Reporter
*The Lutheran, Official publication of the Lutheran Church
of Australia, August 11, 1975 and August 25, 1975.
Christian News, September 22, 1975*

Report on the Convention of The Lutheran Church-Missouri Synod,
Anaheim, California, U.S.A., July 4-11.

PART I

For the opening service of the Missouri Synod's 51st regular convention, under the theme Jesus Christ Is Lord, nearly 4,000 people were packed into one of the spacious halls of the Convention Centre at Anaheim, a Los Angeles suburb famed for its fabulous Disneyland. There were 1,022 voting delegates (half clergy, half laymen), about 500 advisory delegates, and over 2,000 visitors.

Since it was the Fourth of July, the service was preceded by a Patriotic Observance celebrating 200 years of American Independence. It was a solemn moment when the vast throng broke into the stately strains of *America the Beautiful.* When we reached the refrain, "America, America, God shed His grace on thee . . ." nostalgia, elation, and sorrow got the better of me and I simply could not continue. Here was America, devout, God-fearing, Christian. But there was another America: godless, rapacious, intent on various schemes of secular salvation and damnation. And then there was America the innocent giant, so powerful, yet so vulnerable. President Ford had just refused to meet with Solzhenitsyn, in the name of that fantasy, "detente"! How ironic that "Christian" America, menaced by unprecedented Soviet might and malevolence, had to hear its real Fourth of July message from a Soviet Christian — who pulled no punches before an enthusiastic crowd of trade unionists convened by Labor leader George Meany — while her embarrassed President muttered blandly about friendship with a brutally inhuman regime which had for sixty years trampled upon everything sacred to American idealism! As Khrushchev had put it so memorably: "We spit into their eyes — and they think its dew!" If God is indeed to save America, it seems he must first save her from herself.

THREE CRUCIAL ISSUES

In his opening press conference, Synodical President Dr. J.A.O. Preus set out the main problems facing the Synod. They were: (1) Seminex, the opposition seminary established by the former majority of faculty and students of Concordia Seminary, St. Louis; (2) the problem of the eight District Presidents who had authorized ordination of Seminex graduates contrary to Synod's by-laws, and intended to continue to do so; (3) ELIM (Evangelical Lutherans in Mission), the Seminex support organization, which also operates its own mission agency. While pleading for fairness and Christian love, Dr. Preus pointed out that firm decisions had to be made, since "no church can run on organizational anarchy".

The first of these crucial matters was settled on Monday, July 7. Floor Committee 6 (Higher Education) introduced a resolution to "beseech" Seminex "by the mercies of God" to close the institution "in the interest of promoting peace and harmony in our midst". A second resolve provided that if Seminex were to continue, it would "be regarded as any other theological school not affiliated" with the Synod. This had obvious implications for the placement of its graduates.

After some debate including various parliamentary moves, a motion to terminate discussion failed by 613 to 447, a two-thirds majority being required. After further debate, however, the resolution was adopted overwhelmingly.

THE DISTRICT PRESIDENTS

The matter of the District Presidents was contested much more fiercely and protractedly, although in contrast to the previous Convention at New Orleans, there were no wild demonstrations and emotional excesses. Both chairman and delegates were able to preserve a remarkably cool and low-key atmosphere, despite the tremendous tensions. A lady parliamentary expert, the president of the California Society of Parliamentarians, sat next to the chairman's podium, ready to disentangle procedural muddles. She was fondly referred to by President Preus as the "Delphic Oracle".

Already on the Sunday afternoon, the Floor Committee on Constitutional Matters had introduced a detailed resolution "To deal with District Presidents who have ordained or who have authorized ordination of persons who are not properly endorsed." This document distinguishes carefully between what God Himself has established in the Church (e.g. the Office of the Keys), and the human regulations of constitutions and by-laws, made for the sake of public order. District Presidents are dircted "to uphold and abide by the Constitution and by-laws of the Synod".

Further, "If a District President cannot in good conscience uphold the Constitution and By-laws of the Synod, which he has sworn to do at the time of his installation, and . . . if he cannot refrain from ordaining or authorizing the ordination of candidates for the Holy Ministry, who have not received endorsement for ordination through the duly authorized synodical process, then the said District President, for the sake of peace and the good order of the Synod, shall resign from the office of District President". Should he refuse to do so, he is "commended to the pastoral care and discipline of the synodical president"; and "if pastoral care and discipline have failed to secure from a District President involved stated compliance with this resolution, or he has not resigned, the synodical president, after consultation with the Council of Presidents, shall inform the said District at least sixty days before the beginning of the next regularly-scheduled District convention, that a vacancy exists in the office of said District President . . ."

After some preliminary debate, the Chairman of the Council of Presidents (there are 40 Districts) asked that the Council be given one more opportunity to settle the problem in its own circle. Convention agreed to postpone further consideration until after the special Council of Presidents meeting on the Monday night.

LAST MINUTE EFFORTS TO AVOID DIVISION

Those who favored the cause of the eight District Presidents had no doubt taken heart when on Tuesday Convention declined, after spirited debate, the administrative floor committee's resolution to dissolve the English District. Wild cheering from English District supporters among delegates and visitors greeted the decision. Unlike the Synod's geographical Districts, the English District is nation-wide. It had joined the Synod in 1911 on a language basis, at a time when the rest of the Church was still German speaking. In recent years, the English District leadership had been prominent in supporting opposition theology and causes such as "Seminex". Many conservatives voted against amalgamation, because they feared the influx of dissidents into their Districts. At any rate, the Convention by this action proved that it would not act simply as a rubber stamp to approve anything and everything put forward by the floor committees.

Then the District Presidents matter came up once more, and all eight dissidents were given ample opportunity to speak in justification of their stand. The previous night's meeting of Presidents had produced no results. The President of Synod then made a moving last-minute plea. No-one really wanted to pass the resolution in question, he said, but Synod could not continue on a path of anarchy. He reminded the delegates that behind the technical issues, it was really a question of supporting "Seminex". But forget about the past, he continued, no-one was interested in what the Presidents had done or not done, and they were not being asked to apologize. It was solely a question of present and future policy, of principle. Even now, he said, he would be happy to ask for withdrawal of the whole resolution by the committee, if the eight Presidents would give the Synod only one single word, one indication that in future they would abide by Synod's constitution and by-laws. He begged the eight for such a word of assurance. The silence in response was deafening.

TELEVISION CAMERAS COVER PROCEEDINGS

Time had run out and the matter was made the first order of the day for Wednesday. Several Synodical Vice-Presidents then spoke, all in support of the resolution. President George Wollenburg, of the Montana District, argued that allowing District Presidents to violate Synod's constitution and by-laws, far from supporting the principle of congregational autonomy as was claimed, really undercut it by subjecting congregations to arbitrary and capricious rule, contrary to mutually agreed arrangements.

A delegate from the Eastern District presented a petition with some 5,000 signatures in support of the dissident stand.

Tensions mounted as the time for voting approached, and TV cameras and crews appeared on stage, ready to film the drama of this crucial decision. President Preus, mindful of the wild disorders of New Orleans, suggested to the Convention that the TV cameras be excluded, since they seemed to be waiting for some pre-arranged spectacle. But Convention turned this down decisively, and allowed the media to televise the proceedings, on the grounds, as put by one speaker, that the Church had nothing to hide.

EVANGELICAL LUTHERANS IN MISSION

On the same day the third "crunch" issue — ELIM — was decided. The Floor Committee on Theological Matters (No. 3) had prepared a lengthy, firm, but mildly worded resolution which declared that ELIM's support of a competing seminary and a competing mission agency made it in effect a church within a church. These functions were schismatic and in violation of Synod's very first object, the promotion of unity. Those who played "active roles" in these schismatic functions were asked to desist, or else leave the Synod. Finally, all who objected to decision of Synod were asked "by the mercies of God" to "follow our mutually adopted procedures for expressing their dissent".

An amendment to declare also the conservative *Affirm* group as divisive was defeated. It was pointed out that *Affirm* operated neither an opposition seminary nor an opposition mission program. President Preus had again offered, unsuccessfully, to have the resolution withdrawn, if only ELIM leaders would agree to co-operate with the Synod. Upon termination of debate the resolution was adopted, a division of the house showing the vote as 601 to 473. A fifteen minutes recess followed, during which ELIM forces conducted a rally outside the Convention Hall.

OTHER MATTERS BEFORE CONVENTION

* A Sunday night celebration of "special ministries" attracted a capacity crowd of 10,000 to the mammoth indoor stadium. The evening was hosted by Art Linkletter, of "People Are Funny" fame, and Lutheran TV personality Lillian Lehman.

* Synod resolved to "reaffirm its continued desire to establish altar and pulpit fellowship with the Lutheran Church of Australia". Convention also officially declared itself to be in fellowship with the newly-formed Independent Evangelical Lutheran Church of Germany.

* After lively debate it was decided to close the Senior College at Ft. Wayne. This two-year school had channeled the graduates of Synod's dozen junior colleges (providing the first two years of tertiary studies) to the Church's seminaries. Although the decision was based on economic arguments, conservatives were displeased that in the recent past a high proportion of Ft. Wayne graduates had gone to "Seminex".

* The solidly conservative junior college at Ann Arbor, Michigan, was upgraded to a full 4-year school, geared especially to supplying the terminal schools for church workers.

* Finally, the Springfield Seminary was transferred to the new 15-million dollar campus at Ft. Wayne, the city in which Missouri's founder and

first president, Dr. C.F.W. Walther, had originally established this seminary.

* In connection with the Synod's participation in Lutheran Council in the USA efforts to resettle some 10,000 Vietnamese refugees. Convention gave a standing ovation to sponsors, Mr. and Mrs. J. Quinelly (ALC) and their "charge", Mr. Nguyen Trong Lieu, a former presiding judge of the military court at Saigon.

* Recognizing that the Synodical President had labored for years under unprecedented pressures as he sought to carry out the duties of his office, and that the strain inevitably involved also his family. Convention rose for a thunderous round of applause as Mrs. J. Preus was ushered to the platform and presented with a bouquet of flowers on behalf of the Synod. Visibly moved President and Mrs. Preus thanked the delegates.

PART II

DOCTRINAL DIVISION
Theology was not in the forefront at Anaheim. In a sense that was inevitable. New Orleans had made the basic theological decisions. Now Anaheim had to deal with the constitutional crisis brought about by organized opposition to Synod's doctrinal stand. Regrettably speakers from both sides at times gave the impression that the unity of the outward synodical organization was the supreme good, as if the Synod itself were as such the Body of Christ, and separation from it the ultimate tragedy. Such an un-Lutheran attitude, fully exploited by the dissidents, makes it difficult to face up to real doctrinal differences.

But the doctrinal division was never far from the surface of the action. Adding to the tense atmosphere was a sensational decision by a Missouri District official clearing Dr. John Tietjen, the President of Seminex, of all charges of false doctrine. The media had publicized the action just a few days prior to the Convention. Dr. Tietjen had been convicted by the Concordia Seminary Board of Control on several counts of false doctrine and administrative malfeasance, and deposed from office. Now Missouri District Vice-President Pastor O. Gerken had been given the task of deciding Dr. Tietjen's membership in the District, and had acquitted him. The decision will no doubt be appealed.

DR. TIETJEN AND AUSTRALIA
Of special interest to Australian Lutherans is this item from the Gerken decision:

"Dr. Tietjen's understanding of the word 'inerrancy' does not coincide with the Synod's traditional definition of this term, i.e. that the Holy Spirit preserved the biblical writers from making errors in the writing of the Scriptures.

"However, I believe that Dr. Tietjen's understanding of the term does not conflict with the statement of the Evangelical Lutheran Church of Australia /sic/ on this subject" (Then follows an excerpt from *Theses of*

68

Agreement, VIII, 10).

In view of this reference to the Australian Church I felt it my duty to ask Dr. Tietjen at a press conference: "Does this mean that you accept the Australian Church's official 1972 definition of inerrancy in its normal sense of freedom from error and contradiction, factual as well as theological?" (LCA *Report,* 1972, p. 360).

Dr. Tietjen's reply suggested agreement with the Australian position in general, without however answering my specific question in particular.

A secular *reporter* then asked a revealing question of another ELIM leader: "Why is it", he said, "that whenever I ask 'moderates' about how they understand the reports of miracles and history in the Bible, I can never understand their answers, even though I have a high-school education?" The reply was a perfect illustration of the question!

DOUBLE-TALK

Some "moderates" themselves are not happy with the dishonest evasion tactic. Thus the strongly anti-Preus and pro-Seminex *Forum Letter* (May 1975) commented on the April Convocation in St. Louis, which had dealt with the doctrinal issues:

"As one Seminex prof remarked, 'I'm not sure from day to day what our approach is. One day we're going to candidly state our differences and let the devil take the hindmost. The next, we're trying to demonstrate that we believe the same thing old Missouri always believed about Inerrancy and all the rest.' The Seminex reps at the convo tended to take the second tack, as they did at New Orleans in 1971... But Seminex credibility is strengthened by candor, not by pretending there are few if any significant differences. If, for example, the historical-critical method doesn't make that much difference in what one believes about the Bible or how one does theology. Why bother everybody by insisting on using it? . . . In short, one cannot honestly practice historical criticism and be under the Scriptures' in the sense that the Preus group means 'under' . . . If the LCMS is to divide, it would seem preferable to divide in a climate of candor. If a new formation is to take place, it would seem imperative that it not be founded upon evasiveness."

Again and again the "moderates" at Anaheim argued passionately that they accepted the confessional paragraph of Synod's constitution, that they therefore were bound only to the Scriptures and the Confessions, and that the whole argument was about whether additional doctrinal formulations, such as *A Statement of Scriptural and Confessional Principles* (adopted at New Orleans), could be forced on them by Convention decision. Synod replied by endorsing the argument of both its Theological and its Constitutional Commissions that *A Statement* does not add to Synod's doctrinal basis, but merely spells out some of the things taught in the Scriptures and the Confessions.

THE REAL ISSUES

That the constitutional objection was in fact only a cover for the underlying doctrinal disagreements had become clear already in 1972. When Seminex professor Dr. Walter Bartling stated before the Louisiana Pastoral Conference (April 17-20):

"One thing they caught most of us on is were Adam and Eve historical persons, I don't know, I don't think so, it is not important. They caught most of us in some way on most of the points in Preus' *Statement* . . . When you speak of the authority of Scripture it's like Daddy and Momma trying to enforce opinions and constrain belief. The Bible doesn't do that. Don't we have freedom with the aid of God's Spirit to form opinion? There is no certainty we have the original text of Scriptures . . . *Sola Scriptura* is a brainwashing which I forcefully react against. . . I have problems with the virgin birth, real presence, bodily resurrection . . . . I can't bear the burden of Scriptural infallibility..."

And an ELIM-promoted sociological study by Rev. D.W. Melber of the West Texas State University, says straight-out:

"The faculty renounced *A Statement* and responded to it and the investigating committee's report by issuing *Faithful to Our Calling — Faithful to Our Lord,* as their collective and individual confessions of faith" (p. 4). In other words, the objection to *A Statement* is doctrinal!

One can only agree with prominent "moderate" Dr. Paul Bretscher, when he comments in his 1975 book, *After the Purifying* on the "moderates" professions of loyalty to Synod's doctrinal paragraph "without reservation":

"The meaning of this confession differed now from the meaning they themselves had once found in these very same words . . . Those who had in reality been changed by . . . critical study could still insist that they were not deviating from Synod's doctrinal and confessional position. . . . The net effect was one of compromise and insincerity" (p. 102).

LUTHERANS WORLD-WIDE, WAKE UP!

In conclusion, let us take note of an eloquent confessional voice from within the American Lutheran Church, writing in *Lutherans Alert — National,* ALC, pastor Dr. R.H. Redal of Tacoma, Washington, shows the global significance of the controversy in the Missouri Synod:

"Even though our ALC leadership upholds those Lutherans in the Missouri Synod who allow for errors in the Bible, we in *Lutherans Alert-National* want it known to the whole church that we stand with those in the Missouri Synod who want to preserve the historic faith of their church.

"It is also appalling to this writer that those who believe in the doctrine of inerrancy within the ALC do not become more vocal and enter into the same kind of dispute with its leadership as is occurring in the LCMS. All of Lutheranism ought to be involved in this raging controversy. This is no synodical dispute. This is the actual battle for the survival of Christianity. . . This is no day for Christians to sit back in comfortable chairs and yawn in the face of the dispute that is raging over the church, which at this very moment is threatening to engulf it. What we definitely need is a grass roots awakening. Every Christian in the Lutheran Church, no matter of what synod, ought to begin to ask questions of its leadership: Where do you stand in relationship to Holy Scripture?" "Do you believe that the Bible is the Word of God without error in all that it speaks?" "Do you tolerate and teach any other view than that the Bible is totally the Word of God?"

1. It was a solemn moment when the vast throng broke into ____.
2. What could Marquart not continue singing? ____
3. President Ford had just refused to meet with ____.
4. If God is indeed to save America, it seems he must first save her from ____.
5. English District leadership had been prominent in ____.
6. What did George Wollenburg of the Montana District argue ____.
7. A delegate from the English District presented a petition with some ____ signatures.
8. Who conducted a rally outside the Convention Hall? ____
9. A high proportion of Fort Wayne Senior College graduates had gone to ____.
10. The Springfield seminary was transferred to ____.
11. Regrettably speakers from both sides at time gave the impression that ____ was the supreme good.
12. Who acquitted Dr. John Tietjen? ____
13. What did Marquart ask Tietjen at a press conference? ____
14. How did Marquart describe *Forum Letter*? ____
15. The constitutional objection was in fact only a cover for the underlying ____.
16. What did Seminex Professor Walter Bartling testify? ____
17. R. H. Redal of Lutherans Alert-National said "This is the actual battle for ____."

CANDID OBSERVATIONS
Commission on Church Co-operation
Adelaide, May 1975
K.E. Marquart

The Lutheran, September 8, 1975
Christian News, September 22, 1975

As one of the LCA's fifteen official observers I must confess to some mixed reactions. On the one hand I deeply appreciated the generosity of the organizers in not only permitting, but repeatedly urging, full participation on our part in the discussions, even though we were only observers from a non-member church. And the opportunity for personal contact with so many church leaders from all parts of the world was valuable. I was greatly impressed by the passionate Christian concerns of some of the men with whom extended conversations were possible, it was also an unexpected pleasure to meet several friends and acquaintances from former days, now scattered about the globe.

On the other hand there were and are the objective issues, which no amount of personal charm and diplomacy can conjure away.

Lutheran World Federation as Church

To begin with, it was plain as day that the Commission regarded itself as being engaged in the real work of the Church. Fellowship in Word and Sacraments on the part of the co-operating churches was simply taken for granted as self-evident. There is no other way to understand the very motto of the meeting. *Togetherness in Mission,* emblazoned above the gathering, together with a symbol of the Holy Spirit.

The essayist, Dr. James Scherer, of the Lutheran School of Theology at Chicago, used the motto as the title for his paper, and said of the Commission: "We wanted to give a visible, structural expression to the worldwide unity of the Lutheran churches in the midst of their diversity of life-situations". And the Findings Committee included this ringing declaration in the Preamble to its Report: "We are deeply aware of our oneness in confession of faith and in mission, and our coming together has increased our desire to support one another in our common obedience to the missionary calling".

To argue here that the organization which carries out these churchly tasks is, after all, only a federation, is quite beside the point. Church and church fellowship depend not on the niceties of outward arrangements — that would be formalism - but on the substance of what really goes on. Our Australian Lutheran *Document of Union* clinches the point when it says: "We declare that wherever continued co-operation in the preaching of the Gospel and the administration of the Sacraments and worship exists, there we have a witness to the world of unity in the faith and a profession of church fellowship" (Par. 7). That, of course, requires real *doctrinal agreement* about the Gospel and the Sacraments!

Some Vital Issues

It is just this agreement which is quite lacking in the Lutheran World Federation. The Helsinki Assembly of 1963 could not even agree on a joint statement on Justification!

The Adelaide meeting did not directly concern itself with doctrine and theology. Nevertheless, important doctrinal implications came through. For example, the voluminous agenda contains thumbnail sketches of the various member churches receiving aid for various projects. Repeatedly the statement occurs: such and such a church is in altar and pulpit fellowship with the Reformed church of that country. There is no suggestion anywhere that such a state of affairs flies in the face of the Lutheran Confessions, which the LWF claims to uphold in its constitution. Indeed, in the case of two Lutheran churches in Czechoslovakia, we read: "The desire to remain faithful and loyal to the forefathers and to their confessions is still very strong. This, together with other factors, makes it understandable — although in the opinion of many not less regrettable — that both churches have refused to agree to the *Leuenberg Agreement*" (p. 58).

This language is masterfully balanced. Does it mean approval or rejection of the *Leuenberg Concord,* a German document claiming to heal the breach between Lutherans and Reformed especially on the Real Presence, but actually side-stepping the issue? Or does it mean simply that in the LWF all views within member churches have equal rights?

Another vital issue is that of the biblical Gospel versus the unbiblical Social Gospel of the World Council of Churches. Dr. Scherer's paper, while criticizing some excesses, tried to make these opposites into complementary aspects of the one full Gospel! Accepting the slogans of the WCC-sponsored Bangkok Assembly (1973), the essayist argued that "proclamation and development" belong together. Dr. Henry Hamann, Vice-Principal of Luther Seminary, Adelaide, made a strong plea to the Assembly to reconsider this confusion of spiritual and political/social realms, which was basically a confusion of Law and Gospel.

How WCC circles understand "development" was indicated when Australian Council of Churches' General Secretary, Frank Engel, in his greetings to the meeting, warmly commended "Action for World Development" materials, among them *Development News Digest,* published by the Australian Council for Overseas Aid, which is supported by the Australian Council of Churches. The issue offered in Adelaide (March, 1975) was full of the most blatant pro-communist propaganda, including an article explicitly glorifying life in North Vietnam!

"Liberation" - But Only In Africa

Certainly the mood of the CCC meeting in Adelaide was not at all that of WCC-type radicalism. Nevertheless, a certain vulnerability to ideological lopsidedness surfaced even there. A document from Southern Africa took the line that the Gospel includes social/political liberation, and not merely "spiritual freedom", and that even "violence", though generally deplorable, might have to be resorted to. Yet nothing similar was said in connection with the fierce oppression in Eastern Europe. On the contrary, one quotation presented "the social and state reality of the DDR" (the East German regime) as "something that comes from the God who is the Lord over Church and State" by way of "a test period to be followed obediently".

When I drew attention to the glaring contrast, it was pointed out that not being a super-church, the LWF's Commission could do no more than respond to the initiatives of its member churches. And the Eastern European churches had never asked for a discussion of persecution! So the Commission accepted an Africa Area Committee recommendation that it "concurs with the general thrust of the resolutions", while not a single word of protest was uttered officially against the brutal persecution of Christians in Eastern Europe. No doubt it was felt that public action would only worsen the plight of the Christians there. The apparent double standard, however, constantly misleads the public into thinking that Southern Africa is the world's worst problem, when in fact the regimes there are denounced only because it is safe to do so. They are civilized enough not to retaliate too harshly, whereas the communists have no such inhibitions and hence must be treated with due respect!

While my remarks clearly did not please the group as a whole, some churchmen, especially those from certain countries in Asia, expressed their appreciation privately, noting that they faced this kind of ideological bias all the time. They were dismayed that despite the obvious horrors of Hanoi's recent conquests in Indo-China, the Asia Area Committee could not be persuaded even to use such words as "communist" or "persecution". Instead, the language of the resolution tiptoed gingerly from "political changes " to "the question of religious freedom in Indo-China now under a new political and social order"!

Free Chinese churchmen also objected to the phrase "New China", and to the biased and misleading approach of selected "China specialists" convened by the LWF's Department of Studies.

"Faith without God?

Professor Scherer had opposed the idea of "polarization" between "evangelicals" and "ecumenicals". All should remember, he said, that they are brothers in the faith, despite their theological differences. But he gave no indication that the differences are actually about the very central facts and truths of Christianity. For instance, Dr. Hans Asmussen, a former President of the Chancery of the whole Evangelical Church in Germany, writing in the LWF's own official organ, *Lutheran World* (XIII, 2, p. 186), had put it very plainly:

"But this is in fact the picture of wide sectors of our Lutheran Church today; clergymen read aloud the Christmas story, which they consider a fairy tale. They read aloud the Easter story, to which they find access only after several re-interpretations. At the grave, they witness to the resurrection of the dead, which they consider a myth"

How is it possible not to divide or "polarize" when these very foundations are being sold out?

At a private meeting between some leaders of the LWF Commission and members of our own Australian Theological Commission, I tried to pursue this crucial matter further, I asked, in view of the pleas for "togetherness" despite differences, where the line was to be drawn, or if, indeed, a line was to be drawn at all. For example, would a position like Bultmann's — for whom Trinity, Divine Sonship, Virgin Birth, Resurrection, Ascension, and all the rest are just so much myth to be got out of the way — still be considered within the pale? The only answer I received was that of a German Bishop who replied that he had once tried to have Bultmann's position condemned at a German Synod, but that the very conservative theologian Dr. Werner Elert had prevented the condemnation by arguing that after all Bultmann still believed in "justification through faith alone"!

"Faith alone" makes perfect sense when it means: without human works, merits, achievements of any kind. But when the "alone" is taken to mean: without God, without Christ, without doctrine, atonement, resurrection, then the term is pure humbug. It is, in fact, a case of lying and deceiving by God's name.

Conclusion

It is very misleading to speak and act as if outward, organizational world Lutheranism were one big happy family, a "world-wide fellowship of Lutheran churches", all agreed on the basics, though differing in some details. Such a happy state of affairs has not existed for at least 150 years — as the origins of both our former Australian Lutheran Synods ought never cease to remind us! To pretend otherwise is to do a disservice to the cause of true Christian unity in the one Lord and His one faith and one Baptism.

1. Church and church fellowship depend on the substance of what ____.
2. The LWF Helsinki Assembly could not even agree on ____.
3. Not a single word of protest was uttered against the brutal persecution of Christians in ____.
4. What was said about South Africa? ____
5. Free Chinese churchmen objected to ____.
6. What did a former president of the whole Evangelical Church in Germany say about "wide sectors in our Lutheran Church today?"____
7. Werner Elert prevented the condemnation of ____ by arguing he still believed in "justification in through faith alone."

Professor Kurt E. Marquart, Author

ANATOMY OF AN EXPLOSION - MISSOURI IN LUTHERAN PERSPECTIVE

Christian News, June 13, 1977

Concordia Theological Seminary Press, Fort Wayne, Indiana has just published *Anatomy of An Explosion - Missouri In Lutheran Perspective* by Professor Kurt E. Marquart. The 170 page paperback with some 460 footnotes is available from Concordia Theological Seminary, 6600 N. Clinton St., Fort Wayne, Indiana 46825.

Anatomy of An Explosion is the third number in the Concordia Seminary Monograph Series. Editors David P. Scaer and Douglas Judisch comment: "*Anatomy of An Explosion* is an apt title for a monograph describing the conflicting theological forces, which encountered each other in the sixties and seventies of our century. As when black clouds move across a summer sky, the lightning was inevitable. Serious students of the Synodical controversy will certainly give careful study to Professor Marquart's scholarly analysis."

Dr. Robert D. Preus, president of the Fort Wayne seminary, says in the book's foreword: "Because what Prof. Marquart says is true, his judgments (which are not directed against people) are factual and correct. Although always challenging and instructive, Prof. Marquart's book is not at all times easy to read. After all, it is not a novel written for relaxing enjoyment. ... Moreover, he must delineate and clarify the doctrinal issues which directly affected the explosion in Missouri, issues which have been dreadfully obfuscated by liberal and confused theologians inside and outside the Missouri Synod. But, most important of all, Prof. Marquart perceives as his burden also to evaluate according to Scripture and our Lutheran Confessions what has happened and the new doctrines which split the Synod and caused so much turmoil. In everything he is eminently successful."

Marquart recognizes that some Lutheran Church-Missouri Synod conservatives had made mistakes which helped breed liberalism. He acknowledges that Missionary Brux of India "became the victim of official over-reactions." He writes: "Another danger-signal was a certain theological stagnation-despite the valiant efforts of the 'Theological Observer' section of the *Concordia Theological Monthly* to keep readers abreast of European theology" (51). Marquart admits that Dr. Theodore Graebner was right when he said long ago that a short-sighted legalism would "breed radicalism, liberalism, strife, and division" (51).

According to Marquart, "Dynamic movements like neo-Pentecostalism cannot be resisted with mere decrees or prohibitions — though these too have their place. The appeal of cultism is a warning signal that an inner emptiness exists into which demons are want to rush. If people truly un-

76

derstood and appreciated the grandeur of God's gift in His Gospel and Sacraments, no one would pay the slightest attention to all the froth and bother of the 'tongues' 'healings,' or 'Late-Great-Planet-Earth' excitement. But such living appreciation cannot come from books alone, though they are necessary. It is not enough to confess the *Book of Concord* in theory — it needs to be put into practice. Preaching and the Sacraments are to be done aright, not merely thought about. How can we expect Lutheran people to have a high regard for the Gospel and Sacraments, when in our parish life we so often disguise our high 'theory' with Reformed or revivalist practices which suggest a low view of the Means of Grace? If we expect people to have some regard for the Augsburg Confession's Biblical position on the Real Presence (Article X), then we shall have to express and implement this evangelical mystery in our public worship and church life (Article XXIV). In the New Testament as in the Lutheran Confessions the Sacrament is a vital and central part of Christian worship. Our actual practice often suggests the Reformed pietistic notion of the Sacrament as an occasional 'extra.' Solzhenitsyn wrote that the Liturgy he heard and saw celebrated in church during his childhood made such a deep and lasting impression on him that no amount of intellectual argument or personal suffering later was able to erase it. There is no reason why Lutheran worship, taken seriously, should not affect men similarly. But who would expect the same from a rousing chorus of 'Pass It On' — with or without hand-clapping? If we foster a taste for spiritual marijuana, we need not be surprised if many go on to the 'fuller' heroin of Pentecostalism. And if parishioners are not earnestly warned against seeking nourishment from a version like the 'Living Bible,' which deliberately changes the great texts about Baptism and the Holy Supper into mere picture-language, how can we expect them to grasp or retain the sacramental teaching of the New Testament? Nor, of course, are people likely to be inspired in that direction if the Christian mysteries are celebrated with all the fervor of a stock-exchange report — collections being more prevalent than communions — or with the gabby folksiness of daytime television" (65-66).

Marquart exposes the kind of theology tolerated within the Lutheran World Federation and the Lutheran Council in the U.S.A. The Concordia Seminary professor writes: "'What right,' asks Tietjen in his book, 'does any Lutheran church body have to deny the hand of fellowship to those whose espousal of the faith of the Lutheran Confessions marks them as fellow Lutherans?'[234] This is precisely the view of the Lutheran World Federation, which holds that because all member-churches accept the 'Confessional paragraph' of the LWF's constitution, they are thereby professing doctrinal unity and ought to show it by formally acknowledging church-fellowship with all other member churches. [235]

This approach invites at least a threefold objection. "First of all, the whole situation is patently untruthful. What is the meaning of all this solemn talk about the Lutheran Confessions if member-churches of the LWF, in fact, practice official intercommunion with Reformed churches, which deny the Real Presence of Christ's body and blood in the Sacrament? Or why did the LWF go to all the constitutional trouble, at its Helsinki Assembly in 1963, of adding the Apostles', Nicene, and Athanasian Creeds to its 'Confessional paragraph,' if there was not the slightest intention to exclude, curb, or ban even the wildest Bultmannian attacks on these very Creeds? Asmussen, a former president of the chancery of the Evangelical Church in Germany (EKiD), has described the situation as follows: 'But this is in fact the picture of wide sectors of our Lutheran Church today: clergymen read aloud the Christmas story, which they consider a fairytale. They read aloud the Easter story, to which they find access only after several reinterpretations. At the grave, they witness to the resurrection of the dead, which they consider a myth.'[236]

"The 'No Other Gospel' and 'Churchly Gathering' movements in Germany arose to combat the historical-critical assault on the most basic Christian truths. At an international conservative meeting in Sittensen, Germany, a Swedish participant asked an official LWF representative what would happen if the faithful Lutherans would be forced out of the Church of Sweden (a member-church of the LWF). Would the LWF then side with those who represented the doctrinal position of the Lutheran Confessions, or would it dismiss them as a 'sect'? The LWF man could not answer.

The report continues:

> It became clear that in accordance with its whole structure as a federation of existing, historical institutions with a common 'doctrinal basis' — but no doctrinal authority — the LWF could only, in the acute case of a division, side, without regard to truth and confession, with the official institution, which continues the established historical tradition.[237]

"The real value of all the lip-service to the Confessions in that case is nil. Nor are things very different in America. What is the meaning of a 'consensus on the doctrine of the Gospel and the meaning of confessional subscription' being 'sufficient'[238] to warrant co-operation in the Lutheran Council in the USA (LCUSA), if that body's Division of Theological Studies could issue a report[239] advocating room for 'a variety of positions' — including attacks on Christ's Godhead and Atonement? Again, presumably all the seminary faculties of the ALC and the LCA would publicly pledge allegiance to the Lutheran Confessions. Yet their joint publication, *The Lutheran Quarterly*, printed without any public rebuke, a blatant denial of the Holy Trinity and of the Divinity of Christ, which blasphemously portrayed the Transfiguration as 'an occasion on which Jesus, who had deep rapport with his psychic disciples, hypnotized them, and presented them with illusions of Moses, Elijah and the Voice of God, in order to convince them of his unusual messiahship. How can this sort of thing be related meaningfully to any alleged 'consensus' about the 'Gospel' or 'Confessional subscription' or for that matter about any grain of Christian truth, however minimal?

"If bodies like the Lutheran World Federation are neither able nor willing to do anything about the mockeries perpetrated by an unbelieving university 'theology,' why the hollow pretenses about the exalted status of the Bible, the Creeds, and the Confessions? Of course, it will be said, no one who is 'in the know' will have any illusions on this score. Very well, but why mislead the simple? Is this not 'lying and deceiving by God's Name,' contrary to the Second Commandment?" (67-68)

Marquart asks:

"Why did the Missouri Synod become the only major American church-body to turn back the modernist tide?" He replies: "Part of the answer, under God's providence, doubtless lies in the fact that Missouri conservatives could truthfully claim that their position was not merely one strand or school among others, but the solemn, authentic, and original confessional platform on which the Synod had been founded, and which it had consistently maintained since its inception" (78).

The author observes: "All the same, the endless preoccupation with by-laws is a danger-signal. Among Lutherans it is axiomatic that only 'faith' (doctrine, sacraments), not 'order' (administration, government) of itself can be church-divisive. In God's Word and doctrine there can be no yielding, but in outward matters, such as indifferent ceremonies or man-made regulations for good order, the rule is that love shall be supreme and consciences may not be bound. On occasion it may be the Christian duty of the majority to yield to the minority in such matters. Conservatives dare never absolutize the letter of human regulations, but must be ever mindful of their churchly intent. This means too that conservatives should beware of simply echoing liberal charges of 'playing politics' every time an orthodox president of synod restrains the full use of his authority in order to avert greater harm among confused and excited people. 'The salvation of the people is the ultimate law,' says an ancient maxim" (97-98).

Marquart shows just how far some "moderates" in the LCMS have departed from historic Christianity. He notes: "Already in 1962 Dr. Robert Scharlemann had followed 'contemporary German theology' in driving a wedge between the Resurrection and the Empty Tomb. Defending this theology in general and Bultmann in particular, Scharlemann thought it a misunderstanding to see in these views 'a subversion of the Christian faith.'[397] In April 1972 Prof. W. Bartling, then a member of the faculty majority in St. Louis, stated in an address before the Louisiana Pastoral Conference: " I believe that many of my Christian brothers have problems with the virgin birth, real presence, bodily resurrection.... I can't bear the burden of Scriptural infallibility." Even the Lutheran Confessions' doctrine of the two natures of Christ was criticized by River Forest Prof. W. Bouman, and that much more fundamentally than he was willing to admit. [398] The notorious Concordia Publishing House course for high school students, *Out of the Desert*, even went so far as to treat Judaism, Christianity, and Islam as equally valid 'ways' to the same God! 'Moderate' spokesman Paul Bretscher illustrated historical criticism by interpreting the dove and the opened heavens at our Lord's Baptism simply as 'a graphic literary imagery.' [399] In the same essay Bretscher said of Bultmann, who rejected all Christian dogma as so much myth and legend, including the Trinity, the Incarnation, Atonement, Resurrection, and Ascension: '. . . as a Lutheran preacher Bultmann submits altogether to the authority of the Holy Scriptures as the Word of God.... It is not Bultmann's intention to detach the Gospel from the history of Jesus. . .' [400]

"One bizarre glimpse into the historical-critical bankruptcy was provided by Sten H. Stenson's Abingdon Award-winning book *Sense and Nonsense in Religion.* The book 'defended' the validity of Christianity and other religions on the grounds of 'the punlike character of miracle stories and religious legends.' 'Religious' language, in other words, is not to be taken literally, but is comparable to puns or 'witticisms,' which 'are irrelevant to truth and falsity in the usual prepositional sense.'

"Stenson likens 'religious' language 'especially' to the theatre of the absurd (p. 232)! Of course, he applauds Tillich's rejection of all absolutes and Bultmann's notion that 'it was not a historical interest that dominated the Gospel writers... "but the needs of Christian faith and life"' (p. 153). Indeed, Bultmann is here cited to the effect that the evangelist St. John 'while making free use of the tradition creates the figure of Jesus entirely from faith!' Stenson's total relativism is clear from these excerpts:

> If a Jew comes to understand Torah, he will, in a sense, have risen above it and can then throw it away... Likewise, when Christians come to understand Christ they will no longer need to cling to him as, literally, the only way to the Truth. This, among other things, is what the so-called death of God theologians have discovered.
> ... both Judaism and Christianity are anti-idolatrous, self-destructive, and equally true in the manner of religious "wit."[401]

"But what has all this to do with the Missouri Synod? One of the judges who awarded the Abingdon prize was none other than Missouri 'moderate' Martin E. Marty, who gushed: 'It is a fresh presentation of the Christian faith, and of faith itself. I would be proud to hand it to bright people up and down my block and to colleagues in worlds of media or academy!' One is tempted to assume charitably that Marty was simply too busy to study the book he praised so lavishly. But that disturbing little reference to 'faith itself' in addition to 'the Christian faith' suggests that he knew only too well what he was saying.

"What parochial innocence, then, slumbers smugly in the conviction that 'it can't happen here,' that the Missouri Synod's magic touch can somehow tame the wild rapacity of historical criticism into a lamb-like 'discriminating appreciation!' Hence Leigh Jordahl's gentle taunting of Missouri's 'moderates:'

> Do you really believe that you have some special gift and grace so that even if you discard (as you most certainly are) that principle of

an absolutely inerrant Scripture, you can somehow do what no other denomination has so far managed to do: keep your fundamental theological presuppositions even while you engage in a historical-critical methodology that must mean a recognition of relativity and theological pluralism? Can you really, except by the most anti-intellectual gymnastics, adopt a method but purge it of those aspects which you term "negative" by the use of "Lutheran presuppositions?" [402] (pp. 122-124)

Dr. Ralph Reinke, President of Concordia Publishing House, is still defending CPH's *From Out of the Desert* and insists that censors appointed by LCMS President Jacob Preus have approved the course.

LCMS President Preus says he agrees with Reinke. Reinke has been severely critical of *Christian News* for raising objections to *From Out of the Desert*. The LCMS's Dallas convention is being asked to deal with the matter.

Marquart shows how the historical-critical method of interpreting the Bible, the method approved by "moderates," undermines the Holy Scriptures and the Christian faith. He writes: "A perfect illustration of all this is the fate of the Lord's Supper at the hands of the historical-critical method. One Missouri 'moderate,' though he admitted that 'biblical-criticism does change the rules and does change the character of biblical authority,' [413] cheerfully announced that 'what higher criticism has revealed is that we may be confident that the Words of Institution are from Christ. . . . But this is the very thing which historical-criticism has most pointedly subverted! Concerning the Lutheran-Reformed agreement, or rather compromise, on the Sacrament embodied in the so-called 'Arnoldshain Theses,' we are informed that half the participants were 'leading New Testament scholars,' and that it was the historical-critical approach which 'ultimately determined the course of the discussions and the formulation of the Theses.' [415] Yet because of this historical-critical approach it was **'no longer possible to connect the institution of the Supper with the night in which He was betrayed!** In other words, the historical Jesus never instituted the Sacrament; instead, the account was created by the 'faith' of the early Christians after their 'Easter-experience.' Such sinking sand cannot support any firm doctrine of the Sacrament, least of all the Lutheran Church's confident certainty that her sacramental teaching 'rests on a unique, firm, immovable, and indubitable rock of truth in the words of institution recorded in the holy Word of God and so understood, taught, and transmitted by the holy evangelists and apostles, and by their disciples and hearers in turn.' [417]

"And what historical criticism does to the Sacrament, it does in principle to the entire Christian doctrine and to the historical facts in which it is grounded. If the Apostles' Creed were to be reworded to reflect honestly the prevailing critical opinion, it would 'confess' about Christ something like this:

... Who was probably not conceived by the Holy Spirit or born of the Virgin Mary, was almost certainly crucified under Pontius Pilate, dead, and buried; on the third day or so He seems in some sense to have risen again from the dead, and was thought to have ascended into heaven; from thence, if the preceding is valid, he may or may not return.... (126,127).

The seminary professor answers some objections "moderates" have toward orthodoxy.

"Contrary to the tiresome caricature, orthodoxy insists not on the Bible but on Jesus as the crucial watershed for faith. F. Pieper, for instance, roundly rejects the suggestion than an unbeliever must be persuaded first of the inspiration of Scripture and then of salvation in Christ! [422] Orthodoxy recognizes that the Bible is seen in one way before, and in quite another way after one has come to faith in Jesus. For this very reason orthodoxy maintains so insistently the very necessary distinction between apologetics, on the one hand, and theology proper, or Christian doctrine, on the other. [423]

Apologetics seeks merely to clear away the obstacles, that is, the false arguments, which keep unbelievers from giving serious consideration to the claims of God's own Law and Gospel; they alone can smite and heal the sinner. In this apologetic realm it is perfectly valid, indeed necessary, to reason from the common ground of public information and argument which the unbeliever too must acknowledge. But this is merely incidental to the proclamation of Law and Gospel which alone can convert. It is simply a service of love, a missionary accommodation, to deprive the unbeliever of his chief excuses for dismissing Christianity out of hand. It is purely 'pre-evangelism,' to secure at least external engagement with the Gospel, which will then do its own work. For example, if someone refuses to read the New Testament because he has been 'educated' to regard it as a doubtful collection of old legends, it is helpful to demolish this objection by referring to books like London University Prof. J.N.D. Anderson's expert treatment of the Christian case as legal, documentary evidence.[424] Once a person is willing to consider the Christian message, it will win its own victories. No matter what one's previous theory of the Bible, the Gospel has the power to create in the Law-stricken sinner faith, that is, trust in Jesus, the Resurrection and the Life! At the same time the Word documents itself as being God's own. Once a man confesses Jesus as Lord, he cannot in principle reject what Jesus Himself teaches about the Scriptures of the Old and New Testaments. Hence the Bible which seemed, before faith, in the realm of apologetics, to be simply a venerable documentary record, is now, after conversion, known, seen, and confessed as God's own inspired, revealed, immovable, and life-giving Word. That is the realm of theology and Christian doctrine" (128,129).

While LCMS "moderates" claim they are loyal to the Lutheran Confessions, Marquart demonstrates that "moderates" have departed from both the Bible and the Confessions. He observes: "It is not, of course, the Gospel at all, but its mortal enemy, historical criticism which demands the surrender of the Scripture-principle. As one of the main founders of the historical-critical method put it, 'the root of the evil (in theology) is the confusion of Scripture and Word of God.' [429] Historical-criticism has been trying to correct this 'evil' ever since. Missouri 'moderates,' like Krentz [430] and Bretscher, [431] do not hesitate to follow suit. Nor can **Faithful... I** (a Seminex document, Ed.) manage a stronger definition of inspiration than that it 'pertains to the effective power of the Scriptures to bring men and women to salvation through the Gospel.' [432] This, however, is not inspiration at all, but efficacy! And why that vague word 'pertains'? Inspiration 'pertains' to many things, but what precisely is it? The confusion continues: 'We affirm, therefore, that the Scriptures are the inspired Word of God.' Therefore? Because of its Gospel-power? But, in that case, are not creeds, catechisms, hymn-books, and our own sermons equally and in the same sense the inspired Word of God? Indeed, such notions of inspiration were openly defended before President Preus 'Fact Finding Committee!' [433]

"This new, historical-critical view of Scripture and inspiration is no longer that of the Lutheran Confessions. The Confessions do not hesitate at the equation, the Bible IS the Word of God. And they do not take the 'is' with any grain of salt. Thus the Smalcald Articles, for instance, use 'Scripture' and 'Word' quite interchangeably in the paragraphs leading up to the classic assertion of the great Reformation *sola scriptura* principle: 'The Word of God shall establish articles of faith, and no one else, not even an angel' (II, II, 15). The *Formula of Concord* allows no fuzzy confusions on inspiration which might blur the absolute difference between Scripture and all other writings" (130-131).

The author repeatedly defends the inerrancy of the Bible.

"This giving 'God the honor of truthfulness' is the whole point of the much-maligned and misunderstood doctrine of biblical inerrancy. Without inerrancy the Scripture-alone principle becomes an empty pretense. If the sacred text is subject to error, then it is no longer the standard of truth, but is itself in need of one. It is no longer judge but defendant. Historical-critical counter-theology with its fallible Bible resembles an asylum in which the Bible is straitjacketed and subjected to 'treatment' while the patients play doctor and nurses! And it is not a question of how much or how little — the situation is in principle wrong. The *Formula of Concord's* sharp distinction between 'divine and human writings' merely echoes Luther's *Large Catechism* on Baptism: "I and my neighbor and in sum all men are capable of erring and deceiving, but the Word of God can neither err nor deceive!" It is sheer nonsense to try to restrict inerrancy here to certain topics only, such as Baptism or 'the Gospel.' Luther argues obviously from inerrancy to Baptism, not from Baptism to inerrancy! The inerrancy attaches to God's Word as such, not to particular topics only (else why just these and not those?). The critical anti-inerrancy stand should frankly admit that it abandons the Confessions' teaching on this point, indeed the whole scripture-principle; it should not pretend to be subject to the Scriptures and the Confessions.

"The main point to be kept in mind here is that inerrancy is not something over and above, or in addition to the Bible's inspiration and authority. It is simply part and parcel of any bona fide confession that the Bible, as God's Word, is the sole and decisive authority for faith, sola scriptura. Least of all is it some kind of obvious fact or feature which can be established by common sense, and which then 'proves' that the Bible is God's Word. It is an article of faith, given with inspiration itself. Inerrancy is to the Bible roughly as His sinlessness is to Christ. If Christ sinned, then he could be neither Savior, nor Son of God, nor Lord. But we do not 'prove' His divine nature by first 'proving' somehow that He was sinless! On the other hand, the sinlessness of Christ is a kind of test or criterion which shows whether one really accepts Him as God and Savior, or whether one is simply mouthing beautiful, traditional, but meaningless words. Similarly, the most fervent professions of absolute and unconditional submission to the Bible as the inspired Word of God, etc., lose most if not all of their meaning if one at the same time rejects inerrancy. How can I seriously accept something as 'absolutely authoritative' if I also believe it to be mistaken or in error?" (131-132)

Marquart concludes: "The neo-Lutheran 'with-it-ry' is not the theology of the cross that it claims to be, but a cultural cringe to secular values. True, Aristotle, that idol of scholasticism, is generally booed — but mainly because he is out of fashion. The new Aristotles, evil geniuses like Darwin, Marx, and Freud, now set the tone. [456] While elsewhere persecuted Christians taste the cross to the full, we in the West accommodate ourselves more and more to the trendy gods denounced so eloquently, and from bitter experience, by men like Malcolm Muggeridge and Alexander Solzhenitsyn! How shallow is all our comfortable 'relevance!' 'Our business,' wrote C. S. Lewis, 'is to present that which is timeless (the same yesterday, today, and tomorrow) in the particular language of our own age.' Is that not precisely what our new, 'critical' theology is all about? Quite the contrary. Lewis continues:

> The bad preacher does exactly the opposite: he takes the ideas of our own age and tricks them out in the traditional language of Christianity. Thus, for example, he may think about the Beveridge Report (the basis of the British social welfare system) and talk about the coming of the Kingdom. The core of his thought is merely contemporary; only the superficies is traditional. But your teaching must be timeless at its heart and wear a modern dress. [457]

"But without contempt of the world we cannot love, much less proclaim the eternal things of God. Worldly 'theology' leads instead to a despising of that very suffering and cross which opens our eyes to the priceless grandeur of the 'visible and lowlier' things of God! Is it our respect for suffering or our love of convenience that makes us so serenely indifferent to the torments of millions of our fellow believers? In East Germany in August 1976 Pastor Oskar Bruesewitz burned himself to death in a futile attempt to draw the world's attention to the fearful oppression inflicted especially on young Christians under militant Marxism. He hoped no doubt by his own sacrifice to secure some relief for the weak lambs in his flock and elsewhere. Meanwhile in New York and Washington other pastors used their freedom of action to speak out boldly — for the killing of the unborn in the name of 'civil rights!' And in Minneapolis they explored the ultimate possibilities of self-indulgence through pornographic exercises in 'human sexuality!' But, of course, it is all a matter of interpretation: 'In the beginning was the Flesh . . . .' [458]" (138,139).

Marquart writes in the book's epilogue: "That the 'moderate' theology runs afoul of 'old Missouri's' most cherished convictions is so plain that it is really beyond dispute. More important are the wider implications of the Biblical and Confessional Principles. After all, whether something is genuinely 'Missourian' or not is really of no theological interest except as it clarifies what is genuinely Lutheran; just as the question of what is really 'Lutheran' is trivial and sectarian unless its intention is to make clear what is genuinely Christian" (141).

1. Who published Marquart's *Anatomy of an Explosion?* ____
2. Robert Preus wrote that Marquart's judgments are ____.
3. What did Solzhenitsyn write about the liturgy? ____
4. "The Living Bible" deliberately changes ____.
5. What did EKID President Hans Asmussen say about wide sectors of the Lutheran Church? ____
6. The endless preoccupation with by-laws is a ____.
7. What did Concordia Seminary Professor Walter Bartling tell the Louisiana Pastoral Conference? ____
8. Professor W. Bouman criticized ____.
9. The CPH course From Out of the Desert criticized ____.
10. CPH President Ralph Reinke was critical of *Christian News* for objecting to ____.
11. Orthodoxy insists not on the Bible but ____ as the crucial watershed for faith.
12. Apologetics seeks to clear away ____.
13. The new historical critical view of Scripture and inspiration is no longer that of ____.
14. Without inerrancy, the Scripture alone principle becomes ____.
15. Inerrancy is to Scripture as sinlessness is to ____.

A Generally Favorable Review
MARQUART'S ANATOMY OF AN EXPLOSION

Missouri In Perspective, July 18, 1977
Christian News, July 25, 1977

A "moderate" reviewing *Anatomy of an Explosion* hardly knows which Kurt Marquart to take on, the serious Marquart who seems to understand what "moderates" are thinking theologically and then challenges them on the basis of serious scholarship, or the Marquart who lapses into foolish generalizations and distortions, such as his assertion that the "moderate" view equates the Gospel with "secular permissiveness."

But then, not even a "moderate" review should take on the author without first exploring what the author has to offer, and in the case of *Anatomy* that is significant. What Marquart has to offer is some of the better "conservative" theology extant as it relates to the current Lutheran Church—Missouri Synod controversy.

Marquart believes that the theological position affirmed by today's "conservatives" not only represents the authentic Missouri Synod position but also the authentic position of Luther, the Lutheran Confessions, and the other reformers at their best. The seventeenth century era of Lutheran Orthodoxy represents in Marquart's view an authentic understanding of the sixteenth century Reformation, not a corruption of it as it is seen by many church historians.

Thus Marquart provides both a recount of controversies that have affected Lutheranism from the post-Reformation period, through the migration of the anti-rationalists and anti-Prussian Unionists who formed the Missouri Synod, through to today's "moderate"- "conservative" tensions. Particularly pivotal in this discussion are the questions of church fellowship with alleged errorists and of the inerrancy of the Scriptures.

On the issue of church fellowship, Marquart seems to have two main goals: one, to prove that new ecumenical trends, affecting the Missouri Synod since 1945, would lead ultimately to a sell-out on the Synod's doctrinal position, and two, to debunk Dr. John Tietjen's historical study, *Which Way to Lutheran Unity?* On both fronts, he maintains, "moderates" fail to recognize that the other Lutherans only pay "lip service" to the Confessions while allowing "undisturbed liberty" to do anything members want to with the Confessions. In the process, Marquart has harsh words for the Lutheran World Federation, the Lutheran Council in the USA, the Lutheran Church in America, the American Lutheran Church, the St. Louis seminary, and a dozen or so LCMS members, for all of whom Confessional subscription was a mere "formality," he says.

On the question of Scriptural inerrancy, Marquart provides enough historical background and theology to shake most "moderates" out of our comfortable clichés and to re-study the issue. Marquart is especially convincing in his argumentation that Walther, Pieper, and most of Synod through the early 1950's held to a strict view of inerrancy. Somewhat less convincing is his documentation that Luther and the Lutheran Confessions are rooted in the same view. His analogy of the inerrancy of the human/divine Scriptures to the sinlessness of the human/divine Christ provokes thought, if not agreement. (Is an error in the Bible the equivalent of a sin by Jesus, or maybe a stomach-ache?)

Marquart saves some of his strongest judgments for proponents of historical-critical methodology, arguing that confessional subscription rules out use of the method. Citing at length from both LCMS and non-LCMS proponents of the methodology, Marquart concludes, "Historical criticism, to be true to itself, must keep itself unfettered by any authority save that of human reason. But this very feature has condemned the method to ultimate sterility and bankruptcy." But, while demonstrating other instances where historical criticism has led to abuses, Marquart has a hard time coming up with instances where criticism as practiced at Seminex has demonstrated the same sterility. Some of Marquart's danger signals are useful, but the fact that he repeatedly uses Seminex Professor Edgar Krentz's work to support his warnings should have indicated that historical critics at Seminex are as aware as he of potential abuse.

Another question that Marquart should have asked himself was whether Lutherans need to adopt the same condemnatory attitude towards other Christians that the Confessions ofttimes display, in order to be faithful to the doctrine of the Confessions. In other words, can Lutherans have a give-and-take relationship with, say, Reformed Christians in discussions of the Lord's Supper without selling out the doctrine of the Real Presence? (Indeed, worthy of additional study would be the way in which careful historical-critical study has brought many other Christians closer to the Lutheran position on issues like the Real Presence or Justification by Grace through Faith.)

In spite of Marquart's over-all effort to be well-documented and carefully reasoned in his argumentation, there are several annoyances, not the least of which is his repeated implying that those who do not share the "Old Lutheran" views of LCMS "conservatives" are less interested in pure doctrine and the Scriptures than they. His working assumption seems to be that those who disagree are, by definition, less faithful. That will annoy many "moderates."

Also annoying is his occasional misrepresentation of "moderates," such as his suggestion that our view of the Gospel is "secular permissiveness," that we place human reason over the Scriptures, or that by not absolutizing certain doctrinal formulations we do not believe the Word of God is an absolute.

Other lesser annoyances include an attack on "pastors with twanging guitars," his repeated insistence on British spelling (defence, programme, behaviour, fervour, haemorrhage, etc.) while writing for an American audience, and too many glaring typographical errors, along with some of the worst page make-up and printing imaginable.

One other factor in the book is more than an annoyance. In his foreword, Concordia Seminary (Fort Wayne) President Robert Preus—while giving *Anatomy* some well-deserved praise—suggests that because of Professor Marquart's long years in Australia "he was the ideal person to tell the story. He was uninvolved in the events and so had little occasion to form prejudices or animosity toward any of the principal actors in the drama." For those who have been reading Marquart's regular contributions to *Christian News*, suggestions that he was an unbiased outsider do not ring true. Further, says Dr. Preus, Marquart "was far enough from all that happened to be unhurt and unaffected personally by others 'hurts'." In saying that, Dr. Preus perhaps tips off the greatest weakness of the "conservative" movement, an insensitivity to the hurts of others.

On balance, however. Anatomy is a capable, thorough, and well-written statement of the "conservative" theological position. A clear improvement on the slip-shod theology of many of the right-wing newsletters, it will force many "moderates" to re-examine their own position in the light of the Scriptures, the Confessions, and their own history. And any book that sparks new study is clearly an asset.

1. *Missouri In Perspective* was published by the ____ in the LCMS.
2. Marquart has harsh words for ____.
3. Marquart is especially convincing that ____.
4. What will annoy many "moderates" about Marquart? ____
5. According to *Missouri In Perspective* the greatest weakness of the conservative movement is____.

INTEGRITY BAROMETER: FALLING

From the Concordia Theological Quarterly, April, 1978.
Christian News, May 15, 1978

It is always interesting and often instructive to hear veteran church-men reminisce about important events in which they themselves have participated. Such recollections are so much more colorful than the dull official minutes and other bureaucratic leavings among which historians are forced to fossick. A case in point is the forthright and spirited critique, "Observations on Parts of Dr. Nelson's Lutheranism in North America, 1914-1970" *(Lutheran Quarterly,* May, 1977), by Dr. Fredrik Schiotz, for-mer President of the Evangelical Lutheran Church, of The American Lutheran Church, and of the Lutheran World Federation.

By far the most important issue raised by Dr. Schiotz in his article is that of the very nature of Lutheran churchmanship today. The upshot of Schiotz's argumentation is startling, if not to say shattering. For it means, to put it bluntly, that theological, doctrinal honesty is not partic-ularity relevant in our ecumenical era, dominated by the will-to-union. What is at stake here, be it clearly understood, is not the personal ethics of Dr. Schiotz. He is obviously quite sincere in his belief that the supreme good of pan-Lutheran union demands and justifies the sort of policies he defends and advocates. The point rather is to address, and assess, the objective merit of his argumentation, which must carry considerable weight, given the author's eminently representative status in world Lutheranism.

Schiotz is miffed at Clifford Nelson's claim that he, Schiotz, made, within the short span of one decade, a complete "about face . . . with re-gard to inerrancy." What is astounding however is Schiotz's line of ar-gument. He does not deny that in 1966 he publicly took the "old Lutheran" position on Scripture and inerrancy, or that in 1966 he was defending the opposite, "neo-Lutheran" view. But he explains that he had held the neo-Lutheran view all along, even while for the sake of peace he had been publicly proclaiming the "old Lutheran" view, which he did not believe. He suggests also that doctrinal candor is a luxury in which the-ological professors may indulge, but which administrators must some-times forego. Here are his own words:

> In Dr. Nelson's discussion of Lutheran unity efforts, he is preemi-nently the theological professor. He follows the straight line of what he terms the "neo-Lutheran" view with regard to scripture. My posi-tion had to be that of an administrator. . . . I had to pay very careful attention to the thinking of our-people. . . . In my own mind I did not conclude that Dr. Nelson's position was wrong theologically, but it be-came a question of timing. Since the constitution charged the president with the responsibility to watch over the peace of the church, timing was of the essence. I had not forgotten the debacle in 1948 when the convention was frightened and thoroughly rejected consideration of

World Council of Churches membership. . . .

In my speaking of the ULCA's attitude regarding the Word as "liberal" I was announcing the prevailing attitude of the Church Council, most of the pastors, and the cross-section of lay people in the congregations. My own attitude was represented by the United Testimony.

Such a defense is really more damaging than the original accusation. There is no disgrace in an honest change of mind. But for the first officer of a church-body to pretend to hold one doctrine while subverting it behind the scenes in favor of another, quite contradictory doctrine (Schiotz: "Thus, there was emerging in the church among the younger pastors a consensus that refused to settle for a fundamentalist interpretation of the meaning of inerrancy.") amounts surely to a complete abandonment of the ordinary and accepted canons of integrity.

To justify his dissimulation Dr. Schiotz appeals from the ALC's constitution, which teaches biblical inerrancy, to the United Testimony on Faith and Life, which deftly, manages to create the impression of teaching inerrancy without actually doing so. Because the United Testimony was the earlier and basic document (1952), Schiotz argues, he was entitled to set aside (he calls it "interpret") the strict inerrancy language of the Constitution in favor of the loose language of the United Testimony. The argument is as tricky as it is false. In the first place, the strict inerrancy language of the ALC's Constitution goes back beyond the United Testimony to the even more basic Minneapolis Theses of 1925 and 1930. On Dr. Schiotz's own admission public opinion in the uniting churches was such in 1952 that the United Testimony would have been roundly rejected had it been openly presented and understood as a repudiation of the Minneapolis Theses' strict stand on inerrancy! And secondly, Dr. Schiotz himself concedes that Clifford Nelson's account of the rise of the "neo-Lutheran" view of Scripture is "substantially . . . accurate." If so, then Dr. Schiotz must know very well that the ALC's constitutional formulation on inerrancy, taken from the Minneapolis Theses, was deliberately designed to counter and rule out the ULCA view embraced by Schiotz, secretly at first and later in public. Why does he assume that the Constitution required the President "to watch over the peace of the church" but not to uphold its solemn confession of inerrancy?

What is alarming is that such pragmatic disdain of doctrine is accepted as perfectly normal in ever wider circles today. Nor is it merely tolerated as a regrettable administrative necessity. It is perceived rather as a positive virtue, *viz.* "dealing pastorally"!

Now, of course, there is such a thing as pastoral tact and wisdom. No pastor worth his salt would normally accost a prospective convert with a discourse on predestination or a blistering attack on Freemasonry. Nathan used discretion to lead King David to repentance. Richard Wurmbrand once disarmed a morose atheist in a Rumanian Communist prison by saying, "Atheism is a sacred word to us Christians, for the first Christians were called atheists in ancient Rome!" There is obviously a vast gulf between the missionary largeness of heart of a good pastor and the petty, brittle rule-book mentality of the bureaucratic pedant. But taking into account the hierarchy of Christian truths or the state of mind of the person to whom they are to be applied, is one thing. It is quite another to resort to outright misrepresentation, or even to mislead whole church-bodies by playing fast and loose with the language and intent of solemn, public doctrinal definitions and pronouncements. Even among politicians it was until recently considered honorable to tender one's resignation if one's principles had changed or even if they had only fallen into disfavor.

The great crash in the Missouri Synod must stand as an awesome warning of what happens to the greasy sort of "pastoral dealing" if and when the lavish promissory notes of its inflated theological currency can no longer evade the demand for payment. Dr. Schiotz has chosen to describe the LCMS New Orleans (1973) Convention as giving "evidence of a big city-like, ward political machine at work. What a jolt that was! For me such highly unevangelical action revealed that whoever was responsible for it was blind to the meaning of the Gospel. This was the natural Adam gone wild." On the contrary, New Orleans was basically the repudiation of a church-political establishment which had frittered away its credibility. After a generation of pussy-footing, people were sick and tired of all the touching speeches and all the "pastoral dealing." They were fed up with gutlessness dressed up as Gospel-sweetness. They had been deceived, manipulated, and exploited long enough. The day of reckoning had arrived, and all the heady, windy, and evasive neo-Lutheran rhetoric was weighed and found wanting. A chastened, sobered church demanded a return to basic honesty in theology and church practice.

Dr. Schiotz's apologia raises for American Lutherans in acute form the watershed issue posed by the old-Lutheran/neo-Lutheran conflict: that of theological integrity and credibility. No doubt Dr. Schiotz intended, for instance, to give a genuinely pastoral and evangelical speech to the assembled delegates at New Orleans. But when in the course of his emotional address he suggested that the ALC's United Testimony—which by then he was in the habit of taking in a neo-Lutheran sense—reality took the same stand on inerrancy as the well-known Missourian conservative, Dr. Robert Preus (LCMS *Proceedings,* 1969, p. 74), Dr. Schiotz was clearly transgressing the bounds of truth. No amount of personal goodwill and sincerity can remove from such tactics the stigma of disingenuousness. When the zeal for outward church-union becomes so all-consuming as to override dogma and confession, then the rule of Christ is replaced by the whims of men. Since objective standards and controls are thereby abolished, truth becomes indistinguishable from falsehood, pastoral leadership from political manipulation, and Christian unity from bureaucratic empire-building.

There is only one way out of this morass of nihilism, and that is unyielding insistence on the objective givens: the pure teaching of Christ's Gospel and the right administration of His holy Sacraments. Especially we pastors need daily to abjure the corrupting allurements of success-orientation and to shoulder faithfully the sacred yoke of our office as servants of Christ and stewards of the mysteries of God. Let us leave

grinning ambiguities to the White Houses of this world.
K. Marquart

1. Frederik Schiotz claimed that he made a complete change with regard to ____.
2. The strict inerrancy language in the ALC's United Testimony and Faith goes back to ____.
3. Even among politicians it was until recently considered honorable to ____.
4. New Orleans was basically ____.
5. A sober minded church demanded return to ____.
6. The only way out of the morass of nihilism is ____.
7. Let us leave grinning ambiguities to the ____.

REACTIONS TO THE OFFICIAL RESULTS OF INTER-LUTHERAN (LCUSA) THEOLOGICAL DISCUSSIONS SINCE 1972

The Concordia Theological Quarterly, October, 1978
Christian News, December 11, 1978

Mere Lutheran union in America or even globally is small change in the lofty perspectives of Pastor Richard Neuhaus' *Forum Letter,* fervently heralding the ecumenical millennium right now if not sooner. Still, Neuhaus has generally been benignly tolerant of LCUSA, so long at least as that body seemed destined to herd the maverick LCMS safely into the ecumenical corral. But now something has gone very wrong, and *Forum Letter* does not like it a bit. "Lutheran Differences Reinforced," grumbled its leading caption for June 30. The reference was to a report issued by LCUSA's Theological Studies Division on official inter-synodical discussions held between 1972 and 1977.

The report is entitled "The Function of Doctrine and Theology in Light of the Unity of the Church" (FODT for short). It is worthy of very careful study. Every pastor in the ALC, the LCA, and the LCMS should have received a copy.

The reason for Neuhaus' displeasure is curious. He does not challenge the veracity of the report. What offends him, it appears, is not that differences between the churches are misstated, but the very fact that they *are* stated at all. To paraphrase a famous epigram: "How odd of FODT to vent dissent"! Such is Neuhaus' confidence in the theology of the ALC and the LCA that he seems to take it for granted that a public ventilation of that theology by its own practitioners will tend to reinforce "the suspicions and arguments against ALC and LCA that Preus' party has always nurtured . . . . In terms of rehabilitating stereotypes, the present document is an unquestionable success."

Anyone rushing headlong into the FODT document itself, however, his appetite whetted by Neuhaus' piquant suggestions, may soon find himself yawning. That would be a mistake. Bureaucratic committee reports simply are a *genre* very different from the racy readability of *Forum Letter.* One must make due allowances for the difference if one is to gauge the true import of the calm surface prose. One will look in vain in such documents for vulgar excitement, e.g., "The place is on fire; everybody out!" To catch such a message one needs to keep one's eyes open for judicious understatements like, "General evacuation may indeed be indicated, should responsible efforts to control the present combustion prove only marginally effective."

Given the limitations of the accepted dialogical idiom—and without a certain disciplined restraint fruitful controversial discussions would not be possible at all—the FODT report is extraordinarily candid and revealing. It frankly admits, for instance, that unlike the Missouri Synod's spokesmen, ALC and LCA representatives generally favored the historical-critical approach to Scripture. This is explicitly acknowledged to involve the issue of *"the legitimacy of affirming the existence of discrepancies, contradictions, mistaken notions, or diverse theologies within the Scriptures"* (pp. 7-8; emphases added). Yes, "diverse theologies"! In other words, there is no such thing as *Christian doctrine — only* Pauline, Johannine, Lucan, etc. "theologies"! Neuhaus of course has known this all along: "Basically, there are no surprises," he says, "and that is not surprising." Why then begrudge Lutheranism a "full public disclosure," as we say nowadays, of such non-surprises?

One can only describe as a total lapse from objectivity Neuhaus' interpretation-in-a-nutshell: "The [FODT] document makes explicit what it admits everyone expected in advance, that Missouri dissents from the understanding of doctrine, theology, and the Church that prevails in two-thirds of American Lutheranism." This deft public relations projection defies the dogmatic, theological realities. It suggests the existence of a more or less stable and standard US Lutheran "understanding of doctrine, theology, and the Church," unfairly torpedoed, however, by a petulant Missouri Synod stubbornly pursuing its own eccentric ways. But what if the real facts are altogether different? What if it could be shown that the real problem is not Missouri's dissent from "two-thirds of American Lutheranism" but the latter's dissent from the recognized criteria or standards of Lutheranism? As it happens, one need not go beyond the FODT report itself to make this very point. Since the issue is one of great moment, the relevant wording of the Report should be carefully noted, with due realization that the formulation before us is not some partisan "Missourian" confection but was stipulated to by official representatives of all three church-bodies under the auspices of the Division of Theological Studies of LCUSA (p. 8):

> Representatives of the LCMS emphasize that the entire doctrinal content of the Lutheran confessional writings, including the implications of confessional statements dealing with the nature and interpretation of Holy Scripture, is accepted and remains valid today because it is drawn from the Word of God —that is, because it is a faithful exposition of Holy Scripture. On the other hand, some representatives of the other two church bodies, while affirming their continuing commitment to the gospel of Jesus Christ as witnessed to in the Lutheran confessional writings, tend to emphasize the historical character of those writings and to maintain the possibility of dissent from confessional positions that do not deal directly with the gospel itself, such as some aspects of the confessional positions on the fall of humanity into sin and the nature and interpretation of Holy Scripture.

If "two-thirds of American Lutheranism" really do in principle defend dissent from the doctrinal content of the Lutheran Confessions on such issues as the very nature of Holy Scripture and the fall into sin (no doubt the historicity of Genesis in general and of Adam in particular is the main

94

sticking point here), then surely this cannot simply be waved aside as "not surprising"! At the very least we should then hear no more of the glib propaganda untruth that while all parties accept and subscribe to "the Scriptures and the Lutheran Confessions," the problem is that Missouri insists on yet other documents in addition to these, and that it is these peculiarly Missourian specialties which are causing all the trouble.

Neuhaus notes that by no means all Missouri Synod pastors or people agree with their Synod's official stand. Sad to say, he is right on this score, although his numbers are inflated. Genuinely informed opponents of the Missouri Synod's official doctrinal position are difficult to find, in most cases Missourians who imagine themselves to be opposed to their Synod turn out to be simply well-meaning, conservative Lutherans whose normal human sympathies have been taken advantage of. But of the real doctrinal issues they are blissfully innocent. This deplorable spectacle attests the success of ELIMAELC'S well-nigh cynical strategy of avoiding and evading a thorough ventilation of the precise theological matters in dispute, and of concentrating instead on endless sob stories about alleged injustices with which to exploit Christian sentiments.

That *Forum Letter* should overestimate the dissent within Missouri is not really surprising. But why is there no suggestion at all of any internal dissent from the "prevail [ing]" direction of the other "two thirds of American Lutheranism," the ALC and LCA? Certainly anyone who knows enough about the situation not to be surprised at the FODT report must realize that at any rate the radicalized theologians taking part in the LCUSA talks do not by any stretch of the imagination represent the rank and file clergy, not to mention the laity, of the ALC and the LCA. The tragic chasm between pulpit and lecture-hall, pastors and professors, church and seminary, is after all a characteristic curse bequeathed to theology in and through historical criticism. One cannot permanently cultivate the divine covenant of Christ in the parishes and the legacy of the Rationalist Enlightenment in the seminaries. Nor can such church-destroying schizophrenia be conjured away with "practical" trickeries, scholarly obscurities, or liturgical escapisms. Returning now to the FODT report, let us consider a paragraph like the one on page 6:

> The ALC and LCA representatives also affirm the reliability and truthfulness of the Scriptures, but they link those characteristics with the purpose of the Scriptures—their gospel-hearing function. This view sees the Scriptures as completely reliable in communicating all the promises of God to humankind, not to the exclusion of history but through it. The concern is that this central message of the Scriptures not be clouded, called into question, or confused in its application by creating false tests of faith.

There can be little doubt that this kind of language, standing by itself, would win overwhelming votes of confidence, and not only in the ALC and the LCA but also in the Missouri Synod. But now let us add a bit of context. The immediately preceding paragraph of FODT reads as follows (p. 5):

> The LCMS representatives argue that a less-than-complete commitment to the Scriptures, an uncertainty about their truthfulness, a hesitancy or disagreement with regard to some of their contents, will endanger the proclamation of the gospel. The question is not simply how far the Scriptures should be trusted in what they say about Christ, but really whether the Christ we confess is the Christ of Scripture or a Christ constructed according to some human standard.

If *this* is the context—more precisely: the alternative—then the ALC/LCA formulation becomes considerably more dubious. An affirmation of the "reliability and truthfulness of the Scriptures," which when decoded turns out to mean something more akin to "less-than-complete commitment to the Scriptures, an uncertainty about their truthfulness, a hesitancy or disagreement with regard to some of their contents," is bound to seem somehow fraudulent, and not only to Missourians. The broader ecclesiastical context moreover is distinctly ominous. LCA theologian Philip Hefner, for example, was able to state in a recent LWF sponsored study that there is for his church "a certain authority in modern thought *per se*," hence a "dual authority of doctrine and modern thinking," with the "proper relation of the two . . . as yet an unresolved problem."[1]

The final sentence of the FODT paragraph under consideration states: "The concern is that this central message of the Scriptures not be clouded, called into question, or confused in its application by creating false tests of faith." (FODT, p. 6). A Christ-centered approach to Scripture is, to be sure, a deeply Lutheran attitude. But what are these "false tests of faith"? A wide variety of answers is possible here. For example, the official publication of the LCA's predecessor body, the ULCA, at one time used to print, with full approval, statements by Reinhold Niebuhr like these: "The young men are accused, among other things, of not believing in the virgin birth of Jesus or in his 'physical resurrection' or ascension. Are these beliefs really *tests of the quality of faith?*" (emphases added).[2]

More recently LCA theologian John Reumann, in a glowing editorial commendation of the English translation of Hans Conzelmann's famous essay, *Jesus*, described Conzelmann's theological position as "an Evangelical (Lutheran Reformation) 'theology of the word.' Hence the emphasis on preaching (proclamation) as that which contemporizes Jesus for us today."[3]

Yet Reumann admits at the same time that Conzelmann represents the "Bultmann school" and assumes, for example, "the general non-historicity of the Fourth Gospel." Worse yet, in the essay itself Conzelmann describes the opening chapters of Matthew's and Luke's Gospels as "cycles of legends," treats even the Davidic descent of Jesus as doubtful, and regards the Baptismal accounts as legendary. Further, according to Conzelmann's essay, Jesus did not claim to be the Son of God —this title being originally understood "adoptionistically" in any case—and had no

96

intention of establishing any church! The account of the Last Supper is a "cultic legend," and so on. How many pastors and members of the ALC and LCA would agree that this sort of thing is "an Evangelical (Lutheran Reformation) theology of the word"'? Certainly nowhere near Neuhaus's "two thirds of American Lutheranism," most of whom would surely be horrified if they thought that their seminary professors were even toying with such notions.

It is the great merit of the LCUSA discussions, as reflected in this significant FODT report, to have begun the daring process of facing up to the real issues posed for Lutherans by today's theological climate. And once one has gazed at the depth and enormity of the problems, one cannot simply shut the lid, as it were, and pretend that it is all a question of a few little interpretations of a few little Bible-texts. Some doctrinal differences may well prove to be irresolvable in the end. But surely no one has a right simply to give up without trying. Projected solutions are at this stage clearly premature; first the real nature of the problem needs to be traced with the utmost honesty and precision. If LCUSA's theological discussions can avoid church-political short-circuiting and can patiently lead the Lutheran churches of America into a clear understanding of today's theological options and their various implications and ramifications—and the FODT report is a promising token in this direction — they will have given the churches something of infinitely greater value than all those impressive ecumenical displays which still leave consciences uninformed and doubting. The outcome is beyond the control of men; it is up to the church's Head, who can give far more than we can ask or think.

NOTES

1. John Reumann, ed. *The Church Emerging: A U.S. Lutheran Case Study,* (Philadelphia: Fortress Press, 1977), p. 150.
2. *The Lutheran,* December, 1955, p. 18.
3. J. Raymond Lord, tr., *Jesus* (Philadelphia: Fortress Press, 1973), p. x; Hans Conzelmann, "Jesus Christus," *Die Religion in Geschichte und Gegenwart: Handwoerterbuch fuer Theologie und Religionswissenschaft,* ed. Kurt Galling et al. (Tuebingen: J. C. B. Mohr, III (1959), cols. 619-53.

K. Marquart
(From *The Concordia Theological Quarterly*, October, 1978.
Concordia Theological Seminary, Ft. Wayne, Indiana).

1. Unlike the Missouri Synod's spokesman, the ALC and LCA representatives generally favored ____.
2. There is no such thing, according to LCUSA, as ____ doctrines only ____ theologies.
3. The main sticking point is the historicity of ____ and ____ in particular.
4. Neuhaus is right about ____.
5. Hans Conselmann described the opening chapters of Matthew's and Luke's Gospel as ____.
6. John Reumann described Conselmann's theological position as ____.

"NEW LUTHERAN CHURCH" WILL NOT BE LUTHERAN SAYS LCMS PROFESSOR

Christian News, December 12, 1983

"The 'New Lutheran Church.' will be new, but it will not be Lutheran" says Professor Kurt Marquart of The Lutheran Church-Missouri Synod's Concordia Seminary, Ft. Wayne, Indiana, in an article appearing in the Christmas, 1983 *Affirm*.

The Lutheran Church in America, the American Lutheran Church, and the Association of Evangelical Lutheran Churches are currently involved in discussions leading toward the formation of a new Lutheran Church by 1988. Some conservatives have been complaining that this new Lutheran Church will be broad enough to include those who deny such basic doctrines as the deity, virgin birth and resurrection of Jesus Christ. Some of the theologians on the 70 member Commission For a New Lutheran Church have attacked fundamental doctrines of the Christian faith and are outspoken defenders of the killing of unborn infants. (The April 25, 1983 *Christian News* and *The Christian News Encyclopedia* documents the theological position of members of the CNLC).

Marquart says in *Affirm* that the 'New Lutheran Church' "will embrace Lutheran elements, yes, but as such it is casting aside the constraints of the Book of Concord, hence does not wish to be Lutheran. Good people? Yes, there are good people on bad roller-coasters. And humanly speaking the ride into disaster cannot now be stopped. Yet ecclesial crashes are also times of gracious divine visitations. They are occasions not for smug self-satisfaction, but for penitent faith and renewal on all hands, with the fervent prayer that God would bring together the confessing remnants everywhere which belong together. 'She's dear to Me, the Worthy Maid'!"

Marquart quotes Richard Koenig, who left the Lutheran Church-Missouri Synod and joined the Lutheran Church in America, as writing with "refreshing candor": "Not only are there decided differences in outlook, piety, and organizational style among the three churches, but together they harbor some unresolved theological problems. First, Lutherans of the AELC, ALC, and LCA seem uncertain about a replacement for the scriptural principle even if they quote the Bible as if it were yet sole source and norm for all church teaching and practice."

Although the present constitution of the American Lutheran Church still refers to the Bible as "inerrant," the *CNLC* has announced that the "New Lutheran Church" will no longer say that the Bible is "inerrant." Marquart notes: "Clifford Nelson has long ago publicized the fact that the strong 'inerrancy' — language got into the present ALC constitution as a church-political attempt to 'hold the line,' even while the seminaries were being overtaken by the 'neo-Lutheran,' i.e. historical-critical, denial of inerrancy. More startling is ALC ex-president Fredrick Schiotz' claim, in response to Nelson's presentation, that he, as president, had really

98

agreed with the 'neo-Lutheran' view, but had maintained the contrary, old view in public, lest people become alarmed! ... This policy of 'benevolent deceit' is evidently being continued by the New Lutheran Church, though without the word 'inerrancy.' Any language suggesting serious submission to Holy Scripture as the Word of God, and to the Book of Concord as the right confession of it, is in the circumstances a cruel hoax upon those who would flee if they beheld unveiled the face of historical-critical unbelief."

According to Marquart, "the LCA's John Reumann has not hesitated to brand the Christology of the Augsburg Confession's Article III as Nicene-Chalcedonian tradition rather than biblical truth..." (See *The Christian News Encyclopedia* for an analysis of Reumann's anti-Christian theology. Reumann was one of the leading spokesman of the Roman Catholic-Lutheran dialogue which concluded that Roman Catholics and Lutherans are now in basic agreement on the doctrine of justification).

1. "The New Lutheran Church" will be new but not ____.
2. The New Lutheran Church will no longer say that the Bible is ____.
3. The LCA's John Reumann has not hesitated to brand the Christology of the Augsburg Confession as ____ rather than ____ truth.

THE EX-LUTHERAN MERGER

Affirm 1983
Christian News, December 12, 1983

1. *THEOLOGY ECLIPSED*

The journal *Dialog* is to be commended for raising the issue of theology in connection with the three-way merger. The Spring, 1981, number of *Dialog* brought an array of articles on the subject, some of which criticized very pointedly the purely organizational, non-theological approach embodied in the official proposals. Richard Neuhaus, for instance, asked pointblank: "But what does this merger proposal have to do with achieving theological agreement? Indeed, what does it have to do with theology?" In his own paper, *Forum Letter* (May 27, 1983, p. 8), Neuhaus quoted Carl Braaten: "Theologians in the Lutheran churches are now basically moonlighters. Bureaucrats run the budget and decide what kind of theology, if any, they want. As often as not they will find theologians on the periphery of the church's life to say the things they want said." Maintaining an incisive and courageous battle against the Marxist/political exploitation of "mainline" churches, Neuhaus warns against the managerial model of the church as "an organization pushing religion as McDonalds is an organization pushing hamburgers." (September 23, 1983, p. 2).

In the Spring, 1983, issue of *Dialog,* Gerhard O. Forde, of Luther Northwestern Theological Seminary in St. Paul, wrote an incisive and pessimistic article, "The Place of Theology in the Church," which pursues this question further. Forde argues that the church's agenda is set more and more not by theology, but by "a whole host of bureaucratic concerns: statistics, control, programs, popular causes, something called 'the needs' of people, and above all, I suppose, 'cash flow.'" But theology also has itself to blame, says Forde. On the one hand there is an abstract "academic" theology, which has lost its ties to fonts, pulpits, and altars, and is therefore irrelevant to the church. On the other hand, where the tough-minded demands for correct theology were given up, the churches and their clergy were reduced to the undignified posture of currying popular favor. "The clergy turned from dogmatics to what was supposedly 'practical' and 'devotional.' Thus began the long descent of theology from its lofty heights to the level of greeting-card sentimentality." Forde's stinging phrases are aimed at the general American church situation, which certainly has not left Missouri untouched either.

2. *ANGLICAN-LUTHERAN FELLOWSHIP:*
A CASE IN POINT

With great public fanfare the ALC the LCA and the AELC, have implemented joint Communion services with the Episcopal church, designated as "interim Eucharistic sharing." The agreed statements and the essays of the "Lutheran-Episcopal Dialogue" do not document dogmatic unanimity, but rather a thoroughgoing "pluralism." How was it possible to accept even an "interim" altar-fellowship with a church, which has always included one strand of conviction expressed in the infamous Black Rubric of 1552: ". . . and the natural Body and Blood of our Savior Christ are in Heaven and not here; it being against the truth of Christ's natural body to be at one time in more places than one"? (John Brett Langstaff, *The Holy Communion in Great Britain and America,* Oxford University Press, 1919. p. 86).

The real trouble today is much more radical. Nothing could show it more clearly than the sermon preached by Dr. John Shelby Spong, Episcopal bishop of Newark, N.J., at "the inauguration service of interim shared Eucharistic fellowship between Lutherans and Episcopalians in New Jersey, held October 31, 1982," and reprinted in *The Christian Century* (June 8-15, 1983). Said Bishop Spong:

> every doctrine of infallibility — whether of the papacy, or of the Scriptures, or of any sacred tradition, or of any individual experience — will inevitably have to be forgotten....
>
> Christianity for the first time in its 2,000-year history is floating free in a sea of relativity, unable to maintain any of its traditional authority claims.
>
> The Ecumenical Movement on deep levels symbolizes this relativity...
>
> The church of the future will have to learn to embrace relativity as a virtue and to dismiss certainty as a vice. . . .
>
> The ecumenical journey will carry modern Christians to a fearful, anxious future, where all will be forced to lay down narrow claims and to embrace the openness of this new day. When the Christians of the world can do this, then perhaps in that larger community of faith, worshipers and believers will include the Jews, the Muslims, the Buddhists, the Hindus. They will come. I trust, with equal claims to being children of the one God equally created in that God's image, equally loved and sought in that God's plan for salvation....This is the vision to which the ecumenical movement ultimately points the church.

This is the frightful reality which is accepted and legitimized in "interim Eucharistic sharing," on the basis of a few diplomatic excuses and evasions which make up the "dialogue" papers. The theological abysses having been papered over, the way is clear for practical implementation by way of the inevitable bureaucratic "Guidelines" (see *Lutheran Perspective,* 29 November, 1982). In these tragi-comic "guidelines" it suddenly becomes important that "concelebration — two ministers speaking the Eucharistic prayer (be) avoided, because it conflicts with Lutheran tradition." On the other hand, a Eucharistic prayer should be included, because Anglican practice requires it. There must be approval by bishops of both parties, and "ministers from both traditions should be present at the altar." What matters is that official protocol be observed, so that the mummery may appear legitimate. Both kinds of functionaries must by all means appear at the altar. That one of them happens to advocate Buddhist relativism, as in the case of the Anglican bishop of Newark, matters not at all. How Luther would have thundered against this sacrilege!

3. *GOSPEL MINUS TRINITY EQUALS-WHAT?*

It should be clear by now how thoroughly dishonest is the constant pretense that a basic or generic sort of confessional agreement is already a fact among U.S. Lutheran churches, and that this given unity is mischievously sabotaged by Missouri's sectarian insistence on its own special inventions above and beyond the common faith of the Lutheran Confessions! So Carl Braaten, for instance, speaks of Missouri's insistence "that other Lutherans accept their novelistic *[sic]* idiosyncrasies as the condition of altar and pulpit fellowship." In his editorial introduction to *The New Church Debate: Issues Facing American Lutheranism* (Philadelphia: Fortress, 1983), this same Carl Braaten, however, indicates that much more is at stake than a dispute about polity:

> In the initial draft of the Task Force on Theology, for example, the parts dealing with "Confession of Faith" and "The Nature and Mission of the Church" have carefully excluded all reference to God as Father, and to Jesus as his Son, even when dealing explicitly with the doctrine of the Trinity. The documents refer to some of the functions of the Triune God, but have quietly avoided using the proper name of the Triune God as "Father, Son, and Holy Spirit." This is the standard name of God in Lutheran piety, in the Eucharistic cult, in the ecumenical creeds and in the apostolic canon. Mary Daly's book, *Beyond God the Father,* has caught the imagination of many who struggle for the liberation of women: some believe they can trace their oppression in the church to its Christian roots in the Trinitarian name of God as Father, Son, and Holy Spirit. Obviously, the task force has concurred in this judgment without benefit of serious theological examination (p. 13).

But the trouble goes far deeper than feminism. Warren Quanbeck, then an influential theologian of the ALC, *(The Sixteenth Century Journal,* VIII, 1977. 4. p. 53). wrote:

> The study of language and of the historical development of dogma have shown us that we cannot distinguish as sharply as the reformers did between divine and human origin of doctrines and institutions. We now see the doctrine of the Trinity and Christological definitions as children of mixed parentage, their mother the prophetic-apostolic tradition of the Scriptures and the Christian community, their father the Hellenistic philosophical tradition.

And the LCA's John Reumann has not hesitated to brand the Christology of the Augsburg Confession's Article III as Nicene-Chalcedonian tradition rather than biblical truth *(Lutheran World Report,* IX, 1980. Compare the splendid review by Prof H. Hummel in *Concordia Journal,*

September, 1983). The LCA's controversial Robert Jenson *(The Triune Identity,* Fortress, 1982, p. 186) has written:

> That there are any dogmas at all, much less the drastically particularizing dogma of Nicaea and Constantinople, means among other things that there must be church discipline. What bishop, ordaining his annual crop of Buddhists and Mother-Goddess cultists, wants to think about that?

4. *THE CONFESSIONS REPUDIATED*

Gerhard Forde valiantly challenges the merging bodies: "The basic theological issue for the new church, however, is the place and the future of Lutheran confessional theology in this country." It seems likely, however, that by the time of the actual merger in or after 1988, the question will be academic. For there is before the merging bodies the recommendation of its "Reformed/Lutheran Dialogue" committee, to establish full church-fellowship with the Presbyterian/Reformed partner churches. Since, admittedly, "differences remain" (a standard formula, appearing also in the Lutheran/Roman Catholic Dialogue, which is also urging church-fellowship), it is clear that we are dealing not with an honest settlement, but with a diplomatic formula in the tradition of the Leuenberg Concord (Europe, 1973). To declare church-fellowship on such a basis is to surrender what the Book of Concord understands by the Sacrament and by the Church. As every theologian knows, this is a public abandonment of the Formula of Concord, and thus of the authentic meaning of the Augsburg Confession. (But it is a typically bureaucratic idea that what "really" unites churches is common church-government, by-laws etc., rather than "mere" fellowship at the altar.)

The standard AELC formulation is that the Lutheran church is not really a church but a "confessional movement" within a larger church, that is, one school of thought among others. This thinking goes back not to the Book of Concord, which it in fact violently opposes, but to the Prussian Union of the last century, which dreamt of an "evangelical church" transcending the confessional differences between the Lutheran and Reformed churches (see H. Sasse's writings, and H. Gensichen; *We Condemn,* CPH, 1967).

The tragedy is that even those who deplore the plunge into relativism seem determined to abet it when it comes to the crunch. Thus Gerhard Forde allows ecumenical fervor to override sober theological judgment when he writes: "The Confessions never demand separation. That is not a Lutheran game . . . The Formula of Concord, surely, is interested in bringing concord, not in setting up criteria for separation." In fact, and for the record, the Formula of Concord itself quite clearly says things like these:

> This symbol [the Augsburg Confession] distinguishes our reformed churches from the papacy and from other condemned sects and heresies. We appeal to it just as in the ancient church it was traditional

and customary for later synods and Christian bishops and teachers to appeal and confess adherence to the Nicene Creed...

On the contrary, these controversies deal with weighty and important matters, and they are of such a nature that the opinions of the erring party cannot be tolerated in the church of God, much less be excused and defended *(Solid Declaration,* Rule and Norm, 5, and Introduction, 9).

It is fraud and robbery to excise the words "purely" and "rightly" from Augsburg Confession VII, and to advertise something less as the "true unity of the church"!

5. *GONE: THE SCRIPTURE FOUNDATION*

The confessional crisis has its direct source of course in the crisis of biblical authority, brought about by historical criticism. The AELC's Richard Koenig reports with refreshing candor:

Not only are there decided differences in outlook, piety, and organizational style among the three churches, but together they harbor some unresolved theological problems. First, Lutherans of the AELC, ALC, and LCA seem uncertain about a replacement for the scriptural principle even if they quote the Bible as if it were yet sole source and norm for all church teaching and practice *(Dialog,* Spring 1981, p. 163).

Here, and not in some alleged sectarian exaggeration about inerrancy (see Valparaiso's *Cresset* of November, 1982; "Two Cheers for the New Lutheran Church") lies the unbridgeable gulf between our churches. The ifferences are clearly indicated in LCUSA's official "FODT" Report of 1978, to which President Bohlmann refers in his clear-headed and sobering article, "Missouri and other Lutherans: our diverging courses," in the Reformation, 1983, issue of *The Lutheran Witness.*

According to the LCA's Philip Hefner, writing in the American contribution to the LWF's world-wide ecclesiology-study, the LCA acknowledges "a certain authority in modern thought per se." Hefner therefore speaks of "this dual authority of doctrine and modern thinking" and says that the "proper relation of the two is as yet an unresolved problem" (John Reumann, ed., *The Church Emerging, A U.S. Lutheran Case Study,* Fortress, 1977, p. 150).

All this must be borne in mind when bureaucratic "public relations" seeks to give the impression that the omission of the word "inerrancy" in the proposed new constitutional statement is an improvement, or that the suggested new wording is a "strong statement on 'Word'" *(Lutheran Standard,* October 21, 1983. p. 21).

Clifford Nelson has long ago publicized the fact that the strong "inerrancy"-language got into the present ALC constitution as a church-political attempt to "hold the line," even while the seminaries were being overtaken by the "neo-Lutheran," i.e. historical-critical, denial of inerrancy. More startling is ALC ex-president Fredrik Schiotz' claim, in response to Nelson's presentation, that he, as president, had really agreed with the "neo-Lutheran" view, but had maintained the contrary, old view in public, lest people become alarmed! (See "Observations on Parts of Dr. Nelson's Lutheranism in North America, 1914-1970," *Lutheran Quarterly,* May, 1977). This policy of "benevolent deceit" is evidently being continued by the New Lutheran Church, though without the word "inerrancy." Any language suggesting serious submission to Holy Scripture as the Word of God, and to the Book of Concord as the right confession of it is in the circumstances a cruel hoax upon those who would flee if they beheld unveiled the face of historical-critical unbelief even so, the awful truth is dawning here and there. Pastor James Hanson writes in the ALC's own *Lutheran Standard:*

"I am a slave to Scripture," Luther declared. "My conscience is captive to the Word of God." . . .

The church I grew up in was a slave to Scripture. . . .

The resolutions and agendas of our church conventions are far more politically focused than scripturally based. This is a reversal of Worms. Whereas Luther made a political meeting the occasion for a statement of faith, we made our faith meetings occasions for political statements... To me, the phrase. "I am a slave to Scripture" is a word of judgment. It is so because, quite frankly. I'm not. And we're not. Not at the present time. Yet [it] is also a word of hope. Because Luther was such a slave, I can be one too. And you can. We can *(Lutheran Standard,* 21 October 1983, pp. 8-9).

The "New Lutheran Church" will be new, but it will not be Lutheran. It will embrace Lutheran elements, yes, but as such it is casting aside the constraints of the Book of Concord, hence does not wish to be Lutheran. Good people? Yes, there are good people on bad rollercoasters. And humanly speaking the ride into disaster cannot now be stopped. Yet ecclesial crashes are also times of gracious divine visitations. They are occasions not for smug self-satisfaction, but for penitent faith and renewal on all hands, with the fervent prayer that God would bring together the confessing remnants everywhere which belong together. "She's dear to Me, the Worthy Maid."'

Dr. Kurt Marquart
Concordia Theological Seminary
Ft. Wayne. Indiana

1. *Dialog* is to be commended for ____.
2. The ALC, LCA, and AELC implemented joint Communion service with ____.
3. Dr. John Shelby Spong, Episcopal bishop of Newark, N.J. in his sermon at the inauguration service of Eucharistic fellowship of interim shared Communion between Lutherans and Episcopalians said ____.
4. What did Carl Braaten say about the Trinity? ____
5. How did John Reumann brand the Christology of the Augsburg Con-

fession? ____

6. A typically bureaucratic idea is that what "really" unites churches is ____.

7. The confessional crisis has its direct source in ____.

8. The "New Lutheran Church" will be new but it will not be ____.

APOSTASY IN VALPARAISO'S *CRESSET*

Noted in Brief
Affirm, June, 1985
Christian News, July 1, 1985

This column by Prof. Marquart includes a critical analysis of an article which appeared in the Cresset. The present item deals only with the doctrinal error involved. The author of the Cresset article is on the Missouri Synod clergy roster. The matter, therefore, is under discussion with him by the proper synodical officials. The present article is not intended to interfere in any way with the procedure and the discussion. If a future Cresset article indicates a change of doctrinal position, Affirm will take note of it.

Mahayana Lutherans?

Zwingli, as is well known, expected to hold sweet converse in heaven with pagan Greek philosophers. Similar sentiments influenced the Roman Catholic Council of Trent (1545-1563). Andrada, for instance, held that good pagans too can have faith, righteousness, and salvation, and that only a "hideous enemy of humanity" would regard the natural knowledge of God as not leading to salvation (See M. Chemnitz, *Examination of the Council of Trent,* Vol. I, pp. 392 ff., 426). Contrary to popular impressions, Vatican II then did not really break new ground in allowing saving truth also to pagan religions. It merely hatched the eggs laid already at Trent.

Luther's Reformation took an altogether different stand: "But outside the Christian church (that is, where the Gospel is not) there is no forgiveness, and hence no holiness... Therefore they remain in eternal wrath and damnation, for they do not have the Lord Christ . . ." (*Large Catechism,* Creed, 56,66).

The difference is exactly that between the "theology of glory" and the "theology of the Cross" (see *Luther's Works,* Vol. 31, pp. 38 ff.). The former is guided by human philosophy, that is, worldly wisdom, which of course flatters man. The latter prizes only the saving Word and gift of God in His Son, and lets go of everything else.

Heedless of all this, many modern Lutherans are drawn to what seems to them the more generous position of Vatican II: Christ alone gained the possibility of salvation for all men, but it is accessible also through the non-Christian religions. These Lutherans have forgotten that everything here turns on the Law/Gospel distinction. Of course churches which cannot see any radical difference between Law and Gospel, will reason like this: "If pagans have *some* natural knowledge of God, then why not enough for salvation?" But as soon as Law and Gospel are properly distinguished, it is clear that the natural knowledge fails not in degree ("not enough")—but in kind (it is all Law, Rom. 1 and 2, which cannot save, Rom. 3:20).

And to say that non-Christian religions offer not only natural knowledge but also saving grace is to separate grace from the means of grace. As Luther saw, this is what Rome and the anabaptists have in common: "They separate forgiveness of sins from the Word."

Apostasy in Valparaiso's Cresset

But even Vatican II universalism does not go far enough, according to an incredible piece in the September, 1984, issue of Valparaiso University's *Cresset*. The article is entitled "Does God have many names?" and argues throughout for a positive answer to this question. This wording of the issue is based on the title of John Hick's 1982 book, *God Has Many Names.* Hick is a non-Christian philosopher who edited *The Myth of God Incarnate* (1977), which started a major row in Britain.

Hick claimed that "Buddhology and christology [sic] developed in comparable ways," so that two strictly human beings, Gautama and Jesus, came later to be regarded as more than human. Christology, like "Buddhology," then is "essentially poetic and symbolic language."

This blasphemy is, with minor scholarly slaps on the wrist, presented as a possible "model" in the *Cresset* piece. And what makes the whole thing so serious is that the article was written not by some visiting scholar from the wilder vistas of ecumania, but by Theodore M. Ludwig, a professor of theology at Valparaiso, and a member of the Missouri Synod's ministerium.

Ludwig's basic criticism of Hick's relativism and pluralism is not, as one might have thought, that this flies in the face of the Savior's own express words, such as St. John 14:6: "No one comes to the Father except through Me." No, for Ludwig the trouble is this:

> By giving up the claim to finality and absoluteness of Christianity, at the same time something vital to all religions is relativized: the claim of each religion to ultimacy.

The problem, then, according to Ludwig, is not that Christianity's divine truth-claims are violated, but that the "model" in question "fails to take the truth-claims of the various religions seriously!"

The Vatican II idea of Christ's saving work being available through non-Christian religions too, which anticipate and are "fulfilled" in Christianity, is criticized on similar grounds: "If we hold Christianity as the final and absolute religion, other religions cannot be approached as equals, however we may respect them." Secular notions about "equality" and "pluralism" clearly set the agenda here. The First Commandment is sacrificed to the First Amendment.

There is then, after all, agreement between Christ and Belial, between the temple of God and idols (II Cor. 6:14 ff.), and the "table of demons" offers essentially the same salvation as the Table of the Lord (I Cor. 10:20,21)! For Ludwig expressly holds that Christianity is "not the exclusive possessor of truth and salvation." Indeed, there must be dialogue among the religions, and "its goal is not to convert but to share and to challenge and to contribute in a common quest for understanding the Mystery." God is held to "[reveal] himself in the Scriptures and in human culture and religion." One "must accept in a basic way the pluralism of religions; if other religions are met as basically inferior, something other than dialogue takes place in the meeting."

A Crisis in the Church

Ludwig and his mentors are wrong in implying that their new approach comes from our increased historical knowledge and sophistication, as compared with those of past ages. Faith and unbelief have contended with each other from time immemorial. Luther's strong convictions were not due simply to the naiveté of the times. What the *Apology* says about the Renaissance popes shows that the views of Bultmann and Hick were as "viable" in the sixteenth century as in ours: "Many openly ridicule all religions, or if they accept anything, accept only what agrees with human reason and regard the rest as mythology, like the tragedies of the poets" (VII/VIII,27).

What is new *is that* the Bultmann/Hick views are, with minor modifications, publicly held up *as theological* options within the ministerium of the Missouri Synod. The *Cresset article* errs not in some grey area of application, but *in the deepest foundations of Christian doctrine.* And it is not a question of "overstatements" which could be "fixed up" with a few judicious rephrasing's or explanations. The attack on Christian "exclusivism" is really an attack on the central New Testament confession that Jesus is Lord. The Christian confession is to be replaced ("reinterpreted") by something like Alexander Pope's "Universal Prayer ," much beloved of Freemasonry:

> Father of all! In every age,
> In every clime adored,
> By saint, by savage, and by sage:
> Jehovah, Jove, or Lord!
> Or, in earthier doggerel:
> We all believe in one true God:
> Jew, Christian, Turk, and Hottentot!

Whether they know it or not this is the ultimate destination towards which the historically-critically infected merging Lutheran churches are moving. The goal was clearly described by Episcopal Bishop John Shelby Spong of New Jersey, at the formal inauguration of "interim Eucharistic fellowship" between the (merging) Lutherans and the Episcopalians there on October 31, 1982. Dr. Spong said that the church of the future would have to "learn to embrace relativity as a virtue and to dismiss certainty as a vice." The "ecumenical journey," as outlined by the bishop, aims at "that larger community of faith," in which "worshipers and believers will include the Jews, the Muslims, the Buddhists, the Hindus."

No pubic, official protest against this has been lodged by the merging Lutheran bodies. The latters' "openness" and "pluralism" appear to extend therefore beyond unionism and heresy to apostasy and syncretism, that is, to paganism itself. If this is so, the title "Mahayana Lutherans" may well apply. The term, which means "Greater Vehicle," is used to distinguish "main-line" Buddhism from the more traditional minority.

Now, however, the *Cresset* piece has publicly raised the "Mahayana" banner within the ranks of the confessionally committed Missouri Synod. So *long as this public scandal remains officially uncorrected and unrepudiated, our church and ministry as a whole share co-responsibility for it.* In the days of C.F.W. Walther doctrinal purity and unity were *the* top priorities of our Synod, the chief reasons for its existence. If our frenzied modern busy-ness dictates other priorities, perhaps we need to stop in our tracks and heed the Savior's words to Martha: "You are worried and upset about many things, but only one thing is needed" (St. Luke 10:41-42).

Prof. Kurt Marquart
Concordia Theological Seminary
Ft. Wayne, Indiana

Editor's Note: LCMS President Ralph Bohlmann was displeased when Christian News sent "Does God Have Many Names?" by Theodore Ludwig in the September 1985 Cresset to almost all of the churches in the Lutheran Church-Missouri Synod. The January 14, 1985 Christian News published these articles: "LCMS Officials Keep Ludwig on 1985 LCMS Clergy Roster – No Retraction of Valparaiso Cresset Article Attacking Christianity," "Ask the President," "The 'Success' of Valparaiso's Jewish-Christian Dialogue – LCMS Professor Claims Christianity Is Not the Only True Religion," "Still No Evidence of Liberalism? Will Action Now BE taken?", "Does VU Teach That Christ is the Only Way," "Does God Have Many Names" by Theodore M. Ludwig reprinted from the September 1984 Cresset. Robert Schnabel, VU President, Publisher, James Neuchterlein, editor. Neuchterlein later worked with Richard Neuhaus on First Things founded by Neuhaus, a Universalist who said unconverted Jews are in heaven and that no one is in Hell. When Neuhaus died, he was highly praised by Paul McCain of CPH and David Benke in the Concordia Journal of Concordia Seminary, St. Louis. Neuhaus and his close friend Robert Wilken, who also joined the Roman Catholic Church, cheated Marquart out of becoming the editor of the Seminarian of Concordia Seminary, St. Louis.

1. Zwingli expected to hold sweet converse in heaven with ____.
2. Similar sentiment influenced the Roman Catholic ____.
3. Vatican II did not break new ground in allowing saving truth to ____.
4. The Lutheran Reformation took an altogether ____.
5. The "theology of glory" is guided by ____.
6. The "theology of the cross" prizes only ____.
7. What did Valparaiso University Professor Theodore Ludwig argue? ____.
8. What is new is that the Bultmann/Hick views are publicly held up op-

tions within ____.

9. The attack on Christian exclusiveness is really an attack on ____.

10. The historically-critically infected merging Lutheran church are ____.

SANTA CLAUS THEOLOGY

Christian News, March 31, 1986

In 1897 little Virginia O'Hanlon was devastated when her playmates told her that there was no Santa Claus. On her father's advice, she wrote to the *New York Sun,* where Francis P. Church composed a famous editorial, which has been reprinted at Christmastime ever since. Church wrote, among other things:

Yes, Virginia, there is a Santa Claus. He exists as certainly as love and generosity and devotion exist, and you know that they abound and give to your life its highest beauty and joy . . . Nobody sees Santa Claus, but that is no sign that there is no Santa Claus. The most real things in the world are those that neither children nor men can see.

Liberal theology argues exactly like that for the reality of God, Christ, Buddha, or whatever. If the experience of love, beauty, and joy is the real proof of religious truth, then of course God and Santa, Easter Bunny and Resurrection, Hinduism and Methodism, are all equally true — and equally false. For the organization-minded it is then simply a question of choosing whatever vocabulary ("pitch") can best pull the heart-strings, and the purse-strings, of any given "target audience." That is what the "religion business" boils down to in a pragmatic age.

Liberal Lutherans, too, are spinning Santa Claus theologies when they talk about a "Trinity" which is "simply the Father and the man Jesus and their Spirit as the Spirit of the believing community"

(Braaten/Jenson, *Christian Dogmatics* (1984), vol. I. p. 155); a "Christ" whose "pre-existence . . . in a spirit realm in which the Word 'lives' prior to entering human history" can no longer be taken literally (Paul Jersild, *Invitation to Faith* (Augsburg. 1978], p. 99): or a "real presence of Christ in the Sacrament" which not only the Lutheran Church but also the Reformed churches have always "strongly affirmed," and which therefore should divide these churches no longer! (*Lutheran-Reformed* Dialogue, *Series III [1981-1983],* p. 16).

In the twilight zone of "religious language" all things are possible. (Why then would anyone settle for Rudolf Bultmann when he could just as well have Rudolf the Red-nosed Reindeer?)

Theoretical difficulties aside, there is a serious moral problem.

Francis Church did not set out to deceive anyone with his piece of whimsy. He could count on his readers' common sense to take up his paean to Santa Claus in the spirit in which it was written. The case would have been altogether different had the newspaper depended economically on readers who, having their illusions about Santa shattered, would have taken their custom elsewhere. In that case the only honorable course would Professor Kurt Marquart have been to say plainly: "No, Virginia, there is no Santa Claus. So far as this newspaper is concerned."

In paying lip-service to traditional Christian themes, knowing full well that these beliefs are ridiculed by professorial elites in seminaries, church politicians are taking advantage of the unsuspecting sheep of Christ, whose sacrifices support the seminaries. The differences between orthodoxy and heterodoxy are of course dogmatical. But the fraudulent use of traditional Christian language is a deep-seated *ethical* cancer in contemporary church-life. Honest people of all stripes, and church leaders above all must see it as a primary obligation to root out all doubletalk and to restore basic integrity and credibility to theological discourse. It is one thing to take liberties with Santa Claus, but quite another to lie and deceive by God's Name (Second Commandment. Catechism).

***

When Better Is Worse

When looser, less orthodox language about Scripture, is replaced by stricter, more orthodox language in a church constitution, is that not a welcome improvement? Not necessarily. It depends on the situation.

Case A: Two basically orthodox churches unite, and a constitutional paragraph about Scripture is proposed. The language is found to contain loopholes to accommodate unorthodox views. The challenge is faced, and the official language tightened to exclude the unorthodox views. This clearly represents a gain for honest churchmanship.

But consider *Case B:* Two or more basically liberal doctrinally indifferent churches merge, and develop a statement about Scripture. Its language is very permissive, in order to accommodate the unorthodox views held by the faculties of all participating seminaries. Some pious pastors and laymen are alarmed and demand more traditional language. In order to prevent grassroots disquiet and defections on the issue, the merging churches thereupon adopt more traditional language about Scripture, even though the seminary faculties will continue exactly as before. In this case honest churchmanship would have been served better by formulations which openly reflect the liberal theology of the seminaries.

Case B describes the situation of the New Lutheran Church. Some conservatives rejoice that at its September, 1985 meeting the Commission for a New Lutheran Church adopted more traditional language about Scripture for the new constitution. The crucial paragraph now reads:

The canonical Scriptures of the Old and New Testaments are the written Word of God. Inspired by God's Spirit speaking through their authors they record and announce God's revelation centering in Jesus Christ . . .

This is certainly stronger than the February 1985 version:

The Word of God is the canonical Scriptures of the Old and New Testaments. Inspired by God's Spirit speaking through their authors, they are the record and witness of God's revelation centering in Jesus Christ.

That in turn was stronger than the February 1984 version:

The Word of God is the Sacred Scriptures because, inspired by God's Spirit speaking through their authors, they are the record and witness of God's revelation centering in Jesus Christ.

At the February 1984 meeting the chairman of the subcommittee handling this matter was asked why the wording. "The Word of God is the sacred Scriptures, inspired by God's Spirit, the record and witness of God's revelation," had been rejected. He replied that "the committee had done so because it wanted to say *in what sense* Scripture could be called the Word of God" (S. Nafzger, *Concordia Journal,* Sept. 1984. p. 167). But now that a stronger wording is being proposed, does anyone really imagine that historical-critical theologians will no longer interpret it as simply a way of speaking in which "Scriptures could be called the Word of God"?

One can only admire the valiant souls who fought long and hard to improve the new church's Scripture paragraph. In the end, after the ALC Convention itself asked for stronger language, the Commission had to yield. All this is no doubt very encouraging to the conservative elements within the merging churches. Their victory, however, is an empty one, unless it can be translated into doctrinal discipline and an honest abandonment of the historical-critical destruction of biblical authority at the seminaries.

Since all the participating seminaries are thoroughly addicted to historical criticism, a change here would require a collective Damascus Road experience of unprecedented proportions. (Concordia Seminary in St. Louis was retrieved not by conversion but by separation). What the efforts of the conservatives will really amount to therefore, as so often in church history, is simply improved public relations for the liberal establishment. The conservatives get their constitutional language, and the liberals get to interpret it in the seminaries and publications of the church, while continuing to teach just as they please.

The well-meant efforts of ALC conservatives are foredoomed to futility by history. The ALC's own strong "inerrancy" and "infallibility" language was a dead letter already when it was being written into the constitution. The ALC historian Clifford Nelson wrote: "By 1956, when the proposed constitution of the new American Lutheran Church was voted on by the Evangelical Lutheran Church, several if not most of its professors of theology were teaching a view of Scripture at variance with the statement on the Bible in the new constitution. That is, while church administrators sought to uphold 'old Lutheranism,' many college and seminary professors were teaching "neo-Lutheranism" (*Lutheranism in North America 1914-1970.* p. 164).

Former ALC-president Fredrik Schiotz even admitted that he himself had privately favored the "neo-Lutheran" view of Scripture, but had publicly maintained the old view, for church-political reasons *(Lutheran Quarterly,* May, 1977). It is hardly surprising therefore that its Task Force on Theology recommended to the Commission for a New Lutheran Church in September 1983 "that the words inerrant and infallible not be included" in any constitutional statement on Scripture. But without inerrancy and infallibility the notion of "inspiration" is an empty chimera.

Having given up any chance of a serious confession of Scripture as the very Word of God, the Task Force muttered pathetically: "we want to make as strong a statement as possible about the authority and use of the Scriptures."

So long as the defective merchandise is not replaced, improved packaging and labelling merely compound the offense. "Any language sug-

114

gesting serious submission to Holy Scripture as the Word of God and to the Book of Concord as the right confession of it, is in the circumstances a cruel hoax upon those who would flee if they beheld unveiled the face of historical-critical unbelief" *(Affirm,* Christmas, 1983).

Prof. Kurt Marquart
Concordia Theological Seminary
Fort Wayne, Indiana

1. The religion business in a pragmatic age boils down to ____.
2. What does the Braaten/Jenson *Christian Dogmatics* teach about Christ? ____
3. All the participating seminaries are addicted to ____.
4. Without inerrancy and infallibility, "inspiration" is a ____.
5. All the participating seminaries are thoroughly addicted to ____.

LEVELS OF FELLOWSHIP

Christian News, May 9, 1988
From AFFIRM

Editor's Note: The first part of Professor Marquart's article was inadvertently omitted from the February, 1988 issue of AFFIRM and only the concluding section was printed. The omitted section is printed below. We are confident that what Prof. Marquart has said will be a significant contribution to the "levels of fellowship" discussion.

What are we to make of the trial balloon of "levels of fellowship," which has suddenly received so much publicity in the Missouri Synod? Several observations suggest themselves:

In the first place, the phrase is capable of a perfectly innocent interpretation. It might mean no more than the obvious fact that the one fellowship of the church needs to be expressed appropriately at every applicable level, such as that of the individual, the public minister, the congregation, the District, the Synod, and the global fellowship of confessional Lutheran churches.

But this is surely too obvious, too trivially true. Something else must be meant, especially if it is to provide an alternative to the old, and now allegedly untenable, "all-or-nothing" view.

Actually, the whole talk about "all-or-nothing" is not really true to the facts. It is a scarecrow, meant to suggest that the strict view of fellowship would prevent us from "doing anything together" with others. In point of fact the confessional Lutheran church both in Europe and in this country always knew how to distinguish church-fellowship from other necessary forms of co-operation. Indeed, our forefathers, with their straightforward ways, no doubt got a whole lot more actual theological discussing done than we manage in our urbane "dialogues," over the inevitable wine and cheese!

Nor was the strict view of church-fellowship a Missouri invention. It was the common Lutheran stand, in principle, shared also by the American Lutheran Conference's *Minneapolis Theses*. "All-or-nothing" is a propaganda device which expresses the traditional distaste of unionists and sentimentalists for the churchly integrity of Old Lutheranism.

Secondly, the origin of "levels of fellowship" thinking inspires no confidence. It was strongly advocated by representatives of National Lutheran Council synods (now "ELCA"), and rejected by the Missouri Synod. In an LCMS/National Lutheran Council essay of 1961, Dr. Martin Franzmann wrote: "There seems to have been great variety in the organizational manifestations of unity in the New Testament church; but is there any evidence that there was anything like an organizational recognition of fractional obedience to the one Lord?"

"Consensus in Ignorance and Poverty of Doctrine"
Thirdly, even more ominous is the use of "levels of fellowship" language in a 1985 LCMS District resolution, which included these points:

"4. Decisions regarding the exercise of fellowship on the local level are best made at the local level."
"9. There is a growing recognition that an 'all-or-nothing', 'either/or' approach to fellowship is inadequate."
"10. Christian relationships differ at various levels: international, national, church body, Synod, district, congregation, and individual, and may require diverse and appropriate responses."

This is "selective fellowship," which, as Dr. Hermann Sasse wrote, "atomises the church" *(We Confess the Church,* p. 67).

Our Synod has always understood itself as one confessing and confessional church — not as a conglomeration of 6,000 independent sects, each with its own "foreign policy," that is, fellowship arrangements. Sasse's further comments, on the same page, about perceived local agreements, are also to the point: "What is regarded as a consensus in doctrine may in fact be a consensus in ignorance and poverty of doctrine." And then: "There are even those who suppose that they can establish degrees of unity. The degrees match the levels of agreement reached so far in the discussions. The consensus one tries to read out of Article VII [of the Augsburg Confession] is in all such cases a purely human arrangement."

Fourthly, some seem to think that the old understanding of church fellowship leads to hatred or unfriendliness. They may in fact carry childhood memories of Irish and German schoolboys throwing rocks or worse at each other on the way to their respective parochial schools!

But it is terribly naive to blame that sort of thing on conscientious obedience to the New Testament warnings against false doctrine. Few Lutheran churchmen of our time have taken their confession more seriously, and at greater personal cost, than Dr. H. Sasse. Without ever compromising on church-fellowship, he enjoyed the respect and friendship of many, also of leading men, in other churches. He wrote:

"To search for a new and closer relation between these [Lutheran, Reformed, and Union] churches would be both thinkable and praiseworthy. But, [whatever] one might call such a relation, the expression 'church fellowship' for it is impossible, since this has a fixed meaning in the teaching and church law of the Lutheran church (and not only of that church), a meaning going back to the earliest church and one deeply rooted in the New Testament" *(This Is My Body,* Appendix, p. 352).

Fifthly, church-fellowship is not a matter of church-political convenience, like "diplomatic recognition." It is pulpit and altar fellowship and does not come in bits and pieces. It is a seamless garment, either given whole, or refused whole. To suggest that all is well so long as President Bohlmann and Bishop Chilstrom avoid each other's altars — while local pastors (and pastoresses?) exchange pulpits and altars at will — is to put a monstrous caricature in the place of the real church. Of course more is expected of leaders than of those whom they must lead in Christ. But participation in the Sacrament of the Altar makes the same confession in one case as in the other, and every public minister of the Word must be expected to know what that means.

It means a good deal more, for instance, than saying that one repents and believes in the "Real Presence," in whatever sense. The Sacrament of Christian unity (I Cor. 10:17) is the most solemn public confession of the Gospel (I Cor. 11:26, compare Apology 24:35). Continuing steadfastly in "the Apostles' doctrine" and in "the breaking of bread" belong together (Acts 2:42). Compare also Gal. 1:8.9, and Rom. 16:17 with the hint (v. 16) of the Lord's Supper as context. A Christian's spiritual identity is not purely private or atomistic. It is shaped not simply by what he thinks or says he believes at a given moment, but chiefly by the altar (and its pulpit!) at which he regularly confesses:

"By his partaking of the Sacrament in a church a Christian declares that the confession of that church is his confession. Since a man cannot at the same time hold two differing confessions, he cannot communicate in two churches of differing confessions. If anyone does this nevertheless, he denies his own confession or has none at all" (W. Elert, *Eucharist and Church Fellowship in the First Four Centuries*, p. 182).

1. Was the strict view of church-fellowship a Missouri invention? ____
2. Hermann Sasse wrote that "selective fellowship" ____ the church.
3. By his partaking of the Sacrament in a church a Christian declares that the confession of that church is ____.

AVOIDANCE OF CONFESSIONAL CRISIS

Christian News, December 31, 1990

How was it possible to gather all the boards and commissions of the Synod to consider the "big picture," and yet not even raise the question of how to cope with our deepest problems? For example: On 19 Feb. 1988 the CTCR stated: "We continue to recognize the present situation in regard to fellowship practices within the Synod as a crisis in our Synod's confessional unity." Or: In its report to the Wichita Convention (1989 Convention Workbook. 58, 64-6S) the CTCR offered serious warnings against the theology of Missouri Synod "charismatic" pastors. How and when will these crises be faced? Where do they fit into the "big picture"?

And why the continued official hobnobbing and joint worship with the ELCA bishops, who, whatever their personal qualities, are official representatives of a union church ("Interim Eucharistic Sharing" with the Episcopal Church, and full pulpit and altar fellowship through the Lutheran World Federation with Reformed and Union churches in Europe)? How is it possible for confessional Lutherans to discuss not basic differences but "ways to help pastors and congregations be more effective in ministry" (*Lutheran Witness*. Oct. '90) with the official representatives of a church which "ordains" women, contrary to the Word of God, and whose chief dogmatics text denies the Holy Trinity (Braaten-Jenson, *Christian Dogmatics* I, 155)?

The Wichita Convention's re-definition of circuit counselors may give us a clue to what is going on.

Confessional ties were weakened, and organizational ties strengthened. Among duties taken out were: "b. He shall inquire whether the congregations are zealously guarding the purity of doctrine, not tolerating errors or schismatic tendencies. . . d. He shall inquire what means are being used to guard against the evil influence of sects and organizations which endanger the spiritual life of the congregation." Instead of merely reporting on the work of Synod and urging adequate support, the new language has:

"He shall be conversant with and supportive of Synod-wide and District resolutions and programs and shall be responsible for communicating them to the congregations of the Circuit" (1989 Proceedings, 137-138). Are we no longer endangered by sects and errors? Is "zealously guarding the purity of doctrine" no longer necessary?

It is clear what the spirit of the time is: awkward details and particulars of our precious dogmatic and sacramental heritage must not be allowed to interfere with the "compatible relationships" necessary for the smooth functioning of the organization. Instead, we stress "resolutions and programs," to be promoted by an ever-growing army of loyal functionaries, with "mission-driven" rhetoric. This latter is the "apple-pie-and-motherhood" theme in the church, which opens purse-strings and shuts up critics.

Will there be more of the same for Pittsburgh, 1992? Or will we finally take our doctrinal crisis seriously?

K. Marquart
Concordia Theological Seminary
Ft. Wayne, IN

1. ELCA's Braaten-Jenson's *Christian Dogmatics* denies ____.
2. At the LCMS's Wichita Convention, confessional ties were ____ and organized ties were ____.

"The Church and Her Fellowship, Ministry, and Governance"
FEMALE PASTORS SHOULD
NOT BE RECOGNIZED

Christian News, February 25, 1991

"According to the revealed will of God, women cannot occupy the office of the Gospel ministry. Whatever else may and must be said on the subject — and that is a great deal — the inspired apostolic prohibitions in 1 Cor. 14:34 and I Tim. 2:12 make it impossible to recognize female pastors anywhere within the one, holy, catholic, and **apostolic** church" writes Concordia Seminary, Ft. Wayne, Indiana Professor Kurt Marquart in the recently published *The Church and Her Fellowship, Ministry, And Governance.*

Pentecostal and charismatic churches have long rejected what the Bible teaches about the ordination of women. Today most major Protestant denominations, including the Evangelical Lutheran Church in America and the Southern Baptist convention have women pastors.

Marquart's 263 page book is Volume IX in a new *Confessional Lutheran Dogmatics* edited by Dr. Robert Preus. Preus writes in the general introduction to *Confessional Lutheran Dogmatics*:

"For some time those of us in the Lutheran Church who have interested ourselves in the Lutheran Confessions and actually taught them and done research in these great symbolic writings have recognized the need for a dogmatics book based upon the outline and thought patterns of the Lutheran Confessions. Such a book which has never been written before, except for Leonard Hutter's little *Compendium Locorum Theologicorum*, would address the theologians, Lutheran and hopefully others, of our day with a truly confessional answer to the theological issues which we are facing in Christianity and in our Lutheran Zion today. We were in no way interested in replacing in our Lutheran Church-Missouri Synod Francis Pieper's monumental *Christian Dogmatics* as a textbook which has served students in our church body and others for three generations. Such an intention would have been unnecessary and unproductive. The authors of the various monographs, which will appear in this series entitled *Confessional Lutheran Dogmatics*, come at their respective subjects from somewhat different vantage points and backgrounds and personal predilections as they do dogmatics. It was decided, therefore, to issue a series of dogmatics treatises on the primary articles of faith usually taken up in traditional dogmatics since the 16th century, (e.g. the Augsburg Confession; Philip Melanchthon's *Loci communes*: Martin Chemnitz's *Loci theologici*, etc.)

"But why the approach from the Lutheran Confessions? Are not these musty old creeds and symbols irrelevant to our day, and would not a series of monographs written from the point of view of confessional Lutheran theology be equally irrelevant to the theological issues confronting the church today? It is because we must respond with an emphatic no to such a question that we presume to issue the forthcoming volumes. The Confessions whose theology is taken directly from the Scriptures are relevant to our day just as the Scriptures themselves which are always 'profitable for doctrine, for reproof, for correction, for instruction in righteousness' (2 Tim. 3:16). There is a real call and a need for just the kind of dogmatics book here proposed, that is, a *Confessional Lutheran Dogmatics*."

"The Confessions always lead deeper into the Scriptures, especially as new issues arise in new cultures and succeeding generations which must be faced only with theology drawn from the Scriptures and patterned after the Lutheran Confessions.

"The forthcoming volumes are dedicated to Dr. Francis Pieper, a great confessional Lutheran dogmatician of our church, in the hope and prayer that they will help to achieve what he did so much to accomplish in his day; namely, doctrinal unity and consensus in the doctrine of the Gospel and all its articles among all Lutherans and a firm confessional Lutheran identity so sorely needed in our day."

Marquart says in the preface:

"The treatment which follows intends simply to display some of the incomparable evangelical treasures of the Church of the Augsburg Confession, so that these may shine in their own light. The work is frankly animated by the conviction that it is just the characteristically Lutheran ecclesiology of the cross — as distinct from the alternative paradigms of Eastern Orthodoxy and Roman Catholicism on the one hand, and of Zwingli/Calvinism on the other — which reproduces the New Testament substance with unique fidelity."

Marquart has been serving as a counselor to Preus in his case with Dr. Ralph Bohlmann, president of The Lutheran Church-Missouri Synod. Bohlmann contends that pastors who maintain that the Bible does not oppose the ordination of women should be allowed to remain on the clergy roster of the LCMS. * Preus has been a strong opponent of the ordination of women and insists the Bible teaches that women should not serve as pastors of Christian congregations.

Marquart writes in *The Church*:

"A church which ordains women into the public ministry of Word and Sacraments, thereby certifies itself to be un-apostolic and anti-apostolic. Behind the apostle stands of course the Lord Himself. Despite the prominence, exemplary devotion, and courage of women in His cause and service (ML 27:55-56), and despite the temporal priority of women as witnesses to His Resurrection (Mk. 16:1-8; Jn. 20 : 1 ff.), Christ appointed not a single woman as His apostle. If the reason for this be sought in the Jewish legal system, in which a woman could not be a **shaliach** for instance, then such considerations do not apply in the case of the 'apostle to the Gentiles,' since priestesses of all kinds were well entrenched, culturally, in the Greco-Roman world. The facts remain that in Jesus, God became a man, not a woman; that His chosen apostolate, in, with, and under which our public ministry was divinely instituted, included no women, not even those very near and dear to Him; and that by express apostolic command the public ministers of the Gospel, that is, those who in this special way 'do not represent their own persons but the person of Christ....in Christ's place and stead' (Ap. VIWIII.28), must be qualified men, not women.

"The apostolic prohibitions on this score must not be put on a par with transitory, culture-dependent directives like those about Mosaic proprieties (Acts 15:29) and head coverings (I Cor. 11). The first case is clearly one of missionary accommodation (Acts 15:21), and in the second Paul appeals ultimately to the church's 'custom' (suneitheiat, I Cor. 11:16). The immutable principle behind changing customs like those to do with head coverings, is that of 'headship,' or the 'kephalei-structure' (I Cor. 11:3, cf. Eph. 5:23), built into the creation itself.

"As a divine institution the public ministry is by definition culture-invariant in its essence. The headship principle either applies here, in this clear-cut case, or else it cannot be applied at all. 'The main application of I Cor. 14:33b-35 and I Tim. 2:11-15! in the contemporary church is that women are not to exercise those functions in the local congregation which would involve them in the exercise of authority inherent in the authoritative public teaching office (i.e. the office of pastor).' This implies that there could, no doubt even should, be other applications of the basic headship/subordination principle. It is after all in the nature of Christian faith and love to seek to please God as much, and not as little, as possible. Only, in most other cases we are not dealing with the unambiguous theological category of a divine institution — there is a doctrine of the ministry, but there is no such thing as a 'doctrine of head-coverings,' for example! — and to that extent further applications will be less conclusive, and more subject to individual judgment, in the spirit of Rom. 14:19-23.

"Although the ordination of women was not an issue in Luther's day, he grasped the theological import of the question more keenly than did some of the later theologians. Luther was well aware of the prominent leadership positions occupied by certain women in the Old Testament, and he taunted the anti-clerical fanatics for having overlooked these examples seemingly favorable to their cause. 'But in the New Testament,' he wrote, 'the Holy Spirit, speaking through St. Paul, ordained that women should be silent in the churches and assemblies (I Cor. 14:34), and said that this is the Lord's commandment.' On the underlying headship/subordination principle Luther wrote: 'The gospel, however, does not abrogate this natural law, but confirms it as the ordinance and creation of God.'

"In opposing the ordination of women, modern Lutherans should take care not to align themselves with the misogynist ethos of the celibacy-oriented Roman Catholic hierarchy, and of its imitators among 'Anglo-Catholics': 'Daniel says that it is characteristic of Antichrist's kingdom to despise women (11:37)' (Ap. XXIII. 25). G. Stoeckhardt was on the right track when he spoke of womanly 'reserve' and 'decorousness' — thereby suggesting that what was at stake in I Cor. 14 was not an ontological inferiority of women, but their distinctively feminine modesty and dignity. On the other hand, it is patent nonsense to argue that modern church-life is too male oriented and needs to be made more appealing to women. On the contrary, religion in modern Western society is already a predominantly female affair, and is becoming more so. It is important to understand that the real push for female pastors comes not from any sort of biblical considerations at all, but from a militant, and essentially secular, feminism.

"To talk of the New Testament as 'an intrinsically oppressive text,' even renaming it 'the Second Testament' – clearly in order to deny it finality — is to abandon all pretense of Christian exegesis or interpretation. The glib deployment of Gal. 3:28 ('there is neither male nor female') against the express apostolic prohibition of female pastors, points in the same direction, for it logically entails also a total interchangeability of the sexes in marriage — in other words, same sex 'marriages!' **Some do not hesitate to go to such lengths, and patronizingly dismiss St. Paul's condemnations of sodomy as the culture-bound judgment of 'a faithful apostle and a profound interpreter of the central message of the gospel, yet one who was also a fallible and historically-conditioned human being.' To discard at will so crystal-clear a piece of consistent prophetic-apostolic teaching is to throw the whole Bible to the winds."

1. Today most major denominations have _____ pastors.
2. According to the revealed will of God, women cannot occupy the office of _____.
3. Should Francis Pieper's *Christian Dogmatics* be replaced? _____
4. Marquart served as counselor to Robert Preus in his case with _____.
5. Christ appointed not a singular woman as His _____.
6. Religion in Western society is already predominately a _____ affair.

*Editor's Note: Dr. Ralph Bohlmann said he began changing his position opposing the ordination of women when his daughter asked him for scriptural reasons why she could not become a pastor he found none. His daughter attended Eden Seminary of the United Church of Christ. She was installed as the pastor of a United Church of Christ in Jacksonville, Illinois where she lives with her lesbian partner. When the UCC was formed in 1958, it adopted a non-Trinitarian Statement of Faith which the Unitarians said they found acceptable. Rev. Lynn Bohlmann is a champion of same-sex marriage and has preached in a Unitarian church. There is plenty of room on the LCMS clergy roster for those who support the ordination of women even though the LCMS officially opposes women serving as pastors.

**The U.S. Supreme Court in 2015 approved same-sex marriage. The July 13, 2015 *Christian News* noted that a Religious News Service story in the July 4, 2015 *St. Louis Post-Dispatch* reported; "Americans have moved to accept gay marriage with astonishing swiftness – almost 60 percent of Americans approve, with the younger generation set to drive that figure even higher."

LUTHERAN CONFESSIONAL REVIEW

Volume 2, Number 1, Summer 1991
Christian News, October 7, 1991

The next volume in the series *Confessional Lutheran Dogmatics* is now available. Kurt Marquart's *The Church and Her Fellowship, Ministry and Governance* deals with the most pressing theological issues of our day. Lutherans in America are struggling to articulate correctly the doctrines of church and ministry. The Lutheran Church—Missouri Synod finds itself in the embarrassing position of having contradicted in practice, if not also in theory, Article XIV of the Augsburg Confession with its "lay worker" resolution passed by the last synodical convention. This issue has forced the Missouri Synod to address issues which have been simmering for years. It is unclear at this point how or when the LCMS will return to its confessional roots and affirm, in both theory and practice, the complete scriptural and confessional understanding of the Office of the Holy Ministry. A proliferation of so-called "commissioned ministries" does nothing to improve the situation. It seems that for every possible task in the church there soon appears yet another "commissioned ministry." Even our vocabulary is confused and confusing.

The Evangelical Lutheran Church in America has difficulties with this issue as well. The ELCA's three predecessor church bodies brought their distinct understandings of the doctrines of church and ministry to the new church. The spread of a feminist theology, combined with the current discussions regarding pulpit and altar fellowship with the Episcopalians, added to an inadequate understanding of the normative character of the Scriptures and Confessions, provides all the ingredients for substantial disagreements on the doctrine of church and ministry within the ELCA.

The greatest challenge facing all Lutheran church bodies is the influx of a generic evangelical Protestantism, often cloaked in the guise of a "church growth" movement. This movement, perhaps more than any other single factor, threatens the Lutheran church in America with theological dangers as great as any faced since the time of the 16th century Reformation. Lutheranism's theological integrity is at stake. Pragmatic "new measures" for an American Lutheranism (a la Schmucker) are sweeping across the entire spectrum of Lutheranism in this country, from the WELS to the ELCA. The piety of the laity is being formed, more often than not, by a generic Protestant fundamentalism mixed with a hearty dose of good old-fashioned pietistic "enthusiasm" via radio and television. Many Lutheran church bureaucrats, pastors and laymen choose to ignore these trends and label them as ways of being more "effective" or as methods for pursuing the "mission" of the Church.

An informed clergy and laity is the key to combatting these dangerous trends in the Lutheran Church. Imitating fundamentalist and evangelical churches in style will eventually destroy the substance of what it means to be an orthodox, confessional Lutheran church. To imitate the "style" of a church body which is at odds with confessional Lutheran theology and practice is to invite disaster. To surrender that which distinguishes the Evangelical Lutheran Church from other groups is to surrender the apostolic and catholic doctrine which the Evangelical Church of the Augsburg Confession wishes never to abandon and from which she never intends to deviate. This is a time of confession, as critical as the time of the Leipzig and Augsburg interims in the 16th century. The Lutheran Church at the end of the 20th century needs again to embrace the insight of Matthias Flacius that "Nothing is an adiaphoron when confession and offense are involved." [Nihil *est adiaphoron in casu confessionis et scandali].*

It is in the midst of this present theological crisis in the Lutheran Church that Marquart provides his careful discussion of many crucial issues. With a careful use of historic sources, Marquart addresses such pressing issues as the Mission of the Church, the Office of the Holy Ministry, Lay Ministry, Women in the Ministry, Church Fellowship, the History of the Ecumenical Movement and much more.

At a time of confession, as when enemies of the Word of God desire to suppress the pure doctrine of the Holy Gospel the entire community of God, yes, every individual Christian, and especially the ministers of the Word as the leaders of the community of God, are obligated to confess openly, not only by words but through their deeds and actions, the true doctrine and all that pertains to it, according to the Word of God... Hence yielding or conforming in external things, where Christian agreement in doctrine has not previously been achieved... will sadden and scandalize true believers and weaken them in their faith.

—The Formula of Concord, Solid Declaration, X.10-15.

1. The greatest challenge facing all Lutheran church bodies is the influx of _____.

2. An _____ is the key to combatting these dangerous trends in the Lutheran Church.

ROBERT D. PREUS

From the *Handbook of Evangelical Theolgians*, pp. 353-365
Reprinted in the June 19, 1995 *Christian News*

by Kurt E. Marquart

Robert David Preus, Lutheran theologian, churchman, and seminary president, was born on October 16, 1924, in St. Paul, Minnesota, the youngest son of the then governor, Jacob ("Jake") A. O. Preus. It is above all to his parents, under God, that Robert Preus attributes both his love of theology as a living knowledge of God in Christ and his corresponding keen concern for the salvation of a lost humanity through faithful mission work.

Our opening remarks have already sketched Preus as, in broad terms, an evangelical. Perhaps a clarification is in order. We may distinguish at least three layers of meaning in the term *evangelical:* (1) The word was used of those who by virtue of the Reformation had rediscovered the gospel (evangel) of full and free salvation solely through faith in Jesus Christ. [1] (2) In nineteenth-century Germany "evangelical" denoted the Lutheran-Calvinist alliance against the growing influence of Roman Catholicism. [2] (3) In modern America "evangelical" generally denotes an interdenominational but basically Reformed or Arminian conservatism regarding Christ and Holy Scripture. People who hold to this position stress "evangelistic" outreach in the style of, say, Billy Graham, and are often millennialist in orientation.

A glance at Preus's bibliography confirms that he qualifies as an evangelical in what amounts to an overlap of senses (1) and (3). [3] Along with an evident zeal for missions, his work has focused largely on the central core of the gospel—the atonement and justification—and on biblical authority, including inerrancy. While it is true that the confessional, sacramental, churchly dimension associated with sense (1) does not ordinarily characterize sense (3), there have of late been signs that many Christians who are evangelicals in sense (3) are yearning for the wholeness of sense (1). [4] For Preus himself "evangelical" and "confessional" are as a matter of course not opposites but twins. [5]

Preus's life and ministry fall into three very distinct phases: (1) the early years (1924–1957); (2) professorship at Concordia Seminary in St. Louis (1957–1974); and (3) presidency of Concordia Seminary in Springfield (Ill.) and Fort Wayne (1974–1993). Of these the last two will for obvious reasons receive the major emphasis in the present overview. We will find that Preus's story is inextricably intertwined with that of the Lutheran Church–Missouri Synod in our time, and specifically that there are direct correlations between his St. Louis and Springfield–Fort Wayne periods, and the two major theological crises which confronted that church body during those years.

The Early Years

Robert Preus was the second son of Governor Jacob Preus and Idella Haugen Preus to survive infancy. Twin boys had been born in 1910, but lived only a few months. Robert's older brother Jacob ("Jack") was born in 1920. The newborn Robert and his brother Jack were both featured with their father in the *Minneapolis Star* as a part of the 1924 Christmas Seal campaign. Having failed in his bid to succeed the late Senator Knute Nelson in Washington, D.C., the elder Preus retired from politics in 1925, when his second gubernatorial term was up. The family moved to Chicago in 1925, where Jake Preus devoted himself successfully to insurance work. He regarded his cofounding of the Lutheran Brotherhood insurance giant as the crowning achievement of his life.

Young Robert took both his primary and his secondary education in the public schools of his neighborhood. His father was a devout and loving man with intense moral convictions. Having himself scrupulously paid off debts for relatives who found themselves unable to do so, Jake Preus impressed upon his sons the absolute necessity of honest dealings. One incident particularly burnt itself into Robert's memory. Together with some friends young Robert, then nine years old, had stolen from the local Woolworth and then denied his guilt. Thereupon his father told him that his stealing and lying would have to be cured in reform school. The boy was told to pack a few belongings. After doing so, he was taken to the railway station and put on a train. Only at that point did the father relent and take his remorseful son home.

The Preuses numbered among their ancestors in Norway many clergymen, including a headmaster at the Cathedral School in Kristiansand. Herman Amberg Preus (1825–1894), Robert's great-grandfather, immigrated to the United States, where he helped to found the old Norwegian Lutheran Synod in 1853 and eventually became its president. His son, Christian Keyser Preus, became president of Luther College in Decorah, Iowa. When congratulated by a little celebration in front of his house upon his son Jake's inauguration as governor of Minnesota, Christian Preus replied that he was proud—but would have been even prouder had his son been ordained into the ministry! [6] Both of the governor's sons did in fact become pastors, and he was immensely proud of both, writing to Robert in 1944: "Mother and I should be the happiest people in the world if we could raise such fine boys and their father is such a rascal." [7]

After graduating from Luther College with his B.A. degree, Robert entered Luther Theological Seminary in St. Paul, where his uncle Herman Preus served as a professor. This seminary, like Luther College, belonged to the Norwegian Lutheran Church of America, the large merger of 1917. A minority group with leanings toward the Lutheran Church–Missouri Synod had declined to join the merger and formed the Evangelical Lutheran Synod. Both Preus brothers found the seminary atmosphere oppressive, laden with theological compromise, evasion, and indifference. Shortly before graduation, Robert transferred to Bethany Lutheran Seminary, which the Evangelical Lutheran Synod had recently established in Mankato; and in 1947 he became its first graduate.

Ordained in October 1947, Robert Preus served congregations in Mayville, North Dakota, and Bygland, Minnesota, for two years. In 1948 he married Donna Rockman, and the couple were ultimately blessed with ten children and over forty grandchildren. In 1949 he entered the University of Minnesota for further academic work. He then went to the University of Edinburgh, where in 1952 he completed his first doctorate (Ph.D.).

After Edinburgh, Preus was called to the Evangelical Lutheran Synod's Harvard Street Church in Cambridge, Massachusetts. Three years later he accepted a call to serve three small congregations near Fosston, Minnesota. Then came a major change. In 1955 both Jack and Robert had supported the Evangelical Lutheran Synod's suspension of relations with the Missouri Synod on account of the latter's developing liberalism. Later both brothers joined the Missouri Synod, Robert as instructor at Concordia Seminary in St. Louis (1957), and Jack at Concordia Seminary in Springfield (1958). Much has been made of this apparent about-face, as though it meant a surrender of theological integrity to practical church politics. [8] Subsequent history does not bear out this interpretation. The Preus brothers had changed not their theological principles, but their assessment of the Missouri Synod. It is one thing when youthful idealism is strangled by self-seeking; it is quite another when idealism ill-informed is tempered by idealism better informed. A realistic and charitable assumption is that Jack and Robert Preus, upon better acquaintance with the Missouri Synod, decided that the situation there was not hopeless, and that their battle for evangelical, confessional orthodoxy might better be waged in the much larger Missouri Synod. Their move, then, was merely a tactical, not a strategic change. "A foolish consistency," wrote Ralph Waldo Emerson, "is the hobgoblin of little minds."

Professorship at Concordia Seminary (St. Louis)

There can be little doubt that Robert Preus was catapulted into his professorship at Concordia by the studies which culminated in the publication of his doctoral thesis, *The Inspiration of Scripture: A Study of the Theology of the Seventeenth Century Lutheran Dogmaticians.* [9] Nothing like this had been seen in conservative North American Lutheran circles for some time. The book was reissued by the publishing house of the Evangelical Lutheran Synod in 1957, the same year in which Preus was called to the faculty of the Missouri Synod's flagship seminary in St. Louis.

The Lutheran Church–Missouri Synod had been founded in 1847 as the German Evangelical Lutheran Synod of Missouri, Ohio, and Other States. The two world wars no doubt shook the Missouri Synod out of its German ethnic cocoon sooner than would have been the case had the normal forces of gradual acculturation simply run their course. Bear in mind that apart from the Book of Concord (the Lutheran canon of creeds and confessions) itself, few of the standard Lutheran sources had been translated into English from the original Latin or German. The fifty-five-volume American edition of *Luther's Works* had only just begun to appear

129

(1955). The clergy's rapid loss of competence in both German and Latin had made them dependent on English-language theological resources, which naturally did not reflect the distinctive character of the Lutheran Reformation. A classic identity crisis was in the making.

By 1957, when Robert Preus was called to St. Louis as an instructor in symbolics (creeds and confessions) and philosophy, theological ferment among the students there was well advanced, as can be seen from the student journal, the *Seminarian*. Soon the ferment spread to the faculty itself. A stale traditionalism was simply no match for the allurements of the new theologies from abroad, especially Barthianism. Clifford Nelson has captured the atmosphere well:

> Many of these men, who found their way into teaching positions in major colleges and seminaries of the Lutheran churches, including Concordia Seminary (St. Louis), had been exposed to contemporary biblical research (Dodd, Hoskyns, Wright, Albright, Bultmann, G. Bornkamm, von Rad, *et al.*); to contemporary theologians such as Nygren, Aulen, Barth, Brunner, Tillich, and the Niebuhrs; and to the Luther researches of Swedes, Germans, Englishmen, and Americans (notably Wilhelm Pauck and Roland Bainton). One result was that in the course of time students were exposed to a new brand of Lutheranism that was remarkably similar in all schools, whether in Chicago, Philadelphia, the Twin Cities, or St. Louis. [10]

Student unrest at St. Louis came to a head in a series of special presentations and discussions. "The chief questions of the students centered in the extent to which the Scriptures themselves and the Confessions of the Church teach a doctrine of Verbal Inspiration and what the function of that doctrine is." [11] Some of the faculty courageously attempted to hold the line in respect to biblical inspiration.

The new professor and the American edition of his book on inspiration arrived on campus together and made an immediate impact. Scholarly, yet personable and friendly, Preus was well liked by both students and colleagues, even by those who did not agree with his theological orthodoxy. His academic credentials and competence were such that he could not be dismissed as a blinkered establishment hack loyally passing on clichés uncritically inherited from the tribal elders. In this respect Preus resembled another outsider, John Warwick Montgomery, whose work was to appear meteorlike a decade later in the Missouri Synod's firmament. [12]

Preus's book on inspiration supplied welcome ammunition for the traditionalists, then very much on the defensive. The old inspiration doctrine was routinely ridiculed as a scholastic artifice contrived by seventeenth-century dogmaticians from pagan (Aristotelian) philosophical pedantries, and inflicted on the church contrary to the dynamic or Hebrew genius of the Bible and of an existentially reinterpreted Luther. It was of course much easier to bat about caricatures of the old divines than to study them. The Preus volume actually engaged their arguments in detail and at first hand. The treatment was sympathetic, but by no means uncritical. For instance, Preus judiciously analyzes what might be meant by the term "Lutheran scholasticism," and grants some of the critics' charges while refuting others. [13] He grants, too, that the Aristotelian-scholastic mode employed by the old theologians sometimes misled even major figures like Johann Gerhard, David Hollaz, and Johann Baier into a rationalistic departure from sound biblical doctrine, for instance, on predestination. [14]

On the other hand, Preus defends the seventeenth-century divines against the popular charge that they taught a mechanical view of inspiration. Even the early Hermann Sasse was not immune from such misunderstandings. In reply Preus shows that Latin terms like *dictatio* do not have the same narrow meanings as do their English derivatives. Also, "the troublesome word '*dictatio*' cannot possibly have a purely mechanical connotation, [for] the dogmaticians speak of a '*dictatio rerum*' [a dictation of things or subject matter; cf. *dictatio verborum*, a dictation of words]." [15]

All in all, the Preus volume effectively rehabilitated the theological integrity of the old inspiration dogma. Verbal inspiration, inerrancy, and the sufficiency and clarity of Holy Scripture were again shown to make good sense within the continuity of orthodox Christian doctrine from biblical days till the present. In his detailed treatment of an obscure controversy— occasioned by "the renegade Lutheran" Hermann Rathmann's divorcing the external biblical Word from the power of the Holy Spirit— Preus proves biblically and theologically the indissoluble unity between Spirit and Word, and thus the spiritual power of that Word. It is no accident that Preus ventures precisely in this context a critical reference to Karl Barth's proclivity for downplaying the merely external and earthly aspects of the Bible. [16]

It goes without saying that Preus's book and the influence afforded by his teaching position in St. Louis did not settle the simmering controversy. Things had already gone too far for that. Throughout the sixties Concordia Seminary acquired more and more young faculty members who were devoted to historical criticism, and were therefore deaf to the claims of the historic Christian doctrine of inspiration. Fearing the advent of a less compliant synodical administration, the seminary in 1969 called to its presidency John Tietjen, who was identified with the progressive forces. The synod, however, in that same year, elected Jack Preus as its president. Now the die was cast. There followed the dramatic Seminex episode, which has become the subject of several books. [17] Robert Preus was of course deeply involved at every stage. Early in 1972, when confronted with President Tietjen's claim that no one could competently teach at the seminary "without using historical-critical methodology," Preus replied publicly:

When I joined this faculty the so-called historical-critical method was not employed but generally rejected by this faculty. A couple of exegetes might have advocated using certain aspects of it, but this was

131

all. Now after fifteen years, during which the method has been quietly and gradually brought in, we are told that it is impossible to do exegesis at a seminary without using it.

I must respond that as a called teacher at Concordia Seminary, committed to the sacred Scriptures and the Lutheran Confessions, I cannot and will not use the historical-critical method as such for its false basic presuppositions and its false goals and conclusions. I have [said] this privately and publicly and in every possible forum, in joint faculty meetings and before the Council of Presidents, in my classes, in papers delivered throughout the Synod, in periodicals and books, and before our Board of Control. And I intend to do the same in the future in this school or anywhere else with the help of God. [18]

Meanwhile Synod President Jack Preus had just issued a "Statement of Scriptural and Confessional Principles," in which he showed the historical-critical ideology to be incompatible with the Scriptures and the Lutheran confessions. This document was intended to help the seminary's board of control evaluate the hundreds of pages of testimony that Preus's fact-finding committee had gathered from the faculty between December 1970 and March 1971. In September 1972 Preus published his "Report of the Synodical President to the Lutheran Church–Missouri Synod" (the so-called Blue Book), which, without revealing the identities of particular professors, gave copious extracts from their answers to various theological questions. President Preus concluded: "The case now lies before the church. ... It is becoming increasingly clear that we have two theologies. With the influential position the Seminary holds in the church, its views will prevail unless the Synod directs otherwise and sees to it that its directives are implemented."

The synod decided the issue in 1973 at its New Orleans convention when it adopted as its own Jack Preus's "Statement of Scriptural and Confessional Principles." A separate, painstaking resolution dealt with the position held by the majority of the faculty (who were opposed by a minority of five, including Robert Preus). The majority's loose views of biblical authority and clarity, particularly in such matters as the "facticity of miracle accounts and their details; historicity of Adam and Eve as real persons; ... predictive prophecies in the Old Testament which are in fact Messianic; [and] the doctrine of angels" were held to be "in fact false doctrine running counter to the Holy Scriptures, the Lutheran Confessions, and the synodical stance and for that reason 'cannot be tolerated in the church of God, much less be excused and defended' " (the concluding phrase comes directly from the Formula of Concord of 1577).

Amid much theatricality, including demonstrations, armbands, and impromptu sidewalk communion services before television cameras, the Tietjen party argued that the proposed resolution was theologically and procedurally improper. This effort was in vain. The majority at the convention supported the synod president and the old theology. In January 1974 Tietjen was suspended from the seminary presidency. A majority of the faculty and student body chose to declare a moratorium on classes.

When the striking professors failed to return to work by a time stipulated by the board, they were relieved of their positions. The great majority now moved, again with maximum publicity from the media, to premises provided by St. Louis University, a Jesuit school. Thus was formed Concordia Seminary in Exile, or Seminex, which a few years later was absorbed by a number of other schools, including the Lutheran School of Theology at Chicago.

Meanwhile the Concordia campus retained only five professors. Of these Martin Scharlemann became acting president, and Robert Preus chairman of the Department of Historical Theology as well as acting registrar and academic dean. When, as a result of the enormous strains of confrontation and his new responsibilities, Scharlemann became ill, Preus had to take on the position of acting president. Although some had predicted gloom and doom, the institution recovered quickly and is today again flourishing. The judgment of Harold Lindsell, a former editor of *Christianity Today* and himself a Baptist, is worth quoting: "To the best of my knowledge the victory of orthodoxy in the Missouri Synod is the only case of its kind in twentieth-century American Christianity. ... Perhaps the Missouri story will help evangelicals in other places as they wage their own battles for theological orthodoxy." [19] Preus in turn praised Lindsell for sounding the alarm: "History is repeating itself. What happened at the St. Louis seminary prior to 1974 is happening at Fuller Seminary today. And it is happening elsewhere among those who call themselves Evangelicals. ... Harold Lindsell's book, *The Battle for the Bible* ... was right on target as he analyzed what is going on in evangelical circles today." [20]

Personally, the St. Louis years were rich and rewarding ones. The last five of Preus's children were born there. In 1969 he earned his second doctorate, a D.Theol. from the University of Strasbourg. Out of his studies in France came *The Theology of Post-Reformation Lutheranism,* which established Preus as the leading English-language interpreter of the seventeenth-century Lutheran divines. [21] The well-known Swedish scholar Bengt Hägglund has paid a high tribute to this much underrated period: "With respect to its versatile comprehension of theological material and the breadth of its knowledge of the Bible, Lutheran orthodoxy marks the high point in the entire history of theology." [22]

In presenting the theology of the old divines, Preus avoids the false sort of objectivity which, without taking a personal stand, seeks only to dust off this or that quaint little detail. What he presents is in fact largely his own theology. The dogmaticians are criticized, to be sure—but also defended against later thinkers, such as Immanuel Kant, the positivists, and Karl Barth. While Preus stresses the originality and individuality of the classic post-Reformation teachers, he also makes clear their fundamental unity of approach and doctrine. In short, he views their theology not as a series of disconnected snapshots, but as a moving picture, that is, an organic whole.

Although Preus freely criticizes some of the later dogmaticians like Johann Baier and Johann Adam Osiander for their "excessive scholasti-

133

cism," he at once goes on to argue that, contrary to the modern interpretation, there is "no theological cleavage between the period of the Reformation and the period of Lutheran orthodoxy." Indeed, the dogmaticians were as determined as Martin Luther not to allow to reason a *magisterial* (master's) or substantive role in theology. On the other hand, when "Luther spoke of killing and butchering reason, he never meant that God wanted us to be stupid or to think and talk nonsense; he was speaking of the abuse of reason in judging God's revelation." There is, in other words, a ministerial (servant's) use of reason, which seeks not to judge, but only to understand revealed truth. [23]

Among the dogmaticians' notable contributions is their improvement on Thomas Aquinas in the matter of the existence of God. For example, Abraham Calov insists, against Aquinas, that God's existence is not merely a preamble to faith, but "that the very chief article of faith is that God is." [24] Yes, there are reasonable arguments for the existence of God (Rom. 1:20). But they produce philosophy, not faith or theology. Faith is "always based upon a special word or revelation of God." Anything else is mere human opinion or knowledge. "Calov assumes a complete distinction between the theory or opinion of a philosopher and the faith of a Christian. In spite of the fact that they speak of the same thing, faith and philosophy remain in two completely different and distinct categories." Remarkably similar was the conclusion of Etienne Gilson, the great modern interpreter of Thomas Aquinas: "This distinction of orders allows us to understand how the same intellect can know by reason the God of philosophy and know by faith the God of Moses, of Abraham, of Isaac, and of Jacob. ... Philosophy knows that there exists a being that all call God, but no philosophy can suspect the existence of the God of Scripture." [25]

Preus devotes considerable space to the correct understanding of the very nature of theology, as this is argued first by Johann Gerhard, and then, at much greater length, by Abraham Calov. Theology, these teachers insisted, is not a theoretical or speculative science, as Thomas and the scholastics had thought, but a practical, God-given, salvation-oriented skill or aptitude. It is like medicine, which is interested in anatomical and chemical facts not for their own sake, but for the sake of imparting healing to sick people. This practical nature of theology, with its total dependence on the divinely given Word and sacraments, has profound consequences. Preus thoroughly approves this view of theology: "To maintain the practical character of theology against all forms of theological dilettantism, speculation, scientism, and dead orthodoxy is the perennial task of evangelical theology." [26]

Presidency of Concordia Seminary
(Springfield and Fort Wayne)

Robert Preus was to face the practical challenges of theology even more directly after September 15, 1974, the date of his inauguration as the thirteenth president of Concordia Theological Seminary in Springfield. *Time Magazine* commented: "Concordia Seminary of Springfield, Illinois, has an aggressive new president, the Rev. Robert D. Preus—Jack's brother and a conservative with impressive intellectual credentials." [27] Robert's programmatic inaugural address, based on the institution's name, established clear priorities: "Concordia" stands for true, uncompromised unity in regard to all of the articles of the biblical gospel as they are set out in the Book of Concord of 1580. "Theological" means that the divine truth must be the actual stuff of the curriculum; a mere lip service, while secularism is allowed to pervade and corrode all content, is not satisfactory.

"Seminary," finally, implies the implanting and cultivation of spiritual life, not mere intellectualism or even moralism for that matter. "That is what we seek to inculcate here: total commitment, commitment to the highest and greatest work in all the world, ministry, the ministry of the Gospel, the ministry of reconciliation."[28]

Academically, the Springfield seminary had always played second fiddle to St. Louis. It was the "practical" seminary. Continuing the policy of his brother Jack, who had preceded him as president, Robert wished to upgrade the seminary's academic standing without giving up any of its practical, pastoral orientation. Already in his inaugural address he was able to announce the addition of a graduate school, which would grant the doctorate in ministry as well as master's degrees in sacred theology. Preus set out to build an academically and theologically strong faculty. In 1976 the seminary was moved to Fort Wayne, where it had been founded over a hundred years before. It now occupies the beautiful campus designed by Eero Saarinen in the mid-1950s.

The cause of missions was always close to Preus's heart. He served for years on the synodical board of missions, where he stressed concern for a global vision and sound theological underpinnings. Thanks largely to his energetic support, Concordia Seminary in St. Catharines, Ontario, was launched, and theological leadership provided for Lutheran mission work in Haiti. In the 1980s Fort Wayne added a Department of Missions and created centers for Hispanic studies and ministry to the deaf. By 1991 the doctorate in missiology was offered.

In 1974, the year of his inauguration as seminary president, Preus also attended the Lausanne Congress on World Evangelization. He was impressed by the large number of representatives from Africa and Asia. As for the Lausanne Covenant, he found the document to be "as good a statement as one could expect." Theologically, it fell somewhat short of the level of the Berlin Congress of 1966. Specifically, the "means of grace and baptism, as the Spirit's vehicle for evangelization, were simply ignored." [29]

Also occupying Preus's attention at this time was the simmering missiology debate that in 1968 had boiled over within the World Council of Churches. Thundered Donald McGavran, the founder of the Church Growth movement: "They do not believe that it makes an eternal difference whether men accept the Lord Jesus and are baptized in His name. They do not believe that in the Bible we have the authoritative, infallible Word of God. ... Their theology allows them to take neither the Church nor the salvation of men's souls seriously." [30] McGavran's "they" of course included many mainstream Lutherans as well as the mission wing of Missouri's Seminex movement. It was in this context that Preus published, in 1975, a major essay on "The Confessions and the Mission of the Church." [31]

Contrary to fashionable notions of the day, Preus maintained that the church is a spiritual, not a political fellowship. Therefore "the work of the church is the work of the Spirit; and anything which is not clearly the Spirit's work is not the work of the church." The Spirit, Preus continued, gives faith and salvation only through the gospel and the sacraments. To be sure, works of love flow from saving faith. But there are good *theological* reasons why our Confessions do not and really could not advocate corporate, institutional, ecclesiastical activity in the sphere of social and civil affairs, what we today would call social or political action."

Most basic here is the sharp distinction that the Bible and the Reformation make between God's two authorities or governments, the spiritual and the political. While Christians in their various callings are to serve God and their neighbors according to the Ten Commandments, and while the church is to proclaim these commandments to high and low alike, rulers included, "it is," concluded Preus on the basis of the Lutheran confessions, "as members of the church ... who have their specific calling that rulers are given such counsel." Preus employed a similar argument in defending the confessions against the charge of being indifferent to missions. On the contrary, he contended, by freeing the gospel from dependence on works and from entanglements with Caesar, the Reformation liberated the church and her ministry "for mission in the true sense. ... The passion for the Gospel is the passion for souls, and this is the essence of the spirit of mission."

Finally, Preus's article criticized as theologically vacuous and frivolous the "Report on Renewal in Mission" that was put forth by the Uppsala Assembly of the World Council (1968): "The urgency for proclaiming the Gospel is simply not apparent in the Uppsala Report. And this is inexcusable." While advocating ongoing substantive conversations, Preus saw no future for the present ecumenical movement as reflected in the "unevangelical and even heretical" approach of the report. "To identify with a great movement which so tragically buries the Gospel and misses the crucial mission of the church would constitute a compromise and denial of our understanding of the Gospel and the work of Christ's church."

Among the most fruitful of his inter-confessional endeavors was Preus's participation in the three summits of the International Council on Biblical Inerrancy (1978, 1982, 1986). These meetings brought together scholars from various backgrounds, and the disciplined exchange and clarification of ideas were obviously beneficial. Formal agreements were produced by the first and second summits: "The Chicago Statement on Biblical Inerrancy" (1978) and "The Chicago Statement on Biblical Hermeneutics" (1982). [32] The third summit produced no formal statement, but dealt with specific interpretations and applications to current

136

social issues, where confessional differences naturally played their part. [33] Perhaps the most clearly Lutheran contribution to these discussions is embodied in Article II of the statement on hermeneutics: "WE AFFIRM that as Christ is God and Man in one Person, so Scripture is, indivisibly, God's Word in human language. WE DENY that the humble, human form of Scripture entails errancy any more than the humanity of Christ, even in His humiliation, entails sin." [34]

In a similar vein we should note Preus's contribution to the Conference on Biblical Inerrancy sponsored by the six seminaries of the Southern Baptist Convention (1987). His essay was criticized as one-sided by one respondent, and hailed by another as part of "a monumental contribution to the evangelical cause through both scholarship and statesmanship." [35]

In honor of Preus's sixtieth birthday, a festschrift was published by his friends and colleagues. [36] In addition to the local talent, there were contributions by distinguished confessional churchmen and scholars from Australia, Brazil, Germany, Great Britain, and Sweden. The volume paid tribute to Preus for having "striven to tip the balance in favor of theological rather than bureaucratic impulses in the shaping of pastoral training and preparation." This strength, generally appreciated by Preus's teaching colleagues, had its liabilities, however, and nearly proved to be his undoing. Bureaucracies are notoriously fond of safe, rule-driven behavior, and allergic to creative eruptions of substance. Church bureaucracies are no exception.

The catalyst for Preus's difficulties was the Church Growth movement. In an initial burst of enthusiasm reflecting Preus's concern for missions, the Fort Wayne faculty had petitioned the 1977 convention of the Missouri Synod to have each of its subdivisions or districts "make a thorough study of the Church Growth materials." What is more, the districts were to be urged to "organize, equip, and place into action all of the Church Growth principles as needed in the evangelization of our nation and the world under the norms of the Scriptures and the Lutheran Confessions." By the time of the 1986 synodical convention, however, the same faculty, while appreciating the "valuable lessons of common sense" to be learned from Church Growth, asked that "the Synod warn against the Arminian and charismatic nature of the church-growth movement."

This cooling of the initial enthusiasm for Church Growth was inevitable, given Preus's insistence on theological integrity as a necessary condition of all proper mission work. Ever anxious that the seminary be relevant to the church's practical needs, Preus organized a number of public dialogues in which Lutheran advocates of Church Growth played a part. These discussions did not defuse the developing theological tensions, but heightened them. The rift was between the practical men of action and the theologians. The former saw the latter as hopelessly impractical theorists out of touch with modern reality. The latter, in turn, thought that the former were uncritically imbibing theological content along with Church Growth methods. The Fort Wayne faculty became increasingly concerned that the churchly Lutheran heritage was being jettisoned in a vapid, and ultimately futile, flirtation with popular culture.

This debate over substance versus style or, in the context of missiology, gospel versus culture raised in acute form the wider question of the connection between confessional and evangelical. For Preus it had always been axiomatic that if the ancient creeds and the sixteenth-century confessions were truly faithful to the gospel, then one could not be evangelical without being confessional, and vice versa. He bristled at the idea that for the sake of a broad, popular appeal, the confessions might be sidelined into some safe preserve for cultural white elephants. A gospel so liberated from clear doctrinal content and contours would be an insipid mush unworthy of the noble name *evangelical*. There is no generic gospel apart from doctrinal specifics. The New Testament, he asserted, is controversial, not platitudinous.

From the beginning of his presidency Robert Preus had sought ways and means to raise the confessional consciousness of the future clergy. The aim was to counter the cultural predilections for the bland, the banal, and the inoffensive. After the move to Fort Wayne an annual Symposium on the Lutheran Confessions was begun. Here scholars and churchmen of widely different backgrounds could engage each other in the give-and-take of responsible academic debate. Other Preus creations include the International Foundation for Lutheran Confessional Research and the Luther Academy, both dedicated to the pursuit of Reformation related scholarship. The foundation is underwriting the *Confessional Lutheran Dogmatics* series, a projected eleven volumes being compiled under Preus's general editorship. The renewed confessional awareness that developed particularly among the younger clergy of the Missouri Synod in the 1980s was not uniformly welcomed.

It was on a collision course not only with the looser views of the remnants of the Seminex movement, but also with a conservative biblicism mixed with a missionary pragmatism that took its cue from the Church Growth movement. On the one hand, the confessionally minded resisted what they regarded as a slide into a generic Protestant pietism and emotionalism. The pro-expansion forces, on the other hand, were impatient with what they took to be a stubborn clinging to ethnic trivia, which stood in the way of successful mass evangelism in the current American culture. Some administrative types took the view that if only the synod could rid itself of the confessional extremists as it had rid itself of the liberal ones in the 1970s, there would be peace at last.

The focus of the synodical tensions had changed from biblical authority to questions about the nature of the church, the ministry, and the confessions. In 1981 the synodical convention had accepted unchanged a resolution from the Preus-led Fort Wayne faculty which was highly critical of the more liberal members of the Lutheran Council in the U.S.A., namely, the American Lutheran Church and the Lutheran Church in America. [37] Nothing much came of this resolution, and the Lutheran Council in the U.S.A. eventually disappeared with the formation of the new Evangelical Lutheran Church in America, which includes the American Lutheran Church and the Lutheran Church in America, but not the

Lutheran Church–Missouri Synod. By 1989 the Fort Wayne seminary was warning its synodical convention that the Evangelical Lutheran Church in America, which ordained women and practiced interdenominational church fellowship, was really a union church and not confessionally Lutheran. The situation was said to "lend renewed urgency in our region of the world to the question: 'Will Lutheranism everywhere become merely a viewpoint within church bodies that are not in fact Lutheran?' (H. Sasse, *We Confess the Church*, 42)." No action was taken by the convention, since the synodical leadership sought friendly relations with the Evangelical Lutheran Church in America and muted all criticism.

The push for less restrictive practices came not only from the pro–Evangelical Lutheran Church in America forces, but also from those who were under the influence of Church Growth. The latter also demanded lay ministers in public worship, something which went completely against the grain of the confessional Lutheran understanding of the gospel ministry. At the same time bureaucratic pressures brought into question the old Lutheran doctrine of the permanency of the call into the ministry. Preus himself countered with a ringing defense of the old doctrine. [38]

In short, while the Missouri Synod had faced a crisis in the 1970s over biblical authority, it faced in the 1980s a confessional crisis on the nature of the church and the ministry. Fort Wayne was of course by no means the only force for confessionalism. Strong confessional impulses emanated from the St. Louis seminary as well. Yet Preus came to embody this renewed confessional awareness in a special way. A shrewd observer remarked in a pan-Lutheran publication: "Robert Preus would eschew the label 'evangelical catholic,' but he did create and protect a climate on the Fort Wayne campus that fostered a strong confessional theology coupled with a respectable liturgical life." [39]

In view of Preus's worldwide reputation within confessional Lutheranism and beyond, there was considerable shock when he was against his wishes given honorable retirement by the seminary's board of regents in 1989. With the support of many friends, he decided to contest the decision in the church's court system; in the meantime he obtained the help of the civil courts in preventing the appointment of a permanent replacement. The case caused a good deal of turmoil in the Missouri Synod. In response to various defensive actions on Preus's part, the synod's top leadership (the so-called praesidium, consisting of the president and the five vice-presidents) accused him of conduct unbecoming a Christian, and had him removed from the clergy roster. The synod's highest tribunal, the commission on appeals, ultimately reinstated Preus as seminary president (in a 5 to 4 decision) and restored him to the clergy roster (by a vote of 9 to 0). Synodical officials refused to accept this outcome, and sought to bring the matter before the synod's 1992 convention in Pittsburgh. The convention narrowly (by a vote of 580 to 568) defeated the incumbent president, Ralph Bohlmann, and elected Alvin Barry instead. It also abolished the old adjudication-and-appeals system, replacing it with a new conflict-resolution procedure, which gives the impression of having been hastily improvised. The convention did, however, heed its bylaws in not reopening the Preus case. Instead it ratified an agreement according to which Preus was to remain president till May 1993 or a new president was chosen, whichever occurred first. [40] Meanwhile, a mutually acceptable administrator was to handle executive and academic affairs.

The outcome was, of course, a compromise. Yet Preus was essentially vindicated in that the final decision of the commission on appeals was left standing. He was permitted to spend the rest of his productive years doing what he loves best—teaching sacred theology and thus preparing men for the awesome work of stewards of the life-giving mysteries of God (1 Cor. 4:1).

Footnotes

[1] The Lutheran *Book of Concord,* ed. Theodore G. Tappert (Philadelphia: Muhlenberg, 1959), uses this sense of the word when it speaks of "Evangelical churches and schools" (p. 506).

[2] An American transplant of this German usage appears in the title *Evangelical Catechism* (Minneapolis: Augsburg, 1982). Robert Preus castigated this catechism for equivocating not only on the traditional inter-confessional differences (e.g., on the sacraments), but on all articles of faith, including such basics as the virgin birth, miracles, the atonement, the resurrection, the divinity of Christ, and the Trinity: "Nowhere in the entire book which is entitled the *Evangelical Catechism* are we told unequivocally what the Gospel is. How tragic! How utterly tragic!" (*Affirm* 9.8 [April 1983]: 7).

[3] "Robert D. Preus: Bibliography," *Springfielder* 38.2 (Sept. 1974): 95–98; "Robert D. Preus: A Bibliography 1974–1984," *Concordia Theological Quarterly* 49.2–3 (April–July 1985): 83–85. *Concordia Theological Quarterly* is the continuation of the *Springfielder* .

[4] *The Orthodox Evangelicals* , ed. Robert Webber and Donald G. Bloesch (Nashville: Thomas Nelson, 1978).

[5] In the first sentence of his foreword to Kurt E. Marquart, *Anatomy of an Explosion: A Theological Analysis of the Missouri Synod Conflict* (Grand Rapids: Baker, 1978), Preus characterizes the account that http://biblecentre.net/theology/books/het/het327.html (2 of 3) [26/08/2003 10:00:19 a.m.] Logos - Logos Library System R is to follow as "the story of a large, confessional church body gradually, almost imperceptibly but seemingly irrevocably, losing its evangelical and confessional character" (p. iii).

[6] James E. Adams, *Preus of Missouri and the Great Lutheran Civil War* (New York: Harper and Row, 1977), 45–46. A number of other biographical details in this essay are also based on Adams's account.

[7] Ibid., 53.

[8] Adams, *Preus of Missouri* , tends in this direction; see, e.g., pp. 95ff.

[9] Robert D. Preus, *The Inspiration of Scripture: A Study of the Theology of the Seventeenth Century Lutheran Dogmaticians* (London: Oliver and Boyd, 1955). http://biblecentre.net/theology/books/het/het328.html (2 of 3) [26/08/2003 10:00:25 a.m.]

[10] E. Clifford Nelson, *Lutheranism in North America*, 1914–1970 (Minneapolis: Augsburg, 1972), 164–65.

[11] Richard R. Caemmerer, ed., "Essays on the Inspiration of Scripture," *Concordia Theological Monthly* 25.10 (Oct. 1954): 298.

[12] John Warwick Montgomery, *Crisis in Lutheran Theology*, 2 vols. (Grand Rapids: Baker, 1967).

[13] Preus, *Inspiration,* xv.

[14] Ibid., 211.

[15] Ibid., 72–73.

[16] Ibid., 182. Preus was to take on Barth in considerable detail in a series of essays published in *Concordia Theological Monthly* 31.2, 3, 4, 10 (Feb., March, April, Oct. 1960).

[17] For a broad journalistic treatment see Adams, *Preus of Missouri.* Two largely documentary volumes are Marquart, *Anatomy of an Explosion* ; and Board of Control, Concordia Seminary, St. Louis, *Exodus from Concordia: A Report on the 1974 Walkout* (St. Louis: The Board, 1977). More-personal accounts are Frederick W. Danker, *No Room in the Brotherhood: The Preus-Otten Purge of Missouri* (St. Louis: Clayton, 1977); and John H. Tietjen, *Memoirs in Exile: Confessional Hope and Institutional Conflict* (Minneapolis: Augsburg Fortress, 1990). For Robert Preus's empathetic and magnanimous review of the latter see *Logia: A Journal of Lutheran Theology* 1.1 (Oct. 1992): 74–78.

[18] Cited in *Exodus from Concordia* , 33; Preus's remarks originally appeared in *Spectrum* (a Concordia Seminary student publication), 10 March 1972.

[19] Harold Lindsell, *The Bible in the Balance* (Grand Rapids: Zondervan, 1979), 244. http://biblecentre.net/theology/books/het/het331.html (2 of 3) [26/08/2003 10:00:44 a.m.] Logos - Logos Library System R

[20] Robert D. Preus, review of *Biblical Authority* , edited by Jack B. Rogers, in Lindsell, *Bible in the Balance* , 366.

[21] Robert D. Preus, *The Theology of Post-Reformation Lutheranism* , 2 vols. (St. Louis: Concordia, 1970, 1972). Edward Farley, *Ecclesial Reflection: An Anatomy of Theological Method* (Philadelphia: Fortress, 1982), 121n, states that Preus's Inspiration of Scripture and Theology of Post-Reformation Lutheranism are, "on the Lutheran side, the fullest historical studies of the seventeenth-century theologians on Scripture."

[22] Bengt Hägglund, *History of Theology* , trans. Gene J. Lund (St. Louis: Concordia, 1968), 303.

[23] Preus, *Post-Reformation Lutheranism* , 1:41–42. Here is a prime illustration that the allegedly scholastic seventeenth-century divines made independent and creative use of Thomas Aquinas. Their distinction between magisterial and ministerial reason does justice to a crucial aspect of the Christian truth, which undifferentiated talk about faith and reason simply fails to capture (see the sympathetic exposition of Aquinas's view in Norman L. Geisler, *Thomas Aquinas: An Evangelical Appraisal* [Grand Rapids: Baker, 1991], 57–69). The old dogmaticians have left behind a monumental example of just what Geisler suggests needs to be done—pressing Aquinas's superb intellectual equipment into the service of biblical, Reformation theology.

[24] Preus, *Post-Reformation Lutheranism* , 2:38.

[25] Etienne Gilson, *The Philosopher and Theology,* trans. Cecile Gilson (New York: Random House, 1962), 81.

[26] Preus, *Post-Reformation Lutheranism,* 1:194. Preus would later state: "God is not an idea or theory. He is the living Lord of heaven and earth, the Creator and Sustainer of all things, the Redeemer and Savior of all men. One cannot study theology without being caught up by it, changed, born again, without commitment, without faith" ("Inauguration Address,") *Springfielder* 38.2 [Sept. 1974]: 93).

[27] *Time Magazine*, 9 September 1974, p. 67.

[28] Preus, "Inauguration Address," 94.

[29] Robert D. Preus, "Reflections on the International Congress on World Evangelization," *Affirm* , 14 November 1974, p. 6.

[30] Donald A. McGavran, "Church Growth Strategy Continued," *International Review of Missions* 57 (July 1968): 339. See also *The Conciliar-Evangelical Debate: The Crucial Documents* , 1964–1976, ed. Donald A. McGavran (South Pasadena: William Carey Library, 1977); Harvey T. Hoekstra, *The World Council of Churches and the Demise of Evangel-*

ism (Wheaton, Ill.: Tyndale, 1979); and Edward R. Norman, *Christianity and the World Order* (New York: Oxford University Press, 1979).

[31] Robert D. Preus, "The Confessions and the Mission of the Church," *Springfielder* 39.1 (June 1975): 20–39.

[32] For the statement on inerrancy see Lindsell, *Bible in the Balance* , 366–71; for the statement on hermeneutics see *Hermeneutics, Inerrancy, and the Bible: Papers from ICBI Summit II* , ed. Earl D. Radmacher and Robert D. Preus (Grand Rapids: Zondervan, 1984), 881–87.

[33] *Applying the Scriptures: Papers from ICBI Summit III* , ed. Kenneth S. Kantzer (Grand Rapids: Zondervan, 1987). Preus's contribution, "The Living God" (pp. 1–18), deals with soteriological and trinitarian matters.

[34] *Hermeneutics, ed. Radmacher and Preus* , 882.

[35] *Proceedings of the Conference on Biblical Inerrancy* , 1987 (Nashville: Broadman, 1987), 65.

[36] Kurt E. Marquart, John R. Stephenson, and Bjarne W. Teigen, eds., *A Lively Legacy: Essays in Honor of Robert Preus* (Fort Wayne: Concordia Theological Seminary Press, 1985).

[37] The faculty drew attention to an essay in which a leading biblical scholar from the Lutheran Church in America had undermined the whole traditional Christology of the creeds. The faculty's proposal read: "Resolved, That the Synod hereby instruct its President to request the Division of Theological Studies [of the Lutheran Council in the U.S.A.] to place on the division's agenda as a matter of urgency a thorough discussion of the far-reaching implications of historical criticism, as practiced in U.S. Lutheranism, for: (a) the central Christological-Trinitarian core of the Gospel; (b) the very possibility of confessional subscription; and (c) the preamble of LCUSA's constitution, according to which the participating Lutheran church bodies ... see in the three Ecumenical Creeds and in the Confessions of the Lutheran Church ... a pure exposition of the Word of God."

[38] Robert D. Preus, *The Doctrine of the Call in the Confessions and Lutheran Orthodoxy, Luther Academy Monograph* 1 (Fort Wayne: Luther Academy, 1991). This essay, which was read before the 1990 Symposium on the Lutheran Confessions, was printed and sent to all Missouri Synod congregations by Our Savior Church and School of Houston.

[39] John T. Pless, "Previewing Missouri's Convention," *Forum Letter* 21.6 (June 29, 1992): 6.

[40] In April 1993 David Schmiel was installed as the new president.

1. Robert Preus's work was focused largely on ____.
2. Who was the father of Robert Preus?____
3. Robert's great grandfather helped to form ____.
4. Robert Preus was the first graduate of ____.
5. Both Robert and Jack Preus supported the move of the Evangelical Lutheran Synod to suspend fellowship with ____.
6. Robert and Jack Preus decided that their battle for orthodoxy might be better waged in ____.
7. Preus is a certain respect resembled another outsider ____ whose work "meteorlike", came to Missouri a decade later.
8. The early Hermann Sasse was not immune from ____.
9. What did Preus's work on inspiration show?____
10. Throughout the 1960's the St. Louis seminary acquired ____.
11. John Tietjen claimed that no one could competently teach at Concordia Seminary without using ____.

12. What did a "Statement of Scriptural and Confessional Principles show? ____
13. The striking professors were relieved of their positions because ____.
14. What happened at the LCMS's 1973 convention? ____
15. What did Harold Lindsell say about the victory of orthodoxy in the LCMS? ____
16. What did Bengt Hägglund say about Lutheran orthodoxy? ____
17. Preus said that there was no theological cleavage between ____.
18. What is the difference between a magisterial and ministerial use of reason? ____
19. Theology is not a theoretical or speculative science but a ____.
20. What did Time say when Robert Preus was inaugurated president of Concordia Theological Seminary, Ft. Wayne?____
21. ____ was always close to Preus's heart.
22. What is the essence of the spirit for mission? ____
23. Preus participated in three summits of the ____.
24. The most clearly Lutheran contribution to the International Council on Biblical Inerrancy was ____.
25. Bureaucracies are notoriously fond of ____.
26. The Church Growth movement was the catalyst for Preus's ____.
27. The Fort Wayne faculty became increasingly concerned that the Lutheran church heritage ____.
28. Some of Preus's creations at the Ft. Wayne seminary were ____.
29. The Ft. Wayne seminary warned the LCMS that ELCA was ____.
30. In the 1980s the LCMS faced a confessional crisis on the nature of ____.
31. What did the Church Growth movement demand? ____
32. In 1989 Preus was given ____ against his wishes?
33. Why did Preus obtain the help of the civil courts? ____
34. The LCMS's top leadership accused Preus of ____.
35. The LCMS's highest tribunal in a 5-4 decision restored Preus to ____.
36. Synodical officials ____ to accept this outcome and brought the matter to ____.
37. Although incumbent President Ralph Bohlmann was defeated, the convention abolished the old ____ and replaced it with ____.
38. What did Preus say about the Evangelical Catechism published by Augsburg? ____

DR. ROBERT DAVID PREUS
AN APPRECIATION
From A Lively Legacy:
Essays In Honor of Robert Preus

Christian News, August 7, 1989

Robert Preus, pastor, professor, churchmen, and seminary president, is above all a theologian. He is saluted here in this traditional academic way by friends and colleagues on the occasion of his 60th birthday – even though the actual publication falls within the bounds of one calendar year after that event, October 16, 1984.

The remarks which follow must not be understood as presumptuous efforts to anticipate the verdict of history. They are offered as a personal tribute, from a perspective, however, which, to the extent that it succeeds in reflecting a wider consensus, and will eliminate the high esteem in which the jubilarian is held throughout the Orthodox Lutheran Church in our time.

There are of course many things that could be said, but at least three things must be said about the theology of Robert Preus. One is that his theology represents the mainstream of the Orthodox Lutheran legacy. Like the C.F.W. Walther, Robert Preus never tried to be "original" or idiosyncratic in his theology. Nor did he focus narrowly on one or two favorite themes. There is therefore no "Preus school," riding pet hobbyhorses, but only a shared devotion to a common heritage. If there is an "accent," it falls just were St. Paul and the others put it on "Christ alone," against every form of synergism. And as in Walther's case so in Preus's, we find a creative, not uncritical, appropriation of the tradition, rather than the mindless rigidity of stock liberal caricature.

This wide-angle scope is reflected in the essays printed in this book. Apart from their commitment to the substance of the Scriptures and the Confessions, there is no obvious common thread linking the various contributions. None of them, however, whether they deal with Biblical authority or Luther or the church's mission or the "family life" complex of issues, fall outside the domain of concerns marked out by the many-facetted theological work of Robert Preus.

No doubt the leading authority in the Anglo-Saxon realm on 17th century Lutheran Orthodoxy, Preus has helped to rescue English-speaking Lutherans from the paralyzing collective amnesia induced by the lack of effective access to their theological classics. While others, especially his brother J.A.O. Preus, the former president of the Missouri Synod, Professor F. Kramer, and the Rev. Luther Poellot, provided much needed translation of the literary outfit of the early and pivotal figure of the "Second Martin" (Chemnitz), Robert Preus began a comprehensive series, *The Theology of Post-Reformation Lutheranism*, of which two volumes have appeared so far. It is hoped that as the old "sunken treasures" are reclaimed and re-enter the conscious life of the contemporary church, the taste for shapeless mush will quietly fade away.

It is of course the Book of Concord itself which prescriptively defines what Lutheran theology is. But routine lip-service and occasional ceremonial salutes to the Confessions are worse than useless, if their actual content is not known and understood. With this in view, Preus in January of 1978 organized the first symposium on the Lutheran Confessions. This annual "Confessions Congress" has grown into a firm and popular tradition at Concordia Theological Seminary, Ft. Wayne. Inter-synodical and international in participation and attendance, these meetings highlight the theological substance of the Confessions in scholarly analysis, debate, and contemporary application.

The second major point to be made has to do with the contemporary reassertion of the Reformation's Scripture-principle. One may perhaps be pardoned a personal reminiscence here. Those who were students at Concordia Seminary, St. Louis, in the middle and late 50s, will recall the confusion and controversy which attended the question of Biblical inspiration and authority in the wake of the post-World War II "neo-orthodox" *blitzkrieg*. Lip service was paid to inspiration, but that doctrine came increasingly to resemble the context-less grin of Alice's disappearing Cheshire cat. Most of the old framework had been given up, and its champions were despised as "dictation theory" take in scarecrows. Into this tottering world of doubletalk and shilly-shallying, so reminiscent of Yeats 1921 lines,

The best lack all conviction, while the worst
Are full of passionate intensity.

sounded the clear trumpet tones of Robert Preus's first doctoral dissertation, published as *The Inspiration of Scripture* (Edinburg, 1955). Edward Farley has recently described this book and Volume I of Preus' *The Theology of Post-Reformation Lutheranism* (1970) as "the fullest historical studies of the 17th century Lutheran theologians on Scripture."[1]

The enlightning, settling, even liberating effects of Preus's first book were immense, at least for those of us who were as students struggling through the spiritual theological models of those years. And then, in 1957, Preus became an instructor at the St. Louis seminary, where he remained until the drama of 1974. As a faithful professor, and frequent writer and essayist, he did much toward the Missouri Synod's official reassertion, under Pres. J. A. O. Preus of Biblical authority against historical criticism. After the famous "walkout" of the critically inclined faculty majority, Robert Preus was one of the "Faithful Five" who stayed to rebuild. At one point he combined in his person the offices of Acting President, Acting Academic Dean, and Acting Registrar! In that same year he was called to the presidency of Concordia Theological Seminary, then in Springfield, Illinois.

For Preus, after all Orthodox Lutherans, the heart and center of Scripture is Christ. Justification, not inspiration, is the linchpin holding everything else together. It is in this sense that Preus has participated prominently and fruitfully in the work of the International Council on Biblical Inerrancy.[2]

The third and final point to be made here is perhaps the most important. Theology is practical. This is a commonplace in Lutheran Orthodoxy. It means that theology is not like mathematics or physics, but like medicine. Although physicians need technical knowledge, without which mere bedside manner is charlantry, medical knowledge is mastered not for its own sake, but as a part of the art and practice of healing. Theology is like that, except that it's healing resources come from God alone, through His revealed Word and supply eternal, not temporal life. Therefore orthodoxy defines theology as a practical, God-given aptitude, that is, the ability to apply God's law and gospel to people, for the purpose of incorporating them through faith into Christ and his church and tending them there with Word and Sacrament to everlasting life.

Edward Farley notes this old Lutheran understanding, citing in support Gerhard and Calov, via Preus.[3] Farley's own work in this area is nothing less than an autopsy of current "mainline" Protestant seminary education in America. Farley shows that with the collapse of what he calls the "house of authority" under pressure from historical criticism, theology and theological education became fragmented into a welter of independent "scientific" disciplines, which then needed to be supplemented with (basically unrelated) "practical skills." The minister thus becomes no longer a man of God, shaped by his immersion into the theological substance of authoritative texts, but a trained "professional" with marketable "skills." Theological learning turns into a hobby which those so inclined may pursue, but which is basically discouraged by the "reward systems" in a pragmatic, success oriented denominational machineries. Without attending to the underlying theological malaise, says Farley, all my much discussed "curricular reform" remains a purely cosmetic exercise.

Farley's positive prescriptions are unconvincing since he advocates unconditional surrender of historic Christianity's "house of authority," by which he means mainly Scripture is God's Word, transmitting divine doctrine. But only the very naïve can imagine that Orthodox Lutheran seminary education is safely immune from the broad trends identified in Farley's brilliantly depressing diagnosis.

As a foremost representative of the "house of authority," Robert Preus knows very well that without clear-cut God-given truth theology is dead and seminary education bankrupt. He also knows that the "house of authority" exists not for its own sake, but for the sake of the church's divinely mandated mission. This deeply held concern for missions took Preus to Lausanne and in 1974, where he addressed the World Congress on Evangelization. Preus also served on the Missouri Synod Board for Mission Services, and has energetically pursued the cause of upgrading the mission curriculum in the institution of which he is president. In this latter capacity, Preus is striven to tip the balance in favor of theological rather than bureaucratic impulses in the shaping of pastoral training and preparation. For it is of course precisely Lutheran Orthodoxy which cannot remain content as an academic "theory" on a shelf, while "practice" apes the latest sectarian success story.

The essay assumption that the only good orthodoxy is dead orthodoxy is challenged by the theological renewal to which Robert Preus has devoted his life. True, Biblical and Confessional integrity is embattled and lacks the Madison Avenue appeal of all "theology of glory." But has it ever been different in the church? Yet in the faith of the wholesale modern abandonment of the most precious and distinctive treasures of the Church of Augsburg Confession – need one go beyond the U.S. Lutheran Reformed Dialogue Series III, by way of the example? – the faithful old theology of the cross remains at her post and renews her youth like the eagles.

The means of grace and their all decisive, pivotal position are the hallmark of the Lutheran Confession. Let modern social, political, and commercial manipulation depend on the insights of the "behavioral sciences." For theology in the strict sense these insights are of no concern, even when they are trivially true. For the church lives solely and alone from Christ's own pure gospel and sacraments which in turn of course are found not in "cold storage," but in living proclamation and distribution to poor, needy sinners (AC V and VII). To serve as a humble messenger of Him Whose words are spirit and are life (St. John 6:63) has ever been the highest and the only genuine ambition of Lutheran theology. It is this deepest inner vitality of the heritage itself, not any exciting qualities of individual contributions to it, which is the ultimate reference of the "lively" in *A Lively Legacy*.

Footnotes

1 Edward Farley, Ecclesial Reflections: An Anatomy of Theological Method Parenthesis Philadelphia: Fortress Press, 1982 parenthesis, PA. 121, and 10.

2 See Earl D. Radmacher and Robert D. Preus, eds., Hermeneutics, Inerrancy and the Bible (Grand Rapids: Zondervan, 1984).

3 Edward Farley. Theologia: The Fragmentation and Unity of Theological Education (Philadelphia: Fortress Press, (183), p. 46 .n. 32. See also Edward Farley, The Reform of Theological Education as a Theological Task," Theological Education, vol. XVII, no. 2 (Spring 1981), pp. 93-117. The "fallout" from this explosive contribution to the journal of the Association of Theological Schools has not yet abated.

Editor's Note: The special "Preus Sacked" issue of *Christian News*, August 7, 1989, included several news reports of the removal of Robert Preus as president of Concordia Theological Seminary, Ft. Wayne, a comparison chart of the differences between LCMS President Ralph Bohlmann, "Scapping 'the World's Leading Orthodox Theologian'", the Preus Record, and several essays by Robert Preus. Kurt Marquart, who was Preus's chief defender is quoted: "Seminary faculties should not be warrens of cowering rabbits but men of God speaking their convictions regardless of the 'image.'" *CN* called for "A Testimonial for Preus – A State of the Church Conference" where a Twentieth Century Formula of Concord long promoted by Marquart would be considered. The February 25, 1991 *CN* reported: Conservatives throughout the Lutheran Church-

Missouri Synod are disappointed that all of the church's vice-presidents have joined with LCMS President Ralph Bohlmann in accusing Robert Preus for being a persistent liar. The LCMS President and Vice Presidents August Mennicke, Robert King, Robert Sauer, Walter Maier, and Eugene Bunkoske have all charged Preus with 'persistent conduct unbecoming a Christian' and 'a persistent and recurring unbrotherly pattern of untruthfulness and unbrotherly treatment of other Christians.'" King later withdrew his accusations vs. Preus.

Marquart Defends Robert Preus
Christian News, February 25, 1991

"Why Blast Preus and Not liberals," a letter to the LCMS's *Lutheran Witness Reporter Alive* from three witnesses to the latest Bohlmann-Preus meeting, was published in the February 18 *CN* after the *Reporter* indicated that is could not be published by any LCMS publication, at least not in its present form. Pastor William Brege, Professor Kurt Marquart, and Pastor John Stube, the witnesses, wrote in the letter the LCMS publication is refusing to publish: "Is it really credible that the faithful theologian Robert Preus is a greater threat to our Synod's well-being than are all those among us, some in high places, who oppose or undermine our church's biblical and confessional stand, for example, on pulpit and altar fellowship, or on the ordination of women? Is he more dangerous than the whole 'charismatic' infiltration of our church's public ministry? Why then is he alone singled out for such extraordinary public denunciation by the Presidium, as if he were the very troubler of Israel (1 Kings 18:17)."

1. Robert Preus is above all ____.
2. Preus's theology represents ____.
3. Preus never tried to be ____.
4. Robert Preus is the leading authority on ____.
5. The Book of Concord prescriptively defines what ____.
6. In 1978 Preus organized the first symposium on ____.
7. Preus became an instructor at the St. Louis seminary in ____.
8. For Preus and all Orthodox Lutherans the heart and center of Scripture is ____.
9. ____ is the linchpin that holds everything together.
10. Orthodoxy defines theology as a ____ God given aptitude.
11. What took Preus to Lausanne in 1974 to address the World Congress on Evangelization?____
12. Seminary faculties should not be warrens of ____.
13. The president and vice-presidents of the LCMS accused Preus of ____.

ROBERT D. PREUS:
A PERSONAL TRIBUTE

By Professor Kurt Marquart
Christian News, November 13, 1995

Years ago at a party people were talking about what had first drawn them to the study of theology. When his turn came, Robert Preus said, "How about just wanting to know God? I took up theology because I wanted to know the truth about God." That is why Dr. Preus never played academic games with theology. For him it was not an intellectual diversion, to while away long Minnesota winter evenings with cosmic brain-teasers or pedantic word-games. Rather, theology was a life-and-death matter of the authentic voice of God, bestowing love and salvation in His Son and Spirit.

Robert Preus knew well the old standard-bearers of the Reformation Faith: Chemnitz, Gerhard, Calov, and the like. He was the English-speaking world's foremost authority on these "dogmaticians," and stood in fact himself as latter-day champion in their illustrious and apostolic succession. Not that he always agreed with them. He was no mere imitator. But he did not dwell gleefully on the mistakes of his predecessors. With firm churchly tact he would portray the soundness of their basic outlook and intention, and unobtrusively improve and correct what did not pass the test of Scripture and Confession.

With his two earned doctorates— from the Universities of Edinburgh (1952) and Strasbourg (1969) respectively— Robert Preus was a formidable and respected combatant in the scholarly arena. But he wore his learning lightly, and never flaunted it. One felt that he would gladly have given one or both of his degrees to him that hath none. He was too great a man for snobbery or affectation. Humbug he detested, but he could be very patient with plain human frailty.

He dealt easily with people from all walks of life, and could converse naturally and animatedly with scholars and laborers, young and old alike. No dinner table at which he was present, whether as guest or as host, was ever dull. His conversation dipped into philosophy and literature and of course into his own rich experience of life. His vision was global, never parochial, and was sustained even in dark days by a sturdy and childlike faith. His open and considerate manner won him the fierce loyalty of his subordinates. He treated the welfare of students as one of his highest priorities, often "going to bat" for individuals whose troubles had come to his notice.

Most of his theological work focused on the so-called "material" and "formal" principles:
Justification above all, but also Scripture and its inspiration, authority and inerrancy. He resolutely defended the full objectivity of the justifi-

cation of sinners in Christ alone, and its forensic nature, and warned against recent compromises in "dialogues" and the like. He was in his element when teaching, and regretted anything that got in the way of that. He had taught courses or at least lectured on all continents.

But Robert Preus was never an ivory tower academic. His theology had a deeply practical bent. It surged towards implementation, mission, confession. This combination of intellectual power and an indomitable energy and thirst for action suggests in fact a kinship with the temperament of Martin Luther. Various institutions bear the energies — first and foremost of course Concordia Theological Seminary itself, of which Robert Preus was President for over fifteen years. He had also played a crucial part in the survival of Concordia Seminary, St. Louis during the "Seminex" crisis. Help in the founding of a sister institution in St. Catharines, Ontario, was typical of Dr. Preus's vision. Then there are the Luther Academy, the Haiti Mission and Church, and the *Confessional Lutheran Dogmatics* series. Dr. Preus also took an active part in the International Council on Biblical Inerrancy, where he was highly respected and appreciated.

Also like Luther, Robert Preus was fearless in the service of Gospel truth. His own steady course in the church militant in turn inspired courage and devotion in others. In this sacred cause he spent himself unstintingly to the end. In an age of chaos and irresolution he stood unwavering, like a great oak tree defying storm and tempest. Kipling's words come to mind:

If you can keep your head when all about you
Are losing theirs and blaming it on you;
If you can trust yourself when all men doubt you.
But make allowance for their doubting too . . .

Yet this is all too secular. The rugged imagery of the Psalms unveils the hidden ground of faith's invincibility best of all:
"They that trust in the LORD shall be as Mount Zion: which cannot be removed, but abideth forever" (Ps. 125:1).

There are hundreds and thousands of us who know ourselves in Robert Preus's debt for his teaching and example, but also for the warm generosity of his collegiality and friendship. We mourn our loss. Truly, the Lord has given and the Lord has taken away; blessed be the Name of the Lord! But we do not begrudge our brother, teacher, and friend his entry into the ranks of "all the company of heaven," in the very after flow of All Saints' Day, 1995. Dr. Preus hardly ever preached without citing, by heart, appropriate hymn-stanzas, of which he knew many. Here is one to celebrate his memory:

And when the strife is fierce, the warfare long,
Steals on the ear the distant triumph song,
And hearts are brave again and arms are strong. Alleluia!

(LW, 191:5)
K. Marquart

1. What drew Robert Preus to the study of theology? ____
2. Preus was the English speaking leading authority on ____.
3. Preus was no mere ____.
4. What did Robert Preus not flaunt? ____
5. Preus's vision was ____ never ____.
6. Preus played a crucial part in the survival of ____.

LHF BOARD NAMES MARQUART

Christian News, December 25, 1995

Professor Kurt Marquart, Fort Wayne, IN, has been elected Chairman of the Lutheran Heritage Foundation Board of Directors to succeed the late Dr. Robert Preus.

Professor Marquart will assume responsibilities immediately in leading the projects of the LHF in Eastern Europe, Africa, and India. The LHF for the past three years has been involved in translating, publishing and distributing the confessional Lutheran theological works in a variety of languages.

In accepting the position Rev. Marquart said: "I am honored to be asked and am pleased to accept out of respect to the memory of Dr. Preus and in awe of the many accomplishments of the LHF in this short period of existence."

Mr. Richard Hallgren, LHF Board President, said: "We are grateful that Prof Marquart is willing to serve and he is a most logical choice since in his early years he himself barely escaped persecution under atheistic communism. He is also qualified since he speaks Russian and German and has been serving as a theological reviewer of Russian translation work. Having lectured in Latvia and Russia this past summer, he is already acquainted with the personnel working with the LHF in Eastern Europe."

Prof Marquart was born in Tallinn, Estonia in 1934. His family fled from the Soviets in 1941 when he was seven years old. They were living in Vienna and again had to flee when the Soviets entered in 1945.They went to Hanover in northern Germany where they ended up in displaced prison camps. In 1949 they came to America and settled in Nyack, NY.

Mr. Marquart graduated from Concordia Collegiate Institute, Bronxville, NY and from Concordia Seminary, St. Louis, MO, in 1959. He was ordained and installed as Pastor of Trinity Lutheran Church, Weatherford, TX, in July, 1959.

From April, 1961 until November, 1975, he served as Pastor of Redeemer and Good Shepherd Congregations, Toowoomba, Queensland, Australia.

In December, 1975, Prof. Marquart accepted a Call as Associate Professor of systematic and practical theology at Concordia Theological Seminary, then located in Springfield, IL.

The school year of 1981-1982 was spent in London, Ontario, where Prof Marquart pursued sabbatical studies in the philosophy of science, earning the MA degree in philosophy from the University of Western Ontario.

Prof Marquart married the former Barbara Martens of Fort Worth, Texas in 1961. They have five children, all born in Toowoomba, and several grandchildren.

Prof Marquart is the author of numerous articles and books and served until 1992 on the LCMS Commission on Theology and Church Relations.

Rev. Robert Rahn, LHF Executive Director, stated: "Prof Marquart's decision to serve is important as it will indicate to our constituents that the direction and commitment of the LHF as an organization remains firmly fixed. This is also important in an age when organization's deceptively leave their purpose without informing their supporters. The LHF, under the leadership of Prof Marquart, will be true to its stated mission purpose."

The LHF has become the foremost translation organization in the former Soviet Union. LHF offices are open in Riga, Latvia, St. Petersburg, Russia and Tirnopil, Ukraine. The LHF plans to open an office this summer in Novosibirsk, Siberia with a full time Branch Director. Over 75 translators, reviewers, linguists and theologians are involved in the translation process. Over 50 titles have been published to date.

Concurrently with the regular translation and publishing work, the LHF has undertaken its most massive effort to date. In an unequaled, unparalleled and unprecedented effort, the Book of Concord is being published in eight languages simultaneously. Prof. Marquart is reviewing the translation work on the Russian edition which should be published this summer. The Latvian edition will follow soon thereafter. Editions in Ukrainian, Estonian, Swahili, Setswana (African) and Telugu (Indian) will follow in late 96 or early 97.

When the door to Russia opened Prof Marquart was one of the few people fully acquainted with the background of the Russian field. The LHF early on through the efforts of Dr. Preus, took advantage of Prof Marquart's personal knowledge of the situation in Eastern Europe.

Also elected to the Board were Mr. Dean Bell, Hendrum, MN, and The Rev. Daniel Preus, St. Louis, MO. Rev. Preus was selected by the Board to continue the Preus association begun under the Founding Chairman, Dr. Robert Preus.

1. Kurt Marquart succeeded Robert Preus as ____.
2. The Lutheran Heritage Foundation has become ____.

A TRUE DOCTOR OF THEOLOGY

By Professor Kurt Marquart
Christian News, March 25, 1996

Pastor Paul H. Burgdorf has been called Home at the advanced age of 96. His life-span made him an eye-witness to the events of a century unlike any that have gone before. Nor was he merely a passive spectator. Blest with a keen intelligence. Pastor Burgdorf was a lively participant, according to his calling, in the history he observed.

In the Missouri Synod Paul Burgdorf was best known as the editor, for some thirty years, of *The Confessional Lutheran*. This publication arose in response to the loss of confessional substance which our Synod experienced in its hurried "Americanization" in the wake of two world wars. The cultural drift or convergence towards the American Lutheran "mainstream" ensured a share in the crisis about "Lutheran identity." Muddles arose in the understanding of the nature of the church and of church fellowship. Just before the outbreak of World War II the brilliant William Oesch, then a pastor in London, issued three numbers of *The Crucible*, to combat the trend towards pan-Lutheran compromise. When the war ended that project, Paul Burgdorf took up the challenge by founding and editing *The Confessional Lutheran*.

The new (mis)understanding of the church came to expression in *A Statement of 1945*, or, as it is also known, the "Statement of the Forty-Four." That document signaled a fateful switch from an objective, confessional way of thinking about the church to a subjective sentimental one. The question of fellowship was now handled in terms of individuals ("Lutherans" or "Christians") rather than churches. This inability to think in terms of church and churches has cost our Synod dearly, and led to the dissolution of the Synodical Conference. It was the great merit of Paul Burgdorf and those who stood with him, to recognize and resist this confessional peril and sellout. It was a great tragedy for the Missouri Synod that much of the confessional protest went officially unheeded. Unmoved by fear or favor, Paul Burgdorf continued his prophetic witness with courage and dignity. Later events in our church were to prove him right. But he never served the fickle gods of fashion and popularity. To know him was to be drawn beyond the world of shallow appearances to those things that are real and enduring.

As a man Paul Burgdorf was known for his integrity and his ready wit. He also took a keen interest in the well-being of his country. In that "left-hand" realm it was his fate (by his granddaughter's marriage to Mark Thatcher) to come to know Mrs. Margaret Thatcher, as she then was, when she was the British Prime Minister. Her brilliant mind and her grasp of history particularly impressed Paul Burgdorf. And in his own ministry, faithfully contending for the truth of the Divine Word and rightly distinguishing God's holy Law from His life-giving Gospel, Paul Burgdorf embodied Luther's definition of a true Doctor of Theology. May

Light Eternal shine upon him!

1. Pastor Paul Burgdorf was a lively participant in ____.
2. Burgdorf was the editor of ____ for some ___ years.
3. What does Marquart say about William Oesch? ____
4. The "Statement of the Forty-Four" signaled a fateful switch from an ___ to a subjective sentimental one.
5. Burgdorf was known for his ____.
6. Paul Burgdorf embodied Luther's definition of a true ____.

MARQUART OVERTURE SENT TO 2004 LCMS CONVENTION

Christian News, January 19, 2000

"Do Not Let Status And Privilege Override Truth In The Church," an overture written by Dr. Kurt Marquart, the candidate of grass roots conservatives for the presidency of the LCMS, has been submitted to the 2004 convention of The Lutheran Church-Missouri Synod. Unless President Kieschnick uses his authority to stop the publication of the overture in the convention workbook it will come before the convention.

Congregations all over the LCMS are invited to sign the overture and send it to the President of the LCMS.

The LCMS Handbook says that "The principal business of a synodical convention shall be the consideration of reports and overtures." (3.19, a). "Overtures for a convention may be submitted only by a member congregation of the Synod, . . ." (3.19, a. 2.)

"Reports and overtures must be submitted in triplicate to the President of the Synod not later than 18 weeks prior to the opening date of the convention."

"Overtures with reference to a case in which a member has been suspended or expelled and which is at present in the process of or subject to appeal, as well as overtures which, upon advice of legal counsel, may subject the synod or the corporate officers of the synod to civil action for libel or slander, shall not be accepted for convention consideration." (3.19, 2.b.)

"The Synodical President will determine if any overture contains information which is materially in error or contains any apparent misrepresentation of truth or of character. He shall not approve inclusion of any such overture in the convention manual and shall refer any such overture to the District President who has eclasiastical supervision over the entity submitting the overture for action." (3.19, 2.d.)

"The President shall also decide which of the matters accepted for presentation to and consideration by the convention shall be published in the convention manual." (3.19, 2.e.)

"All reports and overtures accepted by the President in accordance with the forgoing paragraph shall be referred by him to convention committees appointed by him in the name of the convention from among voting delegates (By-law 3.13) advisory delegate (By-law 3.09), and advisory representatives (By-law 3.13)."

By-law 3.19 in the LCMS's Handbook is reprinted in its entirety on page 4. Few LCMS congregations including the congregations of organized liberals and conservatives submit overtures to LCMS conventions. Often, conservative and liberal leaders have not informed their congregations about the theological issues facing the LCMS and therefore are unable to persuade them submit any overtures.

Some maintain that the LCMS's Handbook gives the LCMS President too much authority in appointing convention committees and deciding which overtures he does not want to have a convention consider or have published in the convention's manual for all delegates to read. When the LCMS had conservative presidents, conservatives maintained that it was proper for the LCMS President to have so much authority and power. *Christian News* said that it was not proper for any LCMS president, liberal or conservative, to have so much power. *CN* asked: "What will happen if a liberal is elected president? Should he be the one appointing convention committees and deciding which overtures should be published and considered?"

Christian News intends to publish overtures the LCMS President refuses to publish in the convention manual. *CN* will then send these overtures to all convention delegates. One purpose of such publication would be to show delegates that they should not vote for a president who suppresses free speech and refuses, without any valid scriptural reasons, to prevent a convention from considering various overtures.

Dr. Marquart and LCMS President Jerry Kieschnick have differed sharply on the subject of the overture "Do Not Let Status And Privilege Override Truth In the Church."

The LCMS's Commission on Constitutional Matters, appointed to large extent by Kieschnick, has adopted a ruling supported by Kieschnick which many in the LCMS are saying gives him the authority of some "pope." Marquart wrote to Kieschnick: "The increasing reliance on CCM rulings is a deplorable departure from our Synod's confessional foundation. The idea that previous approval by an 'ecclesiastical superior' override prima faci contradiction of our Synod's biblical confession is a deadly instance of what Sasse called 'the institutional lie.'" (Entire letter in *Luther Today*, p. 189. *Luther Today* is available from *Christian News*, $6.95).

Grassroots conservatives have noted that Marquart is about the only LCMS leader who has had the courage to challenge Kieschnick in public. Some fear that if they oppose Kieschnick they might get into difficulty if Kieschnick is re-elected.

Marquart's overture challenging the Kieschnick appointed CCM which LCMS congregations are invited to sign is on p. 7.

Editor's Note: The Marquart overture is on pp. 227-229.

1. Kurt Marquart was the candidate of ____ for LCMS president.
2. Few congregations have been submitting ____.
3. Some maintain that the LCMS's Handbook gives the President too much authority in appointing ____.
4. Who was about the only LCMS leader willing to challenge LCMS President in public? ____

QUESTIONS OF 'DUE PROCESS'

From the April, 1997 Reporter
Christian News, April 28, 1997

It was sad to see—and in the Christmas issue of THE *Lutheran Witness*—the official report of a grave injustice. I refer to the Council of Presidents' refusal first to renew and then to restore the candidate (CRM) status of Rev. Robert Rahn.

Pastor Rahn has served faithfully in our church's ministry for 35 years and is now executive director of the Lutheran Heritage Foundation. A preface by him appears in the new Russian Book of Concord.

His energetic labors were and are indispensable to the completion of this vital project and others like it. At issue here are not the merits of an individual case, but the underlying questions of "due process" (see 1 Tim. 5:19) and of churchly versus bureaucratic structure.

First of all, a simple majority vote can end CRM status, but it takes a three-fourths vote of district presidents present and voting to restore it (Bylaw 2.33). It seems unjust that a simple majority can take away what it cannot give back.

Secondly, since 1986, bylaw 2.31 provides that disposition of a request for reinstatement "shall be at the sole discretion of the Council of Presidents." However, there then existed a strong and independent adjudication and appeals system that could safeguard "due process."

Thirdly, the 1992 convention abolished the adjudication and appeals system and replaced it with administratively selected "dispute resolution" personnel. District presidents serve as "appeals panels" (since 1995), and the non-elected Commission on Constitutional Matters has the final say in all questions of Constitution and Bylaws. Given that setting, "the sole discretion of the Council of Presidents" has real potential for mischief.

Fourthly, if a proven and worthy pastor like Pastor Rahn is denied even candidate (CRM) status—thus making him ineligible for a call—why is it that, for instance, "Church Growth" functionaries, "consultants," publicists and entrepreneurs can continue as full and active members on the synodical roster of the ordained ministry?

Prof Kurt Marquart
Fort Wayne, Ind.
Prof. Marquart is chairman of the
Lutheran Heritage Foundation.—Ed.

1. The LCMS's Council of Presidents refused to restore ____.
2. Robert Rahn was the executive director of ____.
3. The 1992 convention of the LCMS abolished ____.
4. Marquart served as chairman of ____.

LAW/GOSPEL AND "CHURCH GROWTH"
OR
QUO VADIS (WHERE ARE YOU GOING),
LUTHERAN MISSIOLOGY?

Christian News, June 16, 1997

(Originally photographed from pp. 173-188 of *The Beauty and the Bands*, papers presented at Congress on Lutheran Confessions, Itasca, Illinois, April 20-22, 1995, *Christian News*, June 16, 1997)

To confine the issue at once to the limits of a brief paper, I shall focus only on missiology within the Missouri Synod. Neither God's Law nor His Gospel is an impersonal abstraction, or mere information content. The Law is *God* accusing and condemning; the Gospel is *God* forgiving, making alive, and saving sinners. To confess (Matt 10:32) God the Holy Trinity means to confess both the truth and justice of His verdict in the Law (I John 1:19), and the surpassing mercy of His salvation (John 1:14,17; 1 John 2.23; 4:2-15) bestowed and lavished on needy sinners in His evangelical Doctrine and Sacraments (1 John 1:1-4; 5:5-12).

The Gospel dare not be separated from the preparatory work of the Law: "For the Gospel does not preach the forgiveness of sin to indifferent and secure hearts, but to the 'oppressed' or penitent"(Luke 4:18).[1] Indeed:

> Unfortunately, men have learned it only too well; they do whatever they please and take advantage of their freedom, acting as if they will never need or desire to go to confession any more. We quickly understand whatever benefits us, and we grasp with uncommon ease whatever in the Gospel is mild and gentle. But such pigs, as I have said, are unworthy to appear in the presence of the Gospel or to have any part of it. They ought to remain under the pope and submit to being driven and tormented to confess, fast, etc., more than ever before *(LC,* Confession).[2]

If it is true that "one must of course first believe that God is the one who threatens, commands, and frightens, etc.,"[3] then the Augsburg Confession's concern for "dignity in public worship and the cultivation of reverence and devotion"[4] goes far beyond mere matters of good order, decorum, propriety, etc. What is at stake here is the Law's unconditional summons before the awesome Judgment Seat of the Almighty. This call to fear and trembling at the divine diagnosis apart from which the Gospel-cure has no meaning, is frustrated if not totally aborted by the frivolities (FCSD X)[5] of "entertainment evangelism," where a finger-snapping, foot-tapping, thigh slapping, vulgar, familiarity simply breeds contempt. The logical end-point is that dreadful cartoon to the Holy Spirit as laughing gas—a sacrilege that would have been the envy of any former Soviet museum of theism, but is in fact but another charismatic excitement from modern Toronto.

Domestic Evangelism: "Toolbox" and "CMI"

Closer to home now, let us take to hand the *Toolbox* prepared by our Synod's Congregational Services unit, and officially commended by Executive Director Lyle D. Muller.[6] An appendix about the *Church Membership Initiative* concludes with a list of the project's constituent "research data." Item 10 is entitled "Effective Leadership in Growing Congregations."[7] That paper turns out to have been written by Anne Marie Nuechterlein, M.Div., M.Ed., Ph.D., Professor of Contextual Education of Wartburg Theological Seminary (ELCA), Dubuque, Iowa. Dr. Nuechterlein studied the fastest growing congregations (over 15% between 1987 and 1990) of the ELCA. Among her findings was #3: "90% of pastors interviewed reported a positive self-esteem, and 90% of the congregations were perceived to possess positive self-esteem."[8] Then, #21: "Over half of the parishes interviewed had pastors who were actively involved in gay/lesbian issues through Lutherans Concerned, through task forces, and through preaching, teaching, and performing marriages of gays and lesbians."[9]

Any enterprise which incorporates without shame or rebuke such public contempt for the Law of God, thereby declares itself morally and theologically bankrupt. How can official mission agencies promote such "research," and pretend that it is a "tool" or "resource" for "congregations who seek ways to reach people beyond their current membership?"

At the heart of the *Church Membership Initiative* lies the following objective: "To set in motion forces that will result in annual increases in the number of members of Lutheran congregations."[10] Despite occasional lip service to the Confessions, the "forces" have nothing to do with truth or theology, since the unbridgeable chasm between nominal and confessional Lutheranism is clearly taken to matter not one whit. Manipulating "forces" for "annual increases in the number of members of [nominally] Lutheran congregations" fits in very well with synergistic and revivalistic schemes—and with commercial drives for new customers. But the whole idea flies in the face of Article V of the Augsburg Confession, which attributes faith, and thus the life and growth of the Church, only to the holy Means of Grace, and then not subject to human control but "when and where it pleases God."[11]

Here, clearly, it is no longer the preliminary truth of the Law that is at stake, but the ultimate verity of the Gospel itself. Let us remind ourselves that the Gospel in the proper sense, in the sense in which it is opposed to the Law, IS not some meager "principle"[12] for minimizing divine institutions, but a full-bodied dogmatic whole, with justification as its central, not its sole article! (See FC V and the contrast between the First and Second Chief parts of the Catechisms).

The *Church Membership Initiative (CMI)* admits "that some growing congregations use only traditional forms of worship."[13] Yet its advocates maintain a constant clamor for liturgical change, variety, diversity, etc. The theological trouble runs very deep: "UnChurched Lutherans did not leave congregations because of falling away from faith. They left because they moved... they found other interests more compelling... and they felt time was not available."[14] Or, as *CMI* itself puts it in the "Research Summary of Findings": "UnChurched people feel good about their faith."[15] But surely "Congregations that focus on ministry beyond their current membership seem willing to accept the perceptions of the unChurched and work to communicate in ways that are motivational for the unChurched."[16] The preface to the Small Catechism strikes a more sobering note: "It is to be feared that anyone who does not desire to receive the sacrament at least three of four times a year despises the sacrament and is no Christian, just as he is no Christian who does not hear and believe the Gospel."[17]

When serious theological criticism of *CMI* is simply deflected by shifting responsibility to an insurance company (Letters, *Reporter,* November 1994, p. 11), and when it is officially pretended that nothing is wrong (1995 *Convention Workbook,* pp. 31-32, 42-43), it is difficult to avoid the impression of cynicism. Some organizational layers of our Synod apparently just do not care about truth and confession.

Foreign Missions: "African Strategy"

More significant still, both theologically and ecclesially, is the *African Strategy Statement* by Robert M. Roegner, *African Area Secretary* for the LCMS Board of Mission Services.[18] It would of course be sheer presumption on my part to pretend to be able to analyze that important document in the few minutes available to us here. The best I can do is to draw attention to certain issues that ought to be taken up with great care, especially by missionary and theological leaders, but also by everyone who holds with the Augsburg Confession (V, VII, VIII) that the whole life, health, and growth of the Church flow from the purely preached Gospel and from the rightly administered sacraments.

In addressing this topic I need to avoid false impressions. Nothing I say here is meant in any way to denigrate the faithful men and women who have pursued arduous missionary labors in far-away places, and at great risk and cost to themselves. For them, whose shoes I am not worthy to untie, I have nothing but the deepest admiration. What concerns me, rather, is that the support structure here in the "sending" Church be theologically adequate to the task, lest we destroy with one hand what we build with the other.

Perhaps the most helpful way of raising issues that urgently require clarification is to refer to three books that in various respects have either influenced or are relevant to the *Strategy* document. They are by Carl F. George (1991), Roland Allen (1927, 1956, etc.), and David J. Bosch (1991).

(1) Carl George's book. *Prepare Your Church for the Future,* introduces the term and concept "meta-Church," with "its deepest focus on change: pastors changing their minds about how ministry is to be done."[19] It "highlights the lay-led small group as the essential growth center. It's so

important that everything else is to be considered secondary to its promotion and preservation."[20] C. Peter Wagner's Foreword says that the book "may well be the most significant step forward in Church growth theory and practice since Donald McGavran wrote the basic textbook. *Understanding Church Growth,* in 1970."[21] It is, of course, in the *Toolbox* (p. 32). (George's book assumes C. Peter Wagner's "spiritual gifts" scheme. *Toolbox* does not mention the 1994 CTCR document, *Spiritual Gifts.*[22] The theological upshot of that report is that "spiritual gifts" and "inventories," as popularly promoted, also within our Synod, are basically humbug. But heavy bureaucratic editing keeps such spades from being called spades.)

The entire Appendix B of the *African Strategy,* "Church Extension Through Leadership Development," simply takes over the whole "metaChurch" structure, including "zones," "hemispheres," and the "X, C, L, D" algebra for "leaders," without mentioning George or his book(s). Most alarming is the acceptance of George's threefold "celebration—congregation—small group" division, although the treatment here lacks clarity. On the one hand, "celebration," or the "all Church gathering," is distinguished from "congregation—50—100 people," as in George. The description "plenary worship service" occurs under "celebration": "This is where people are fed on the word of God and the sacraments — in the 'divine service' — the place where God comes to serve His people — through His servant, the pastor" — clearly an attempt to "Lutheranize" the alien scheme. Yet on the other hand, "8 and 11 a.m. services" are assigned to the smaller "congregation," without any mention of pastors. Are these the normal Sunday services, while "celebrations" are occasional? Who leads the "congregations" in worship? How exactly is this related to the later statements: "Now there are certain things the pastor cannot delegate, because they are not his to give away! Regular preaching of the Word and the administration of the sacraments cannot be delegated away"? That is about the most clearly Lutheran statement in the entire Appendix. Yet the whole "meta-Church" dynamic pulls in a quite different direction, and to embrace the structure is to embrace the dynamic. Nor is it all reassuring to have "Pastor Cho," * the Korean mega-Church Pentecostalist, cited as mentor. And what is meant by "lay pastors" in Liberia/Ivory Coast?[23]

(2) Let us begin with the "three (or four) self" formula which Allen cites from Henry Venn via the Anglican Bishop Tucker of Uganda: "the foundation of self-extending, self-supporting and self-governing Churches."[24] To this has now been added "self-theologizing".[25] Although that term is inelegant, the reality undeniably goes together with the other "selfs," for how could a Church be self-governing or self-propagating, if it is theologically helpless? Here lies the main trouble, as we shall see more extensively in the next section. There is, of course, nothing wrong with *self*-sustaining Churches as the goal of mission work. What *is* wrong is the assumption that this can be achieved quickly, or by fiat, or by some pre-determined target-date. But the Lord of the Harvest, Who acts "when and where it pleases Him" (AC V), cannot be confined to human sched-

162

ules. Theological, and therefore ecclesial, maturity cannot be forced. God gives His gifts as He wills.

Allen argues eloquently for the almost immediate self-direction and "spontaneous expansion" of missionary Churches. Lutherans, however, need to bear in mind two important qualifications. One is that Allen was writing from within a Church deeply compromised and handicapped by being part and parcel of the (waning) British Imperial establishment. His impassioned attack on colonial arrogance is certainly in order. Yet subsequent history has shown that not even in the political sphere are previous wrongs and neglects righted by the sudden, helter-skelter abdication of responsibility.

More important, however, is a second point Allen argues that a chief obstacle to the spontaneous expansion and self-rule he urges, is the "Fear for the Doctrine," as he puts it in a chapter-title.[26] Allen's approach here is a naive biblicism (as though we could somehow just start where the Book of Acts left off), together with an altogether inadequate view of the nature of Christian doctrine. He writes, for instance: "It is as the complement of experience that Christian Doctrine first took shape the Christian doctrine of the Trinity arose out of attempts to express the experience."[23] That view is quite understandable in a Church as dogmatically unfocused as the Anglican, but its practical prescriptions must differ radically from those flowing out of a serious confessional commitment to the Book of Concord. In short, we cannot follow Allen's missiology-in-a-hurry.

What does it mean, for instance, that *"LCMS World Mission in Africa will not attempt to define actual outward shape or structure of the resulting Church?"*[28] If this means simply that the cumbersome bureaucratic machinery of the West will not be imposed on young Churches, fine and good. However, some might take "actual outward shape" to include also liturgy, the right ordering of the Gospel ministry, and membership in the Lutheran World Federation, for example. To let such things simply evolve higgledy-piggledy according to local option, would in fact be a massive abdication of proper missionary responsibility. Interestingly enough, Allen is actually more "Lutheran" here than some of our own present confusions and hesitations. He writes:

All I can say is that St. Paul certainly did not found Churches without local ministers and sacraments. If the local congregations are in our eyes Churches, then we must acknowledge that, since these Churches have neither ministers nor sacraments, we are creating a new type of Church which has no Biblical authority whatsoever, and is not in harmony with our own Prayer Book, which, following the Bible, takes it for granted that local Churches have local ministers and sacraments. The Prayer Book certainly does not contemplate Churches ministered to by lay catechists and teachers, still less does it contemplate half-a-dozen or a dozen such in the care of a lay catechist; yet that is a common thing in the Mission Field.[29]

For the Anglican *Prayer Book* one may easily substitute here the Augsburg Confession (see esp. Articles V, VII, VIII, XIV, and XXVIII). In the *African Strategy* this whole matter seems nebulous. It is dumbfounding to see that of the four kinds of missionaries constituting the "elements of the evangelization force," three could be either ordained or laymen (though in one case "ordination is preferable"), and the fourth are laymen.[30] Of the six "elements of the missionary support evangelization force," one is "usually an ordained minister," another "usually a lay person," a third (Theological Education by Extension Coordinator!) "need not be ordained," and types four, five, and six are laymen! This conception, on the face of it, has no visible connection to the Lutheran doctrine and understanding of the divine gift of the Gospel-and-Sacraments ministry (1 Cor. 4:1). The seven "Lutheran Missiological Principles"[31] make no express mention of the public ministry at all. Instead, there is talk about "communication," and it is said that "the body of Christ stands in the place of and in the authority of God."[32] The following section does state that "the nature of this mission is that of equipping and sending shepherds,"[33] but on the following page this becomes "a mission that equips and sends other Christians to fulfill the Great Commission."[34] Are the "shepherds" perhaps the "lay preachers" and "evangelists" of Appendices C and D?

Granted that God's children are to confess their faith wherever they are, and especially in places where the Church and her public ministry have not yet been planted. That, however, cannot be the main thrust of the Church's official mission strategy. God Himself did not leave this task to the discretion of individuals or to private volunteers, but established a special office charged with the public proclamation of the Gospel everywhere (Rom. 10:14-16). Luther, cited, with approval, by Walther in *Church and Ministry,* catches the real missiology of the Book of Acts when he writes.

Law/Gospel and "Church Growth"

God, though speaking from heaven to Paul, did not purpose to abrogate the ministry and do something out of the ordinary, but He bade him go into the city to a minister or pastor. There he was to hear and learn what He wanted him to learn God wants us to go and hear the Gospel from those who preach it; there we shall find Him and nowhere else . . .[35]

Chemnitz, the "Second Martin," says the same:

The chief thing of the ministry is that God wants to be present in it with His Spirit, grace, and gifts, and to work effectively through it. But Paul says, Rom. 10:15: "How shall they who are not sent preach" (namely in such a way that faith is engendered by hearing)? But God wants to give increase to the planting and watering of those who have been legitimately called to the ministry and set forth doctrine without guile and faithfully administer whatever belongs to the ministry (I Cor 3:6; 15:58), that both they themselves and others might be saved (I Tim. 4:16).[36]

164

Let us be quite clear whether God's own gift of the Gospel-preaching ministry is at the heart of our mission-strategy, or whether that place is to be given to a generic "communication." If the latter, then this would mean an abandonment of Lutheran missiology. To cite Allen once more, are we for, against, or simply indifferent to what he calls a "fatal inversion?" He writes:

Those little groups of Christians which are sometimes called "Churches" but are not, ought, as I think, to be Churches in the Biblical sense and ought to be instituted and equipped as the Pauline Churches were instituted and equipped, and then the unity of these would represent, and might one day become commonly recognized as, the national Church of the country; but to begin with the national Church and to build that on a foundation of local groups of Christians which are not Churches seems to me a fatal inversion.[37]

(3) The thorniest of our three sub-topics is no doubt that of "contextualization." Moreover, this notion is not argued in the *African Strategy,* but is simply taken for granted as an unquestioned starting-point, axiom, or dogma. The document's very first sentence is:

The Lutheran Church-Missouri Synod (LCMS) World Mission in Africa will establish the Christian Church in its contextualized form among unreached people groups . . .

Of course, at the common sense level it is self-evident that mission work must be properly adapted to its cultural context. But "contextualization" is not a common sense term with self-evident meaning. It is a highly technical notion that bristles with complex details. This is where the overview (pp. 420-432) in Bosch's standard reference is helpful. That treatment in turn occurs within the larger framework of "Elements of an Emerging Ecumenical Missionary Paradigm." A longer excerpt will convey the flavor of the thing:

It is, however, only fairly recently that this essentially contextual nature of the faith has been recognized. For many centuries every deviation from what any group declared to be the orthodox faith was viewed in terms of heterodoxy, even heresy . . . Arianism, Donatism, Pelagianism, Nestorianism, Monophytism, and numerous similar movements were all regarded as doctrinally heterodox, and their adherents excommunicated, persecuted, or banned. The role of cultural, political, and social factors in the genesis of such movements was not recognized . . . In subsequent centuries the formulations of the Council of Trent and various Protestant confessions were employed as shibboleths to determine the difference between acceptable and unacceptable creedal formulations.[38]

Therefore: "Contextual theology truly represents a paradigm shift in theological thinking . . . Contextual theologies claim that they constitute an epistemological break when compared with traditional theologies."[39] While criticizing various extremes, and total relativism, Bosch offers no solutions beyond "creative tension."[40]

Now, if this is what "contextualization" really means, it is altogether inadequate to say no more of it than this:

> *A contextualized church is one that communicates that truth of God's Word in a fashion and that uses methods that are consistent with the culture.* In this system the core meaning does not vary. The Gospel message remains the same regardless of where and to whom it is being preached. The only thing that vanes is the outward form of packaging of the message; i.e., a cultural proclamation or a redemptive analogy.[41]

"Contextualization" is a conceptual predator, and cannot with a few sentences be tamed into a safe house pet, to be left without further ado in charge of the whole farm!

Since "contextualization," in its normal sense, severely devalues traditional confessions—regarding them as conditioned by "Western culture," with which young churches should not be burdened—one looks for firm assurances on this score in the *African Strategy* document. Certainly one cannot quarrel with the solid stance taken at the outset. "It is the view of LCMS World Mission in Africa that missiological principles rooted in reformed theology are incapable of giving birth to communities of Christians that are committed to and view the Holy Scripture from the position expounded in the *Book of Concord.*"[42] Less confidence-inspiring is the fact that the *Book of Concord* then peters out into "Lutheran missiological principles," identified in turn with "Lutheran missiology," which "remains young and undeveloped."

The only other relevant statements I found are: (a) "The TEE [Theological Education by Extension] program should strive to be Biblically and confessionally sound",[43] (b) "... should strive to develop a contextualized Christian Church that is faithful to the Holy Scriptures and views the Holy Scriptures with an understanding that is consistent with the *Book of Concord*",[44] (c) "[membership instruction] Text: Luther's *Small Catechism.*"[45]

The last statement is of course, by far the best. In the first two, one marvels at the weakness and indirection of the language: why should a *theological education* program, of all things, only "strive" to be "Biblically and confessionally sound?" By contrast, the program "must [!] instill a vision of continued growth and outreach,"[46] and the church "must [!] be contextualized."[47] Why should not the aim be an actual understanding *of the Book of Concord,* rather than one merely *consistent* with it?

To say it in the plainest way possible: The proper outcome of confessional Lutheran mission work is confessional Lutheran Churches. To waffle at this point is fatal. To project a "Christian Church in its contextualized form," the "actual outward shape or structure" of which our mission "will not attempt to define,"[48] is, with all due respect, waffling.

A spiritually mature, confessional Lutheran Church will be one, surely, whose leadership can at least (a) work with Holy Scripture in the original languages, (b) understand and confess the *Book of Concord* in conscious contradistinction to other confessions and theologies, and (c) take an informed confessional stand globally/ecumenically, for example, in opposition to the "Lutheran" World Federation. A Church that can apply Law and Gospel only in its own immediate context, but lacks firm and conscious continuity, via the *Book of Concord,* with the orthodox Church of all times and places, cannot truly be said to be "self-theologizing." Genuine confessional maturity obviously will not happen overnight. But it will not happen at all unless it is seriously and prayerfully desired and pursued! "Vision" and "Vision Community"[49] are no substitutes. Nor does it help at all to think of "spiritual maturity" in terms of "reached" vs. "unreached" or "potentially reached" "people groups."[50] These sociological categories have no direct relation to the Biblical, confessional understanding of what a *church* is and ought to be.

The concern for confessionally clear missionary goals and methods is by no means just hypothetical or academic. Consider Udo Etuk's article, "Campus Ministry — Nigerian Style," which appeared in the August, 1994, *Inter-Connections,* the official organ of Missouri Synod campus ministry. This describes and solicits support for the Lutheran ministry of Victory Chapel, the "Protestant" chapel of the University of Uyo, Nigeria. The members come from all sorts of "Protestant" Churches, including the Anglican, Baptist, Pentecostal, Lutheran, Presbyterian, and Methodist. "We are conservative with the Gospel of Jesus Christ but modernists in our modes of worship. We are all things to all students" Baptism, the Lord's Supper, and Confirmation, are "celebrated once a (university] session." For Baptism, "we set out to the river-side." Regular worship is described as follows:

> Preachers are usually the very best from among the ministers, preachers, and evangelists who can deliver the message with power. The liturgy followed is very simple: hymn singing, prayers, praise worship, plenty of choruses (short, simple, spiritual songs) accompanied by dancing, drumming, clapping, and loud hallelujahs!... Speaking in tongues is not discouraged in our worship services. "Deliverance" is an important though not a central feature of this campus ministry. Whenever we have powerful and charismatic men of God to preach our worship venue is usually jam-packed.

It is clear that the virus of "contextualization" is already loose on our mission fields. It is abetted by a naive pietism, which mistakes a generic American "Protestant" missionary culture for something daringly "cross-cultural." Thus the editors of *Inter-Connection* comment patronizingly: "You may sense that some things are very different in Africa and would not necessarily [!] be appropriate in the U.S." As if the problem were Africa, rather than the Baptist, Pentecostal, unionistic, etc.—all thoroughly Western— theologies at issue!

If our missionary trumpet is to give a clear and certain sound (1 Cor. 14:8), then a good deal more will be needed than "dialogue" with "the Lutheran missiological community"[51] — which has already shaped that document! The real need is for a genuine integration of confessional theology and missionary practice. This is the proper and vital concern not of a handful of bureaucrats and academics, but of our entire Synod, and especially our *ministerium* as "the leaders of the community of God" (FC, SD, X, 10).[52]

Notes

1 Theodore Tappert, The Book of Concord (Philadelphia: Fortress Press. 1959), 559.9

2 ibid., 457.5.

3 *Luther's Works,* American Edition, 40 (Philadelphia: Fortress Press), 275.

4 Tappert, 49.6.

5 ibid., 612.9.

6 *Toolbox: A listing of resources to assist congregation who seek ways to reach people beyond their current membership* (St Louis; Congregational Services Unit, Lutheran Church-Missouri Synod, n.d.)

7 ibid., 51.

8 ibid., 16.

9 ibid., 34.

10 ibid., 46.

11 ibid., 31.2.

12 Norman Habel and Shirley Wurst. "The Gospel and Women in the Ministry," *Lutheran Theological Journal* [Australia) (December 1994): 129-134, argue for a "Gospel Principle" that not only allows but even demands the ordination of women as pastors. They also speak of the "Gospel" as our complete liberation from the power of sin, death, and the demands of the law (p 130). Power, curse, condemnation, even compulsion of the Law—yes, from these Christians are free. But that we are free from the demands of the Law is at least misleading Lutheran teaching is not antinomian, but holds that the Creed (or Gospel), which teaches "all that we must expect and receive from God," is given also "in order to help us do what the Ten Commandments require of us" (Tappert, p. 411.2). The Gospel, precisely by giving us salvation *gratis,* frees us for, not *from,* willing obedience to the Law.

13 *Toolbox,* 48.

14 ibid., 47.

15 *Church Membership Initiative* (Appleton, Wisconsin: Aid Association for Lutherans, 1993), 5.

16 *Toolbox,* 48

17 Tappert, 341.

18 Robert M. Roegner, *African Strategy Statement* (St Louis: Board for Mission Services, Lutheran Church-Missouri Synod, December, 1994).

19 Carl George, *Prepare Your Church for the Future* (Grand Rapids: Fleming H. Revell, 1991), 51.

20 ibid., 41.

21 ibid., 9.

22 *Spiritual Gifts* (St. Louis, Commission on Theology and Church Relations, Lutheran Church-Missouri Synod, 1994).

23 *Lutheran Witness, (May,* 1995), 5.

24 Roland Allen, *The Spontaneous Expansion of the Church* (London Word Dominion Press, 1927 [1956]), 34.

25 "When the missionary leaves the field, he wants to leave behind a Church characterized by four (selves.) In their order of importance, it seems to me, the Church will be 1) self-theologizing, 2) self-propagating, 3) self-supporting, and 4) self-governing" (Daniel L. Manson [Board for Mission Services, LCMS). "Mission Strategy

in the Late 20th Century Church Planting Through Leadership Formation." *Interconnections* (LCMS Office of Campus Ministry) [November 1994]; 2).

26 Allen, 55-76.

27 ibid., 54-65.

28 Roegner, 11.

29 Allen, 38-39.

30 Roegner, 18.

31 ibid., 2-3.

32 ibid.

33 ibid.

34 ibid.,4.

35 C.F.W. Walther, *Church and Ministry,* tr. J.T. Mueller (St. Louis Concordia Publishing House, 1987), 193.

36 Martin Chemnitz, *Ministry, Word, and Sacraments: An Enchiridion,* tr. Luther Poellet (St. Louis, Concordia Publishing House, 1981), 29-30.

37 Allen, 39.

38 David Bosch, *Transforming Mission: Paradigm Shifts in Theology of Mission* (Maryknoll, New York, Orbis Books, 1991), 421.

39 ibid., 423.

40 ibid., 431.

41 Roegner, 13.

42 ibid., 2.

43 ibid., 12.

44 ibid., 14.

45 ibid., Appendix C.

46 ibid., 12.

47 ibid., 13.

48 ibid., 11.

49 ibid., 12.

50 ibid., 4.

51 ibid., 2.

52 Tappert, 612.10.

* *Editor's Note: "Recent Pentecostal 'Scandals' in the September 8, 2014 CN reported that "On February 20, 2014, David Yonggi Cho, founder of Yoido Full Gospel Church in Seoul, long billed as the world's largest church, was sentenced to three years in prison for breach of trust and corruption." Cho had a full time staff of 600 to produce one of the largest daily newspapers in Seoul. Some of the articles CN published opposing Cho's anti-Scriptural theology are in the Christian News Encyclopedia.*

1. The Law is God ____ the Gospel is God ____.
2. What was another charismatic excitement from Toronto? ____
3. What objective lies at the heart of the Church Membership Initiative? ____
4. Advocates of the Church Membership Initiative maintain a constant change for ____.
5. "Spiritual gifts" as popularly promoted are basically ____.
6. "Pastor Cho," is ____.
7. Who was the "Second Martin?" ____
8. What would mean an abandonment of Lutheran Missiology? ____
9. "Contextualization" severely devalues ____.
10. The proper outcome of confessional Lutheran mission work is ____.
11. A spiritually mature, confessional Lutheran Church will be one whose leadership ____.
12. The virus of ____ is already loose on our mission fields."
13. The real need is for a genuine ____.

THE CHURCH IN THE TWENTY-FIRST CENTURY: WILL THERE BE A LUTHERAN ONE?

By Professor Kurt Marquart
Presented at the 1998 Symposia on The Lutheran Confessions,
Concordia Seminary, Ft. Wayne, Indiana
Christian News, April 6, 1998

"Why do the heathen rage and the people imagine a vain thing? The kings of the earth set themselves, and the rulers take counsel together, against the LORD, and against His Anointed, saying, Let us break their bands asunder, and cast away their cords from us" (Ps. 2:1-3). That is a fitting and sobering introit, as we make ready to cross the millennial threshold.

Nearly half a millennium ago the *Apology of the Augsburg Confession* took refuge in the true nature of the church despite all contrary appearances, "lest we despair, but know that the church will abide nonetheless" (VII, 9).The German version adds a vivid touch: "the right doctrine and church is often so nearly suppressed and lost, as happened under the papacy, as though there were no church, and it often looks as though she had quite perished."

Is this one of those times? Or is the next century likely to be one?

The topic assigned me hardly calls for an orgy of millennial doom-saying or even prognostication. Instead of "will there be a Lutheran church?" The real question may well be, "will there be a next century or millennium?" That the present motley crowd of bureaucratic corporations labeled "Lutheran," and vaguely pursuing human uplift from Geneva, will drag themselves across the starting-line of the new century, can hardly be doubted. How many of them will also cross the century's finish line, if there is one, is another question.

When Hermann Sasse tried to wake his slumbering fellow Lutherans with the question about the very survival of the Lutheran church,[1] he had in mind something else. What is the meaning of this question? For recipe for success, like the popular sacrilege of "goal-setting," with the goal of Lutheran survival assured by keeping abreast of the most up-to-date trends with a Pandora's box full of clever methods and techniques. What will "survive" in this way may well call itself "Lutheran," but it will have nothing to do with the Lutheran confession, which on the contrary will be happily clappily trampled underfoot to the soft seduction or the raucous savagery of "Christian music."

Of course the "right doctrine and church" will survive—it is built on the Rock and cannot fail. The question is, will we? With us or without us, through us or despite us, God will see His "right doctrine and church" through. Shall we, by God's grace, have apart in this survival? Will our long-suffering Synod and seminaries? The answers to these questions lie hidden in the inscrutable counsels of God. But as the mystery of the election of grace is meant not to paralyze us into inert passivity, but rather to nerve and steel us for the bedlam of the fray (Rom. 8:30,31), so too the mystery of the church.

What matters here is not our assessment of the future, but our faithfulness in the present. Besides, our solemn expert predictions rarely come true. Dr. George Wollenburg, president of our Montana District, has given us an amusing reminder of the follies of futurology. He recalled that in the 1950's and 1960's it was confidently predicted—on the basis of past trends of course—that by the end of the century the Synod would number 4.5 million confirmed members. * "The planning for the future called for building new schools to prepare workers for the future giant church, and a suitable organization. So we did"[2] —especially build the organization, I'd say. It is no good being so intent on the future as to neglect the present—and thereby spoil the future! And here we must beware of the ditch opposite that of "goal-setting." It is true that we cannot "save the church" by our efforts and schemes. It is the Lord Who does all the saving—but we mustn't get in the way of His good and gracious revealed will! Sasse called it "blasphemy" to expect the Holy Spirit to remove the obstacles which we ourselves willfully put in the way of His working. I shall cite that important paragraph shortly.

I propose therefore first to take a closer look at what the "survival of the Lutheran church" really means. Then we ought to take stock of our actual situation, attempting a global overview, with a sort of end-of-century survey of liabilities and assets. We need above all to clear our minds of illusions, in order to ascertain "what is that good, and acceptable, and perfect will of God" (Rom. 12:2). In other words, given a realistic view of our situation now, "what is to be done?" (Lenin)—to quote the opposition. Having tried to see the "big picture," we must then return to the very Holy of Holies of our confession, to re-assure ourselves before God and many why it cannot fail. Truth, especially painful truth, cannot be understood except by going "into the sanctuary of God" (Ps. 73:17).

I.

The question about the survival of Lutheranism, as Sasse formulated it, was shaped by the fateful history of the Reformed-Lutheran Union, Prussia being the prime example. Given the trend of squeezing Lutheran and Reformed churches together into joint structures in which both sets of confessions have validity, the question is: Will there still be Lutheran churches anywhere, or will there by only Lutheran individuals and parishes here and there, within larger churches which as such are not Lutheran? Can the Lutheran confession be a mere "theological direction" or trend within a larger church which as such gives equal rights to other confessions? Is our confession content to be a private interest or hobbyhorse within non-Lutheran churches, or does it define the boundaries of the orthodox church, and demand that church-fellowship observe them?

Perhaps some other confessions can exist as provinces of confessionally mixed churches; the Lutheran confession at any rate cannot. It cannot recognize anything other than the purely preached Gospel and the rightly administered sacraments as constituting "the right doctrine and church," and therefore the boundaries of church fellowship(Augsburg Confession VII, and Formula of Concord, S.D.X., 31).Whatever contradicts the Voice of the Good Shepherd in His pure Gospel and Sacraments, "cannot be tolerated in the church of God, much less be excused and defended" (FC, S.D., Intro., 9); "such teachings are contrary to the expressed Word of God and cannot coexist with it" (Preface to the Book of Concord).

It is the very modesty of the Augsburg Confession which leaves it no more room to maneuver. Everything that could possibly be yielded has been yielded— what is left is indispensable: "It is enough for the true unity of the church that the Gospel be unanimously preached according to its pure understanding, and the sacraments be administered in accordance with the divine Word." How could anybody demand less without disavowing the Church's Founder and Head (St. John 8:31,32)? Other churches demand more than this for ecclesial unity. The Roman Catholic, Eastern Orthodox, and Anglican churches insist on liturgical and canonical conformity, especially in respectof the "historic episcopate," and the Reformed churches maintain that there is a divinely established form of church government or structure. Hence the binary ecumenical formula "Faith and Order." Such "order" our confession regards in principle as belonging to the "human traditions or rites and ceremonies, instituted by men," which need not "be alike everywhere." Non-conformity in such things does not affect the "true unity of the church."

If this is so, then the Lutheran church cannot define herself in terms of outward structure or organization. Her constitution or polity may vary according to circumstances—her confession cannot. Her one unifying bond is her confession, not her constitution. When the confession is lost, her essential identity is lost, and she is no more—even if traditional "judicatories" which Lutheran names and ethnic customs flourish and prosper. That was clearly understood by the founders of our own Synod a century and a half ago. An introduction to the proposed constitution made the point at some length, and it is worth recalling here:

the ministers, named below, of the Lutheran Church came together in order to draft a synodical constitution which would not rest on the Symbolical writings of the church merely in the manner of a signboard, but one which would prove in its whole execution that all parts of it are sustained and permeated in a living way by the uncorrupted confession and the pure doctrine of the church, so that the confessing and teaching church might devote herself to the enabling and promoting of every particular churchly purpose. Hereby a double impropriety should be prevented; the one is that... the Confession is mentioned only externally and incidentally, without it exercising an ordering and shaping influence on the whole constitution and on the church's entire mode of action . .. And this impropriety we find in the constitutions of those existing synods which still pay a certain external respect to the ecclesiastical Confession and formally accept it, although their ecclesiastical practice is blatantly and variously at war with it here and there . . . but also and especially on account of the Schmuckerians, i.e., on account of the so-called Lutheran General Synod, which as is well-known has recently publicly declared its apostasy from the Lutheran, i.e., the churchly, sacramental teaching, and for whom the Confession of the church seems to be something changeable and ambiguous, as if it did not rest on the unchangeable and eternal Word of God—let alone that it should permeate with ordering and quickening effect the entire practice of the church.[3]

There are two intertwining aspects to this understanding of the confession. One is that the confession itself, its evangelical sacramental substance, governs, shapes, and unifies the church. That means that constitutions and outward structures must be held with a light hand, so that they always express and subserve the confession. When they cease to do so, or even counteract the confession, they must be abolished or reformed, regardless of cost. The second aspect is really a refinement of the first, a corollary "nested" within it. If the confession governs the church, then her real boundaries are set by ecclesial communion, that is, pulpit and altar fellowship, not by organizational ties like bylaws, pension funds, or conflict resolution provisions. All these are fine, but they must not be allowed to divide or deny ecclesial communion for the sake of "rites and ceremonies instituted by men." Nor may they impose or pretend the bond of ecclesial communion, when the necessary basis for "the true unity of the church" no longer exists. Church fellowship, then, is not an optional extra. It goes to the heart of everything. In the practice of ecclesial communion the confession is either implemented or mocked and violated. Where there is genuine consensus in the pure Gospel (articles of faith!) and sacraments, there communion may not be withheld. But where dissensus rules, there communion may not be granted. What God has joined together in true confession, mere human constitutions and polities may not put asunder. But what He has solemnly separated (Gospel truth and its opposite, heresy, Rom. 16:17; Gal. 1:6-8), no one has a right to combine into a false spiritual, ecclesiastical union.

The old North American Synodical Conference gave expression precisely to this vision of the decisive priority of the confession over everything else. Its loose outward structure existed only as a platform to enable its member synods to express, deepen, and exercise their doctrinal and sacramental unity, and to commend it to still others. These synods were not required to give up their own structures and merge into some large conglomerate.

It was enough that they practiced pulpit and altar fellowship on the basis of their mutually acknowledged orthodoxy. What mattered was the confessional cause, not organizational empire-building.

A millennium and a half after the Council of Chalcedon (451) Hermann Sasse observed the event with his 21st Letter to Lutheran Pastors. Permit me to cite his concluding sentences, which if anything have grown in poignancy over the past half century:

We have the confidence in the Lord of the church that He, Who raises the dead, can raise also dying and dead churches, just as He has also raised our heart, dead in sin, to faith. But we declare it to be superstition when people fancy that God would do by a miracle that which He has commanded us servants of the church (to do), and which we ever and again fail to do, from laziness and cowardice, from convenience and fear of men. He has commanded the servants of the Word, the shepherds of His flock, for the sake of the eternal truth and for the sake of the souls entrusted to them, to bear witness against false doctrine and to exclude it from the church. We declare it to be blasphemy, when people expect that the Holy Spirit will surely remove the obstacles which we willfully put in the way of His working. We know that no confession ensures the purity of doctrine—what errors have penetrated the churches which actually preserved the Nicene and Chalcedonian creeds, like the churches of the East and Roman Catholicism—but we also know that the doctrine of the church must suffer total ruin, and the Gospel die, where the confession of the truth is forgotten.

To say that, to testify it to the Lutheran church and to Christendom, that is the great task of confessionally faithful Lutherans to-day. It is a thankless task; for the world, also, the Christian, also the "Lutheran" world, does not want to hear this. Today there are only few, and mostly small circles, which still say all this and do not fear the reproach of confessionals and orthodoxy. But on their faithfulness more depends than most of us suspect. We will at any rate not be ashamed to belong to them.

I greet you all with the word which in the liturgy of the Eastern Church introduces the Creed: "Let us love one another, that we may confess in unanimity of faith!"[4]

And let us not forget that less than half a century ago, Franklin Clark Fry, then president of the ULCA, the least confessional of the three major U.S. Lutheran bodies, pronounced: **"Insistence upon agreement in doctrine as a precondition for church fellowship is the distinguishing mark of Lutherans among all Protestants and should never be relaxed."** [5]

There is an important qualification to be added at this point, and precisely in order to assert the radical supremacy of **confession** over organization and constitution. The whole church body as such is, to be sure, the normal unit or object of church fellowship. "Selective fellowship," as a kind of ecclesiastical "local option," makes a mockery of serious confessional boundaries. Something else altogether is the recognition of a status confessions (based on the **causes** confessionis of *Formula of Concord,* Ep. X, 2) against surrounding infidelity. A concrete example from C.F.W. Walther's letters can illustrate the point. In 1869/1870 a theological student in Erlangen John Fackler, corresponded with Walther, and wanted advice about leaving the Bavarian (Lutheran) territorial church on account of its unconfessional nature. Walther strongly urged him to stay and help to restore that church to its original orthodoxy. He wrote in part:

I can advise separation from a degenerated communion which formerly had taken the right stand, only when it is notorious that it has "hardened" (verstockt) itself; and that is notorious only when everything has been tried to lead it back, but in vain . . . would to God that I had this understanding 30 some years ago, then I would likely still be in America, yet not as one who had abandoned his office, but as an exile. I judge the Bavarian church not with Diedrich, according to the abuses occurring there, but according to how it ought to be according to its own principles.

And to Pastor Brunn in Germany Walther wrote:

Although our hot-blooded young Erlangen friends may indeed think that things are moving too slowly, that cannot confuse us. A Lutheran is, so to speak, by nature conservative and can be prevailed upon to break with the conditions into which God has placed him only if he is compelled to act against his conscience. There is after all a great difference between an originally false ecclesial communion and an originally orthodox but degenerated one. To be sure the mere "legality" of the true faith does not make a body orthodox, but the behavior of him who is in such a body is in many ways determined thereby. From a heretical or schismatic communion one must exit without consulting flesh and blood, also from a syncretistically constituted one; it is not so with a church which originally took the right stand, and in which false faith and unbelief still fight for the right to exist. Here it is a matter of leaving the sinking ship, not the one that has sprung a leak. There is probably no grander witness of the truly irenic and conservative disposition of Lutheranism than the Augustana, upon which to be sure an ultimatum like that of the Smalcald Articles had to follow." [6]

Now, if Fackler had visited St. Louis, would—or should— Walther have refused him altar fellowship on the grounds of his membership in the "degenerate" church of Bavaria—when Walther himself had urged him to "stay and do his duty" in it? And if communion was granted to Fackler, who was in a **state of confession** against the Bavarian church, does it follow that it should therefore also be granted to that church as such? Obviously not. I raise this issue because it may well have to be thought through and invoked to cope with the ecclesiastical anomalies and upheavals, for instance in the former Soviet empire, where, thank God, conscientious Lutherans treasure their confessional heritage, and have often risked life and limb under unspeakable conditions, which a soft and self-indulgent West can hardly imagine. Truth remains truth regardless of geographical boundaries. But precisely for that reason genuine confessional bonds of faith and love—not sentimental illusions—must take precedence over legal, organizational niceties.

The solid, established national structures to which we Lutherans have long been accustomed in the Old World, are no more. They still exist as tax-supported entities with dwindling support, to be sure. But hardly any of them have any meaningful relation to the confession. The winds of change are devastating even Roman Catholicism, transforming its monolithic empire, as Hans Liermann argued years ago, in the direction of a commonwealth of churches, with the pope as figurehead. The "Lutheran" World Federation at last year's Hong Kong assembly, took a giant step of "convergence" towards this Vatican strategy. Karl Rahner warned a third of a century ago: "Everywhere it will be diaspora, and diaspora will be everywhere. Nowhere will there exist (Roman) Catholic nations anymore . . . Everywhere non-Christians and anti-Christians will have full equality of rights."[7]

We Lutherans, too, shall everywhere be "New World" Lutherans, that is, diaspora, "free church," without the illusory comfort of staid legal and societal structures and forms inherited from the Constantinian establishment. The twofold challenge will be not to confuse bureaucratic, organizational lines with the boundaries of communion, of church fellowship, but to insist unyieldingly on genuine confessional unity as sole basis and criterion for fellowship. Augustana VII demands nothing less of us.

II.

Now on to liabilities and assets. There is a spectre that has stalked our Lutheran landscape for, lo, these past two centuries, and it is the Reformed-Lutheran union. From small beginnings it is has become an ecclesiastical "black hole," relentlessly ingurgitating everything in its path, and with ever accelerating speed. The example of the "black hole" is particularly fitting because it is based on one of the weakest, least dramatic of the four basic forces of physics, gravity. The strong nuclear force is much more dramatic, but it demonstrates its violent potential only occasionally. Meanwhile, gravity keeps on working unobtrusively, until its immensity in a "black hole" overwhelms all other forces. Such has been the progress of the union, from its humble origins in Prussia and elsewhere to its present global sway in the "Lutheran" World Federation— which had originally been founded, as the Lutheran World Convention, precisely to resist the union and to rescue Lutheranism from its depredations! But the gravity kept on working, despite the occasional, episodic, hence ineffective eruptions of confessional scruples. Sasse has traced the chronology of shame and infamy from 1613, the year of the defection of Elector John Sigismund of Brandenburg to 1933, when Hitler created his short-lived "German Evangelical Church." [8]

After that the pace quickened considerably. In 1948 the union was in effect expanded to the whole of Germany, with the creation of the "Evangelical Church in Germany." This was extended to most of European Lutheranism in the Leuenberg Concord of 1973. A similar development merged most of the Nordic and Baltic Lutheran churches (except for Denmark and Latvia) with the Anglican (that is, originally Reformed) churches of Great Britain and Ireland into one single communion via the

Porvoo Declaration of 1996. Globally the "Lutheran" World Federation adopted the union principle in the form of "Reconciled Diversity" in 1977. The idea of this ecumenical recipe is that all the churches keep their confessions, but the mutual condemnations are dropped. The confessional differences are seen as complementary rather than contradictory, and are embraced as equally legitimate options within the bounds of full church fellowship. Here the LWF has trumped even the Prussian Union, which never dreamt of including Rome as well as Geneva. The newer scheme takes pride in offering an "equal opportunity" unionism. The U.S. branch of the LWF, the Evangelical Lutheran Church of America, has capitulated unconditionally before this massive abandonment of the Lutheran confession.

Perhaps the most baffling aspect of this tragedy for the people of the ELCA and for Lutheranism is the deafening silence with which it was greeted even in our own would-be confessional Synod. With the honorable exception of our confessional president and presidium, no one seems to be particularly shocked or worried. Our media treat it as ho-hum, and our bureaucracy is ever anxious to carry on business as usual. The day after the fateful abandonment of the two highlights of our confession, justification and the sacramental presence, all our Synod's agreements with the ELCA, for instance regarding military chaplaincy, should have been declared null and void. They were all based on the presumption that the ELCA was dejure a Lutheran church. That presumption has now lapsed, since the ELCA is by its own official account no longer a Lutheran church, but part of a union church in which confession and denial of the Sacrament of the Altar in the sense of the Book of Concord (see FC SD VII, 32-33) have equal rights—to say nothing of the outright Unitarianism in the United Church of Christ.

Thirty years ago Sasse described the cancer-like spread of church union without confessional consensus as "the greatest crisis of its history," facing the Lutheran church on the eve of the 450th Reformation Jubilee of 1967. He asked: "And what do our American brethren say? They say nothing. They swoon from admiration of the grandiose achievements of German theology.... And what says and does the venerable Missouri Synod, which still a generation ago was considered the fortress of Lutheran theology? She says nothing, and imitates everything. With fascination, she stares at the giant serpent of the Lutheran World Federation, until it shall have swallowed her. And what can one then expect from the other Lutheran churches of America?"[10]

What is the reason for Missouri's prolonged and disturbing silence? Why have we become so tongue-tied? And when at last we have a sound confessional president, who seeks firmly but patiently to assert the confession, and to curb the dishonesty of unionism at the district and district president level, why does he suffer so much opposition in the very Council of Presidents, which ought unanimously to uphold his hands? How can a whole district announce its own doctrine of open communion, seemingly without any inkling of the confessional implications? How can a whole pressure group brazenly mobilize to seek to destroy and reverse our

Synod's confessional leadership?

Most of these symptoms can be traced to the sea-change singled by the so-called "Statement of the 44" in 1945. Here the whole traditional understanding of the church and church fellowship was scuttled. Before, the object of fellowship were churches, and the criteria were the objective marks of the church, the purely preached Gospel and the rightly administered sacraments. Now the whole notion of orthodox church and confession was dissolved into a sentimental pre-occupation with footloose individuals—so-called "other Christians." The old talk about confessions and confessional differences was replaced with talk about "denominations" and "denominational differences." Confession had dealt with truth, doctrine, theology. "Denomination" suggested mere sociological description. One Missouri writer even referred to confessional differences as mere "denominational tags." Confession still echoed objective divine revelation. "Denominational tags" were clearly "man-made," and could not stand in the way of the divinely commanded fellowship among all "Christians." One prominent theologian even undertook to combine Luther with Schleiermacher in the interests of levels of fellowship"!

This quite naturally paved the way for the project of basing fellowship on felt, experiential kinship, not on the church's marks. Deep called unto deep across confessional boundaries, in great para-church, "inter-denominational" movements like the Evangelical Alliance of 1846, designed to make "the Invisible Church visible," [11] and the Promise Keepers of our day.

The most devastating effect of the collapse of the confessional understanding of the church was the development of an un-Lutheran, but bureaucratically entrenched, missiology which thought it could stitch together an "effective" strategy from bits of McGavran, C. Peter Wagner, Lyle Schaller, Carl George, and the like. When one criticizes this shapeless amalgam one is told that one is opposed to missions. In my little Church Growth book I had pointed out for instance Kent Hunter's uncritical glorification of the Yoido Full Gospel (Pentecostal) Church in Seoul, Korea, and concluded: "Hunter's verbal tributes to the means of grace have a hollow ring" (p. 28).By way of response, Hunter completely ignores the factual, documentary basis of the argument and says: "This is an offence to every missionary who is also an evangelical confessional Christian with a sacramental theology. It is like saying, 'You can't be mission-minded and be committed to Word and Sacrament theology.' How ridiculous!" (pp.150-151, Confessions of a Church Growth Enthusiast. 1997). Later we are told that "church Growth teaching is an ecclesiology" (p. 193. Aha!), and that "evangelical Christians" realize that some areas of Christian teaching "simply cannot be neatly categorized or boxed from the human point of view." Therefore:

Sometimes the academically oriented and systematic mind-sets are so threatened by this new understanding that they quietly ignore it all together. These tendencies are clearly identified in such doctrinal areas as the Office of the pastor, the Priesthood of all Believers, the

178

Charismatic Movement, spiritual gifts ingeneral, certain spiritual gifts like healing or prophecy, castingout demons, etc.

The book bears ringing endorsements from prominent present and former Missouri Synod and district officials. Just what kind of doctrinal mischief is a foot in some corners of the "mission" bureaucracy is clear from a district presentation from the last decade, entitled, "Moving into the '80s: A Mission and Ministry Perspective." One excerpt must suffice:

> We affirm that the whole Church is Christ's mission,. . . that the whole people of God in Christ Jesus may listen and speak to one another; may encourage and support the activity of Christ's Gospel as it is carried on through various denominations and agencies . . . etc.

The derivation from the "Statement of the 44" via the 1965 "Mission Affirmations" of Dr. Martin Luther Kretzmann is fairly clear.

What can a Missouri Synod so programmed through influential layers of its own official leadership, possibly have to say to the global ecumenical crisis of non-confession? Can it understand or care that the "Lutheran" World Federation is not a harmless talk shop but is in fact the main engine for the destruction of the Lutheran confession in the world today?

The August 1997 number of the German publication Lutherische Monatshefte criticized the courageous archbishop of Riga for his "defensive speeches" perceived as "embarrassing" at the Hong Kong General Assembly of the LWF. A tissue was the Latvian Church's refusal to ordain women. The Hong Kong Assembly made a point of appealing to all member churches "at last to make access to the pastoral office possible for women." The article repudiates any suggestion that the withdrawal by the Elbic Church of funds promised to the Church of Latvia constituted "undue pressure." The irony is that the same article quotes at length from outgoing LWF President Brakemeier, who had inveighed against the evils of "market" dominance also in the churches, whereby "not truth but might prevails," with "the deep fissures (Between poor and rich) which run through mankind . . . mirrored in (the LWF's) member churches and on all fields of labor"!

Lest biopsy expire into autopsy, let us leave liabilities and turn to assets.

Since the vital signs of the church indicate integrity of confession rather than church-political power, let me cite, more or less randomly, some "straws in the wind," showing the fate of the Lutheran confession in today's world.

There is, first of all, the remarkable phenomenon of the Luther-Akademie Ratzeburg, founded by German and Scandinavian Lutherans in response and opposition to the 1973 Leuenberg Concord (the LWF approved union-formula for Reformed and "Lutheran" churches in Europe). A perusal of the many volumes of the annual transactions of the Luther-Akademie yields an impressive array of confessional gems in settings of impeccable scholarship.

179

Then there is the extraordinary ecumenical appeal of Luther, for instance among contemporary Roman Catholics. Take the distinguished Roman Catholic scholar Peter Manns, appointed by the Vatican to dialogue with the Lutherans. His charming popular biography of Luther is available in English.[12] His Reformation studies have led Manns to regard Luther as a spiritual father, and indeed one who should be given the title of doctor communis (common doctor of all Christians), hitherto reserved for Thomas Aquinas! (Editor's note, p. 186)

Consider also the startling fact that while many Lutherans are bored with their conventional tidbits of Luther, by far the best treatment of Luther's profound theology of the cross is a recent dissertation written by a Roman Catholic theologian at the Papal Gregorian University in Rome! [13] It is worthy of note that the author, Hubertus Blaumeiser, singles out Hermann Sasse's classic as an "especially well-crafted contribution" (p. 55n).

And then there is the impact of our church's confession in the Slavic world. It has been a great privilege to be made aware of this through our Seminary's Russian Project, and through the enormously important translation work of the Lutheran Heritage Foundation, with which I have the honor to be associated. One brilliant linguist said the Book of Concord gave him the answers he had been looking for all his life, and which the theology of the Eastern Orthodox Church could never give him. An Orthodox bishop even renamed his church the "People's Church of the Augsburg Confession," and was promptly removed for his trouble. His people now worship in the open air, having no church building of their own! In Novosibirsk, the very center of Siberia, a whole seminary has sprung up, by the grace of God, in the context of a burgeoning mission outreach on the full biblical sacramental foundation of the Book of Concord.

A Lutheran Heritage Foundation scholar in Africa, who is translating the Book of Concord into Swahili, recently addressed a conference of African pastors. He reports that especially the younger pastors were virtually angry in their anxiety for these treasures. "Why have you kept this book from us for 150 years?" they asked. Indeed, it is a very short-sighted and paternalistic missiology which thinks that "mission fields" do not need serious theology!

Thank God, also in our own Synod there are signs of a spiritual, confessional awakening, as pastors and people are dissatisfied with clichés and organizational panaceas, and are finding ever more nourishment and delighting the real treasures of salvation, the Bread of Life in its full-orbed incarnational and sacramental splendor. This is reflected also in the publication of solid theological books by Concordia Publishing House, such as Robert Preus's *Justification and Rome*, just off "the press", and the important biblical commentary series, several done by colleagues here.

Such signs bode well for that renewal of preaching and sacramental life which is the indispensable source and foundation for all genuine renewal in the church.

What is the real dynamic at work here? It is not the huffing and puffing of publicity engines or "dollar-diplomacy" which bear such fruit globally. There is at work here the mystery of the Kingdom, the power of the mustard-seed, if you will (St. Mat. 13:31-32). The real missionary magnetism of the Book of Concord, and its remarkable power over the minds and souls of people, lie not in any clever packaging (would that we could do it better!), but in the attraction of that uncorrupted Gospel of Life itself which is there faithfully confessed.

III.

Last year in this place we concentrated on the notion of "adiaphora," literally "indifferent" things, that is, such as "make no difference"— but in a technical, not a popular sense (as though they simply did not matter).They are "indifferent" only in the sense that they are in and of themselves neither commanded nor forbidden in the written Word of God. And we make no distinction in this respect between "universal rites" and "particular rites," as the Apology expressly asserts (VII/VIII, 31). Adiaphora belong totally under and in the service of the pure Gospel and sacraments, and carry no independent weight.

What then is the opposite of an adiaphoron? Take away the a-privative, and you get diaphoron —something different, either for better or for worse. At any rate it makes a difference, it is important, so important in fact that in the Hellenistic Apocrypha to diaphoron to diaphora means "money" (Sir. 27:1; II Macc. 1:35)! Pedantic linguists may note that in Heb. 8:6 the Lord is said to have obtained a "more diaphorous (hence not at all adiaphorous!) liturgy" than Moses.

A related form, ta diapheronta, also from diaphero (be different, excel), is used in Rom. 2:18 and Phil. 1:10, where it means the essentials, the things that really matter, the exact opposite of adiaphora. In the latter text St. Paul prays for the Philippians' growth in knowledge and insight, that they might "ascertain what is essential," or as the Revised English Bible puts it: "enabling you to learn by experience what things really matter." Does that apply also to the contemporary Christian bewildered by all the chaos of ecumenical-melange-cum-millennial-melee, and needing to make some sense of it all? To deny that it does would be to relegate the Bible to irrelevance.

If we pay heed to what "really matters" to St. Paul, we can hardly fail to notice his use of solemn, formulaic "tradition" language at three points in I Corinthians, namely 11:2,11:23, and 15:3. The first text introduces the notion of "the traditions," praising the Corinthians for keeping them just as he "handed them on" to them, but not spelling out any specifics. The instruction that follows about men and women is presented as something additional—perhaps an implication or application, rather than a specification of the express content of "the traditions." The other two texts are direct and concrete: the first refers to St. Paul's solemn transmission to the Corinthians of what he had received from the Lord Himself, namely the Holy Supper; the second speaks of St. Paul's equally solemn transmission— the language is varied chiastically: "received what I handed on" in one case, "handed on what I received" in the other— of the truth of the Lord's death and Resurrection. [15] The stress is on the Resurrection, and the whole sequence sets out the "Gospel" which they had "received" (15:1,2).

The Lord's Resurrection and the Supper of His body and blood, these are the two solemnly specified focal points of the Gospel of Jesus Christ as preached by St. Paul. But is not justification the crux of Paul's preaching? Yes, but for St. Paul it was precisely the Resurrection in which the justification earned on the Cross was "objectively" and officially published to the world, to be individually appropriated by faith alone: He "was delivered for our offences, and was raised again for our justification" (Rom 4:25).See also I Tim. 3:16, about Christ to being "justified in the spirit." As Lamb of God who went to the Cross bearing all the world's sins, Christ could be "justified" only of the world's sins, for He had none of His own!

Hans Kueng, in his answer to Karl Barth on justification, has written very eloquently about the objective justification of the whole world in the Cross and Resurrection.[16] As a competent New Testament scholar he marshals the evidence very cogently. Yet not even he is able to show that all this really tallies with the Council of Trent, which obviously taught nothing of the sort. See the magisterial work of Hubert Jedin [17] on the Roman Catholic side, and Martin Chemnitz's classic Examen on the Lutheran. The Tridentine paradigm has Christ earning not the free gift of salvation as such, but only the opportunity to earn salvation with the aid of divine grace! In other words, the classic Roman Catholic paradigm denies the intensive perfection of Christ's saving work. Calvinism on the other hand affirms the intensive, but denies the extensive perfection of that work. In that view Christ won full and free salvation, but not for all mankind, rather only for the elect. The plain fact is that only the Church of the Augsburg Confession teaches both the intensive and the extensive perfection of Christ's reconciling work—all sins of all men have been fully expiated (II Cor. 5:19-21). All that remains is to receive this gift in faith—and that appropriating faith is itself a gift!

Justification for Christ's sake, sola gratia et sola fide, is for Lutherans as for St. Paul the article by which the church stands or falls. It is the centerpiece which holds all the other articles of the Gospel together. And it more than anything else defines the Lutheran confession vis a vis Rome.

But the Wittenberg Reformation cannot be defined by reference only to the Roman Catholic alternative. The demarcation line against Geneva is just as constitutive for the Lutheran confession. And there everything comes to a head in the mystery of the true presence of the Lord's body and blood in the Sacrament of the Altar. This Calvin denied as much as Zwingli. It is a profound untruth of modern "ecumenical" propaganda that the difference between Calvinism and Lutheranism is purely over the "mode" of Christ's sacramental presence, not over the fact.[18] No, it is that fact which the Lutheran confession affirms, and the Calvinist denies, as the Formula of Concord amply demonstrates in its seventh article. That is why Bishop Perry of the then LCA (Lutheran Church in America) publicly urged that the Formula of Concord be scrapped for the sake of

182

the Lutheran Reformed communion agreement! [19]

In sum, the two constitutive foci for the Church of the Augsburg Confession are justification and the Holy Supper. These stand at the center of her confession, and without them she ceases to be.

We have already noted the deep links between justification and the Resurrection. There is a similar link between the Resurrection and the Supper. Oscar Cullmann has pointed out that the apostolic church understood the Sacrament as a continuation of the Lord's Resurrection appearances, but now invisibly.[20] Christianity's Founding Fact is celebrated every "first" or "Lord's Day" in the Lord's Supper. As the Apology puts it (X, 4): "We are talking about the presence of the living Christ, knowing that 'death no longer has dominion over him.'"

Like Caiaphas before him, who had no idea how profoundly true was his prophecy of one Man dying for the people (St. John 11:50), Rudolf Bultmann uttered a famous phrase, "Christ is risen into the Gospel" which was truer than its author intended. For the Resurrection, though its factual "infrastructure" is accessible to historical investigation, is really and effectually imparted together with all the fullness of its benefits only in the Gospel, which is the "power of God for salvation" (Rom. 1:16). The various forms of that Gospel are the divine "means of salvation," media salutis, and they may be enumerated as the spirit, the water, and the blood (I John 5:8). The "blood," the Holy of Holies of the New Testament (Heb. 10:19; 12:22-24; 13:10), is the culmination or apex of this list. The Gospel is nowhere more concretely concentrated than in that sacred body and blood given and poured out for us and for our salvation!

Einstein brought about a revolution in physics when he realized that space and time were not independent entities, but were relative to each other, as mutually dependent aspects of one single, four-dimensional space-time continuum. Perhaps modern children can understand this as a picture of the way in which the Cross/Resurrection and the Gospel are not two different things which are closely connected somehow, but are two facets or foci of the one great Mystery of Salvation in the Divine-Human Savior! (See the seamless continuity of past and present spirit, water, and blood in Christ, I John 5:6-8). In Baptism we are "co-buried" and "co-raised" with Christ (Col. 2:12), for Baptism "saves . . . by the Resurrection of Jesus Christ" (I Pet. 3:21). And in the Holy Supper we receive the very Sacrifice which won for us forgiveness, life, and salvation, the body of Him in Whom "dwelleth all the fullness of the Godhead bodily"(Col. 2:9); "this is the true God and eternal life" (I John 5:20).

But which of the several confessions actually teaches all this? Certainly not Geneva, despite its laudable zeal for the Bible. Eastern Orthodoxy comes closest in its liturgical links with Christian antiquity, but its conventional theology is marred by synergism and moralism, not to mention the para-Christian cults of departed saints and the Blessed Virgin. The Roman liturgy, too, retains ancient treasures, but is sadly flawed by the sacrificial conception of the mass. Official Roman dogma cruelly distorts and disfigures the Mystery of Salvation. The Lutheran confession exalts this Mystery as does no other, but Lutheran church life has rarely lived up to its official confession—and therein lies the great tragedy of our church. Yet the sources of divine life and renewal, the spirit, the water, and the blood—or to spell it out less mysteriously, the purely preached Gospel and the rightly administered sacraments—ever beckon us back to the Rock whence we were hewn (Is. 51:1; I Cor. 10:3,4). Here lies at once hidden and revealed the divine dynamic that will not let "the right doctrine and church" die. Let me end with the concluding statements of the joint report of the St. Louis and Ft. Wayne departments of systematic theology regarding the Porvoo Declaration:

> With justification out of the way as a stumbling-block to reunion with Rome, and the sacramental presence renegotiated with Canterbury and then Geneva, the way will be clear for "full communion" everywhere, and whatever anyone may choose to make, of the Gospel and sacraments, it will all be fully warranted as apostolic by the "sign" of a joint episcopate.

Where what the Book of Concord confesses about the church as an article of faith is heeded, there the glass beads of illusions and counterfeits will not be allowed to pass for the real treasures of the church. That is the ecumenical stand Lutherans are called upon to take humbly, soberly, and globally. The life-giving truth of Christ must take precedence over everything else—and the very gates of hell shall not prevail against it.

* Editor's Note: "In Defense of M. Becker," a report in the March 23, 2015 Christian News from The Daystar Journal" reported that according to Dan Gilbert, President of the LCMS's N. Illinois District one projection showed that the LCMS will go from 6,000 congregations to 1,000 in thirty years. In 1960 some 86,000 children were being baptized in the LCMS. In 2015 about 20,000 children were being baptized.

Footnotes

1 For instance in "Article VII of the Augsburg Confession in the Present Crisis of Lutheranism" (1961), in Hermann Sasse, *We Confess the Church*, translated and edited by Norman Nagel (St. Louis, Concordia, 1986), pp. 40-41.

2 "A Crisis in the Making," unpublished conference paper, Billings, MT, 25 February 1991, pp. 4-5.

3 Die Verfassung der deutschen evangelisch-lutherischen Synode von Missouri, Ohio, und anderen Staaten, nebst einer Einleitung und erlaeuternden Bemerkungen (St. Louis: 1846), pp. 3-4.

4 In Statu confessionis, ed. Friedrich Wilhelm Hopf. vol. 1 (Berlin and Hamburg: Lutherisches Verlagahaus, 1966), pp. 36-37; my translation).

5 Richard C. Wolf, Documents of Lutheran Unity in America (Philadelphia-Fortress Press, 1966), p. 547.

6 Briefe von C.F.W. Walther, L. Fuerbringer, ed., vol. 2 (St. Louis, Concordia, 1916), pp. 196-197, 194.

7 Cited in H. Sasse, In Statu Confessionis, ed. Friedrich Wilhelm Hopf. vol. 2 (Berlin and Schleswig-Holstein: Verlag Die Spur and Christliche Buchhandels, 1976), p. 325.

8 H. Sasse, Here We Stand, translated and edited by Theodore Tappert. Concordia Heritage Series (St. Louis: Concordia, 1966), pp. 8-9.

9 I have tried to clarify the whole polity/organization problem in "Lutheran Polity in the American context," to be published shortly among the 1997 Luther Academy papers.

10 In Statu, II: 268.

11 Ruth Rouse and Stephen Neill, eds., A History of the Ecumenical Movement 1517-1948 (London: S.P.C.K., 1967), p. 322.

12 Martin Luther: An Illustrated Biography. New York: Crossroad, 1987.

13 Hubertus Blaumeiser, Martin Luther's Kreuzes theologie. Paderbom: Bonifatius, 1995.

14 The Theology of the Cross—Theologia crucis," in Hermann Sasse, We Confess Jesus Christ, tr. Norman Nagel (St. Louis: Concordia, 1984), pp. 36-54.

15 See Wolfhart Pannenberg on the significance of the "formalized nature" of this language, in Terry Miethe, ed., Did Jesus Rise From the Dead? The Resurrection Debate, Gary R. Habermas and Antony G.N. Flew (San Francisco: Harper and Row, 1987), p. 128.

16 Hans Kueng, Justification (Philadelphia: Westminster, 1981), esp. pp. 222-235.

17 A History of the Council of Trent (London: Thomas Nelson, 1961), vol. 2.

18 So for instance James E. Andrews and Joseph A. Burgess, eds., An Invitation To Action. The Lutheran-Reformed Dialogue Series III 1981-1983 (Philadelphia: Fortress, 1984), pp. 114-115.

19 (LCA Bishop) Perry calmly and explicitly repudiated Article Seven of the Formula "(Forum Letter (New York: American Lutheran Publicity Bureau), 16, September 1986).

20 Oscar Cullmann, Early Christian Worship, tr. A. Todd and J. Torrance (Chicago: Regnery, 1953), pp. 14-20.

1. Hermann Sasse tried to wake his slumbering fellow Lutherans with the questions of the very ____.
2. God will see His ____ through.
3. It was predicted in the 1950's and 1960's that on the basis of past trends, the LCMS would have ____ confirmed members by the end of the century.
4. Who does all the saving of the Church? ____
5. The Lutheran Church cannot define herself in terms of ____.
6. The old North American Synodical Conferences gave expression to this vision of the decisive priority of ____.
7. Sasse noted that he who raises the dead can also ____.
8. ULCA President Franklin Clark Fry said that insistence upon ____ agreement was the distinguishing mark of ____ among Protestants.
9. "Selective fellowship" makes a mockery of ____.
10. What did Walther advise Erlangen John Fackler? ____
11. What did the Leuenberg Concord of 1973 do? ____
12. The Evangelical Lutheran Church of America has capitulated unconditionally before ____.
13. The United Church of Christ promotes outright ____.
14. Sasse said the Missouri Synod says ____ and imitates ___.
15. What was scuttled by the "Statement of the 44" in 1945? ____
16. Who glorified the Yoido Full Gospel (Pentecostal) Church in Seoul,

Korea? ____

17. The main engine of the destruction of the Lutheran confession in the world today is ____.
18. The Hong Kong Assembly of the LWF appealed to all churches to ____.
19. The Roman Catholic scholar Peter Manns, appointed by the Vatican to dialogue with Lutherans, said that Luther should be regarded as ____.
20. An Orthodox bishop renamed his church ____.
21. It is short sighted and paternalistic missiology to think that "Mission fields" do not need ____.
22. The Council of Trent denied ____.
23. Calvinism denies ____.
24. The Augsburg Confession teaches both the ____ and ____ perfection of Christ's redeeming work.
25. What is the article by which the Church stands or falls ____.
26. The two constitutive foci of the Church of the Augsburg Confession are ____.
27. The Gospel is nowhere more concretely concentrated than in that ____.
28. The life-giving truth of Christ must take precedence over ____.

Editor's note: "How Shall We Then Live and Die," a series of six lectures the editor prepared for a Memorial Day retreat at Tuscarora Inn & Conference Center, Mt. Bethel, PA, May 22-25 where he promoted *Marquart's Works* in Lecture III (*CN*, May 18, 2015) noted:

Marquart's Works mentions what Marquart said about some of Schaeffer's books promoted by *Christian News*. (*Marquart's Works*, Apologetics, Volume 2, pp. 56-59.)

Doctrine and Life

Contrary to some critics, Bible believing orthodox Christians and true Lutherans emphasize not only truth and doctrine but also proper Christian living.

Peter Manns, a prominent Roman Catholic historian, director of Department of History of Religion at the Institute of European History of the University of Mainz, wrote in his *Martin Luther-An Illustrated Biography*, Crossroad, New York, 1983: "How silly that expression was that for centuries we believed hit the nail on the head: 'To lead a good life one must be Lutheran; to die a good death, Catholic.' Anyone who follows Luther will live well and die even better, for at the end of the dark tunnel stands someone who loves us and to who we can look forward. That is Luther's **ecumenical legacy** for which we give him thanks" (120).

Martin Luther, An Illustrated Biography by Peter Manns was reviewed in the October 3, 1983 *Christian News*.

SEMINARY HOSTS
LUTHERAN/CATHOLIC DIALOGUE

Christian News, April 27, 1998

(Fort) Wayne, IN)—Over 700 people representing the church bodies of the Lutheran Church-Missouri Synod, the Evangelical Lutheran Church of America, and the Roman Catholic Church came to Concordia Theological Seminary (CTS), Fort Wayne, on April 15 to listen and take part in a dialogue that focused on the ecumenical movement.

The evening began with a welcome by Dr. Dean O. Wenthe, President of CTS, who expressed his appreciation in regard to the seriousness by which the present pontiff has taken in regards to doctrine and dogma, in particular, his vigorous efforts on behalf of the Christian vision of life and the sanctity of the unborn.

Dr. Wenthe was followed by Bishop John M. D'Arcy, of the Catholic Diocese of Fort Wayne-South Bend who quoted the words of Pope John Paul II when explaining the inspiration behind the dialogue.

"Pope John Paul II has said that, 'if this was the millennium of the great division then may this next millennium be the millennium of union...if we are not together by the year 2000 then we should at least be closer together,'" quoted Bishop D'Arcy. "And your presence tonight indicates your desire that this be so."

Cardinal Edward I. Cassidy, president of the Catholic Church's Pontifical Council for Promoting Christian Unity, followed with a keynote address titled Commitment to Ecumenism and its Consequences for the Churches and the Faithful.

In his address, Cardinal Cassidy dealt first with the nature of the Catholic Church's commitment to ecumenism, based especially on the teaching of Pope John Paul II in the *Encyclical Ut Unum Sint*.

"The Encyclical should be seen first and foremost as an urgent appeal not only to the bishops, clergy, religious and faithful of the Catholic Church, but to all Christians," said Cardinal Cassidy. "Restoring unity is to be considered a task for all members of the Church, according to the ability of each."

Cardinal Cassidy went on to explain what ecumenism is to the Catholic Church, in the words of Pope John Paul II.

"Ecumenism is not just some sort of appendix which is added to the Church's traditional activity. Rather, ecumenism is an organic part of her life and work, and consequently must pervade all that she is and does. It must be like the fruit borne by a wealthy and flourishing tree which grows to its full stature."

Cardinal Cassidy explained that in order for ecumenism to work, a new mentality in all that concerns other Christians first must take place.

"Pope John Paul II has stated on at least two occasions that it is not enough for Christians simply to tolerate one another. If we are brothers and sisters, then we must love another. We must respect one another and care for one another," said Cardinal Cassidy. "Hence, there can be no place in our minds for the old prejudices, stereotypes, suspicions. The well-being of my brother or sister Christian should be my joy; the difficulties faced by his or her Church my concern. In particular, we should be sensitive to the beliefs and deep convictions of the other, even when we cannot share those same beliefs and convictions."

Another point that Cardinal Cassidy touched on was the serious involvement of theological dialogue.

"There can be no real unity if we remain deeply divided on doctrinal questions. There are those who would have us leave aside the old theological disputes and seek to find a different way ahead by coming together around a Conciliar table," said Cardinal Cassidy. "Nothing, I believe, could be more disastrous for ecumenism. Those essential acts of our faith that we wish so dearly to share, such as full participation in the Eucharist or the mutual recognition of ministers, can never take place until we have overcome our doctrinal divisions on these and other essential articles of the Christian faith."

As far as the consequences of the ecumenical commitment, Cardinal Cassidy explained that the ecumenical task of uniting divided Christians was essentially linked to the need for interior conversion.

"There can be no ecumenism worthy of the name without a change of heart. This change of heart, together with public and private prayer for the unity of Christians is the soul of ecumenism," quoted Cardinal Cassidy from the Second Vatican Council.

Cardinal Cassidy concluded his address by stating that even though much has been achieved in the search for Christian unity, much more could be done, with much still to be achieved.

"What seems important to me is that we look forward with hope and that we do not become discouraged. God works in this world with poor instruments. We are so often afraid. We are chained to memories of the past. We are held back by the divisions within our own communities," concluded Cardinal Cassidy. "We have no need to be afraid of the truth. Our Lord Jesus Christ says to us, as he did to his first disciples, 'Why are you troubled, and why are these doubts rising in your hearts?' (Luke 24:38). Our task is simply 'to let down the nets' (Luke 5:4), to have faith in the Lord Jesus, and to allow ourselves to be guided by his Spirit."

Following Cardinal Cassidy, were responses from Rev. Prof Kurt E . Marquart, associate professor of Systematic Theology at CTS, and Dr. Eugene L. Brand, retired assistant general secretary for ecumenical affairs for the Lutheran World Federation (LWF).

In Rev. Marquart's response, he freely admitted that the ecumenical movement has brought about profound changes for the better, so far as the attitudes of Christians are concerned.

"One cannot today share without horror the accounts within living memory of unbecoming and even shocking hostility among members of different churches. There never was in the New Testament any basis or excuse for such personal animosity," said Rev. Marquart. "The paschal mystery that we just celebrated and are still celebrating should not allow us to treat even our worst enemies, let alone people of diverging convictions, with anything by clarity and compassion. But there is now generally a climate of mutual respect and friendship among members of various churches. For that, one can only be deeply grateful to Almighty God."

While Rev. Marquart admitted that the ecumenical movement has brought forth profound change in attitude, he also spoke of the need to move beyond the introductory stages of ecumenism or greeting card ecumenism and face the hard issues of truth.

"Truth does not refer to any qualitative achievements of our own fallen and fickle human nature, but it refers to that Truth which alone can make us free. The truth as it is in Jesus. Our divine, human Savior, who is Himself, the Way, the Truth, and the Life," explained Rev. Marquart. "That life-giving truth is the one thing needful, the only genuine way and key to the ultimate ecumenical goal of visible unity in full communion."

Along with facing the hard issues of truth, Rev. Marquart was quick to point out that within the ecumenical movement we must not yield to illusions which could cloud our judgments and dissipate our efforts.

As an example, he cited the Protestant Principle, a current, popular belief by many scholars and laypeople that there are no fixed truths of dogma, no absolutes, no permanent creeds, and no infallible authority of any kind.

"How does this relate to ecumenism?" asked Rev. Marquart. "This kind of thinking has led many to believe that what Jesus said and did in the Gospels did not happen or that Christ did not believe that he was the Son of God," explained Rev. Marquart. "The question then of who actually established the sacraments cannot be answered. Or if Jesus did not believe Himself to be the Son of God then we have no ground to believe it either and therefore commit idolatry in praying to Him."

Rev. Marquart ended his remarks by saying that it is "the absence and the dissolution of dogma that stands in the way of true, God-pleasing ecumenism."

"Therefore, it is for us to pursue and press toward the divine truth to the very best of our ability," said Rev. Marquart. "The outcome, however, does not lie in our hands, but in His, who without whom the builders build in vain. To Him be all our humble ecumenical efforts commended."

Dr. Brand, who like Rev. Marquart, stressed the importance of theological dialogue, also emphasized the need for visible unity.

"The world desperately needs one voice from Christ's body on earth," said Dr. Brand. "Unity is a matter of obedience. One must be obedient to the will of God for the unity of the church."

Like Rev. Marquart, who emphasized the need to uphold the truth in all ecumenical pursuits. Dr. Brand went a step further in his assessment.

"Lutherans' passion for the truth has too often been a passion to prove that we are right rather than a humble search with others probing evermore deeply into God's revelation," explained Dr. Brand. "We are not after a super church but a global communion of Christians, which though it has ample room for legitimate diversity, does not deny the deep unity which we share as a result of our one Lord, one Faith, and one Baptism. That unity signals God's will for the whole creation."

The dialogue ended with a question-and-answer period from the audience which was immediately followed with a Vespers service in Kramer Chapel led by the Rev. Matthew Harrison, pastor of Zion Lutheran Church, Fort Wayne.

"The Lutheran/Catholic Dialogue was characterized by a forthright discussion of those issues which are at the center of Christian identity—Christ's person and work, the reliability of Scripture, and the need for both truth and clarity," explained Dr. Dean O. Wenthe. "The clarity of analysis and positive nature of the discussion will serve the Christian community well."

1. What was the "Protestant Principles" Marquart cited? ____
2. Today many within Christendom believe that what Jesus said and did in the Gospels did not ____.
3. What stands in the way of true, God pleasing ecumenism? ____

DOCTRINE AND OUTREACH
Christian News, July 20, 1998

President Kieschnick's concern about "incessant internal purification" distracting us from mission work (January *Reporter*) is, with all due respect, pure fantasy.

If anything, we are plagued by incessant confusion and division about the pure Gospel.

Examples? First, there is the neo-Pentecostal movement in our Synod. As President Kuhn said in his 2001 convention report, "the charismatic movement and the teachings of God's Word are incompatible."

And then there are the lobbies for women's ordination, open communion and various confusions about the Gospel ministry. Instead of "incessant" attempts to correct these aberrations, our real danger is incessant yakkedeyak to evade the issues.

Getting the message straight is logically and theologically prior to getting it out!

Evangelism depends absolutely on the evangel, the content of the Gospel. If synodical trumpets cannot give a clear sound (1 Cor. 14:7,8), they need to be replaced — precisely for the sake of the Church's sacred mission!

Dr. Kurt Marquart
Fort Wayne, Ind.
Reporter, 2003

1. The charismatic movement and the teachings of God's Word are ＿＿＿.
2. If synodical trumpets cannot give a clear message they need to be ＿＿＿.

THE SHAPE AND FOUNDATION OF FAITH
Concordia Seminary, Ft. Wayne, Indiana
January 20, 1999
Christian News, March 15, 1999

Talk about the "structure" of faith may seem pretentious. When Werner Elert published his *Structure [Morphologie] of Lutheranism,* Hermann Sasse fulminated: "There is no such thing as a 'structure' ['Morphologie'] of Lutheranism!" Lutheran "identity," as we like to call it nowadays, is normatively set by the Lutheran Confessions, not by various contingent historical expressions or developments connected with these Confessions. That was Sasse's point. That point is even more urgent today, when it has become essential for the survival of the Church of the Augsburg Confession rightly to distinguish the unchanging confessional verities from mere cultural trappings. This cuts two ways: On the one hand, we need the utmost missionary magnanimity and accommodation to the rich rainbow-palette of the various cultures; on the other hand, nothing of the evangelical-sacramental fullness of the faith may be given up on the specious plea that only "culture" or "style" is at stake.

Has "the faith which was once delivered unto the saints" (Jude 3) a discernible "structure," or, by your leave, shape? Or is it just one thing after another? Is Christian doctrine a higgledy-piggledy of individual articles, which theologians may then arrange in any order or none? St. Paul defines the ordering principle: "For I determined not to know anything among you, save Jesus Christ, and Him crucified" (I Cor. 2:2). Here we have the sum and substance, the heart and center of the Christian "system"—with none of the speculation or constructivism often associated with that dangerous word. The Person and Work of the God-Man is the real content of Holy Scripture, and therefore the true Key to its right interpretation. To confess Jesus is to confess the Most Holy Trinity (St. Mt. 3:13-17; 28:19), and implies and entails at once the Law/Gospel division as fundamental ("The law was given by Moses, but grace and truth came by Jesus Christ," St. John 1:18), and therefore the centrality of justification (what the *Smalcald Articles* [II/I] call "the first and principal article"). And the "One Lord, One Faith, One Baptism" of Eph. 4:5 links the faith's **incarnational** and **sacramental** content so inextricably that one cannot consistently say yes to the one and no to the other! "Glorious-content-under-lowly-appearance" marks the hiddennes of faith's treasures in this present age, and defines true theology as "theology of the cross," utterly opposed to all worldly-wise "theology of glory." The shape of faith then is Trinitarian, cruciform, and sacramental, and all these wholly and simultaneously.

Moreover, the One Lord is indivisible— if we have Him at all, we have Him wholly and altogether. And since faith is no mere human conviction, but is in every case the work and gift of the Spirit of Truth (St. Jn. 16:13), this Spirit-wrought faith is exactly the same in every believer's heart— whatever the contradictions in his fleshly mind or in the doctrine of his heterodox church! This means that every Trinitarian Font, whatever its other entanglements, offers and bestows in the One Baptism the One Lord and His One Faith—no more and no less by divine institution— if it offers the Lord's Baptism at all. It is the most sacred and solemn duty of the Church of the *pure* Gospel and Sacraments to teach, publish, confess, defend and "insist on" (Titus 3:8 RSV) this one and only true and life-giving faith, the faith of all Christians, the truly ecumenical faith of the one holy catholic and apostolic church.

"Next to the article of the Holy Trinity, the greatest mystery in heaven and on earth is the Personal Union, as Paul says, 'Great indeed is the mystery of our religion: God was manifested in the flesh' (I Tim. 3:16)."[1] This suggests a certain hierarchy among the divine truths of faith. We may therefore envisage the Christian doctrine as a great tower, crowned at its apex with the Trinitarian/ Christological mysteries. In post-apostolic times it was this top of the tower that came first to be safeguarded or "dogmatized." Round this sacred pinnacle of Christian truth, battles swirled for centuries, and the relevant decisions of the so called Seven Ecumenical Councils represent the final, sifted, settled truth of the matter. The revealed, divine truth does not change or develop, of course. Only terminology or formulations develop—and this precisely in order to keep the content unchanged.

The second great conflict was about the tower's mid-section, or soteriology, the way in which the Lord's work of salvation is mediated to us. This was the great battle of the Reformation, which convulsed the Western church in the sixteenth century, and resulted not in a single settlement, but in three basic confessional alternatives: the Augsburg Confession (later the whole Book of Concord), the Roman, papal reaction in the Council of Trent, and the various responses of the Zwingli-Calvinist type. If the two great focal points of the Lutheran Book of Concord are justification and the sacramental presence (represented in the Formula of Concord, for instance, by articles I to VI, and X on the one hand, and by articles VII to DC and XI on the other), this may at first seem simply a matter of contingent historical fact, i.e., the double challenge posed by Rome on the one hand and Zurich/Geneva on the other. Yet the inner links between justification and the Lord's Body and Blood are such that the double focus on them can hardly be merely contingent. As we noted last year in this place, St. Paul suggests something of the sort when he deploys parallel solemn tradition/transmission formulas at precisely two concrete points in I Corinthians: in respect of the Lord's death and resurrection (15:3) and of His Body and Blood in His Supper (11:23). Indeed, I would argue, the Four Gospels themselves, in their own ways of course, culminate in the Resurrection and in the Mystery of the Lord's Body and Blood; for without the latter the former would recede into historical remoteness or cosmic abstraction.

Now It's the Underpinnings, or "Prolegomena"

In our day the battle is raging about the tower's foundations. None of the three confessions that issued from the sixteenth century dreamt of questioning the formal authority of Holy Scripture as the Word of God. The radical subversion of that Word was the result of the cultural revolution known as the Enlightenment. First the European state churches and then the various American "denominations" suffered dogmatic evisceration as liberalism/modernism triumphed in one university after another. Rome seemed to escape the devastation, but there too the floodgates were opened at the Second Vatican Council. Indeed Rome more than the Reformation churches was open to the new supremacy of human reason, since its scholastic "theology of glory" has always been in bondage to "natural theology," that is, philosophy. See the latest papal encyclical on faith and reason by John Paul II.

In the wake of the Enlightenment the ("scientific") historical-critical ideology systematically degraded all sacred texts and authorities, and abolished the whole notion of revealed truth or dogma. An "Ecumenical Movement" arising out of this historical context could not but end up stressing outward union rather than inner unity, and bureaucratic-worldly consolidation at the expense of truth. The twin crisis about Scripture and church has drawn also the erstwhile confessional Lutheran churches of the world into its vortex. The defeat of "Seminex" in the Missouri Synod was only a partial and temporary measure, since it was achieved not by unanimous doctrinal confession, but by organizational majority-vote, and without a coherent doctrine of the church (ecclesiology). As Christology was debated in the ancient church and soteriology in the Reformation, so today we are engulfed by a fierce and all-encompassing battle about *prolegomena,* the very ABC's and foundation-stones of Christian dogma, i.e., the nature and authority of the Word of God, and the very possibility of truth, doctrine, and theology.

It is a sobering reminder of the deep spiritual impoverishment and humiliation of our church that she has been unable to confront the post-Enlightenment devastations with a global symbolical Formula of Concord. Instead there is, on the one hand, a "Lutheran" World Federation, which is anything but that. On the other hand, our little family of confessional churches throughout the world has indeed found it necessary to meet various issues via doctrinal statements, some "brief" and some not so brief—yet even we do not have a common global symbolical platform, to do for the Book of Concord what the Formula of Concord once did for the Augsburg Confession. Our various formulations are local, piecemeal, *ad hoc,* and we all suffer from quite blatant invasions by assorted spirits of the times, making themselves impudently comfortable in the very midst of our ecclesial and academic establishments. What is needed to clear the air after four centuries of symbolical silence—and the intervening cultural crises and revolutions— is a binding symbolic decision, both unitive and divisive, at a global level on the two great issues of the times: *de scriptura* (Scripture) and *de ecclesia* (Church). That was the conviction of our German sister church's leading dogmatician, the American-born Dr. William Oesch,[2] and I can only concur.

194

"Postmodernity": Bane, Blessing, or Tease?

And now the Enlightenment itself has fallen into confusion of tongues! This development has been dubbed "post-modernism," hailed by some and damned by others. Thomas C. Oden, who admits to using "the term postmodern in [his] own reclusive way, with a meaning far different from recent pop deconstructionists,"[3] defines the modern era very precisely as the two centuries bracketed by the French Revolution (1789) at one end and the collapse of Marxism in Eastern Europe, and the fall of the Berlin Wall (1989) at the other. Attractive as this tidy scheme no doubt is, it seems to give too much place to politics, to the neglect of the underlying cultural (i.e., philosophical, literary, artistic) elements.[4] Given the dramatic setting of Oden's lectures— Moscow State University, 1991, under the sponsorship of the *former* Department of Atheism, now renamed the Department of the Scientific and Historical Study of Religion and Freethinking—the political orientation is perfectly understandable. Oden diagnosed "mod rot," concluding that "[despite enormous differences, both Soviet and American societies are grieving over the decomposing assumptions of modern nihilistic relativism" (p. 12). His overall evaluation of postmodernity is surprisingly sanguine:

> Above all, postmodern consciousness will be searching for the recovery of the family, for enduring marriages and good environments for the growth and nurture of children. Postmodernity whether East or West will be searching for a way back to the eternal verities that grounded society before the devastations of late modernity. The direction of postmodernity, in short, promises to be an organic approach to incremental change grounded in traditionally tested values (p. 45).

Our own Prof. Gene Veith, while agreeing with Oden up to a point, is much more cautionary:

> Both Christians and modernists believe in truth. Postmodernists do not. Whether modernism or postmodernism will prove the more hospitable to Christianity remains to be seen... Faced with the inherent meaningless of life, modernists impose an order upon it, which they then treat as being objective and universally binding. Postmodernists, on the other hand, live with and affirm the chaos, considering any order to be only provisional and varying from person to person... Rationalism, having failed, is giving way to irrationalism—both are hostile to God's revelation, but in different ways. Modernists did not believe the Bible is true. Postmodernists have cast out the category of truth altogether. In doing so, they have opened up a Pandora's box of New Age religions, syncretism, and moral chaos.[5]

Already Malcolm Muggeridge had noted today's "selective credulity." Veith offers an example: "affluent business executives, successful movie stars, and well-educated young professionals" are the typical clientele drawn to "Scientology," with its absurd story that "aliens from outer space entered our universe millions of years ago and fought a galactic war," etc. Asks Veith: "People who think of themselves as too sophisticated to believe in the Gospel of John can believe in this?" (p. 194). Or take *The Serpent and the Rainbow* (Simon and Schuster, 1985) by Harvard anthropologist/ ethnobotanist Wade Davis. It offers a remarkable illustration of how Western intellectuals, presumably immune to the "obscurantism" of the Christian mysteries, can swoon into sheer helplessness before "authentic" mumbojumbo like that of pagan Haitian voodoo! And here is the very latest example, from next week's (25 Jan. 1999) *U.S. News and World Report:* John Leo reports on a new book by anthropologist David Stoll, which shows that Rigoberta Menchu's alleged autobiography, for which she won the Nobel Prize in 1992, is largely fiction. The literature professors are enraged—at Stoll of course, for having dared to deface a feminist/liberationist icon! Says Leo: "A growing number of professors accept the postmodern notion that there is no such thing as truth, only rhetoric."

If the very existence of truth and reality is at stake, and not merely an abstract "neutrality" or "objectivity," it becomes highly problematical to claim, as my esteemed friend and colleague in St. Louis, Dr. James Voelz does, that "post-modernism, for all its excesses, is not our enemy but a sort of friend, a late 20th century discovery that, in so many ways, the perspective of the early church was right: only believers can truly interpret the sacred books of God."[6] For one thing, post-modernism knows nothing about "truly" interpreting anything, but scorns the whole idea.

Dismantling Truth: Reality in the Post-Modern World is the telling title of a book edited by Hilary Lawson and Lisa Appignanesi (St. Martin's Press, 1989). Writes Hilary Lawson in his introductory piece:

> But at its philosophical core post-modernism is an attack on truth . .. While relativism can be described as the view that truth is paradigm-dependent, post-modernism might be described as the view that meaning is undecidable and therefore truth unattainable. . . All our truths are, in a sense, fictions—they are the stories we choose to believe (pp. x, xii, xxviii).

In a way the issue grows out of the old rivalry between the natural sciences and the humanities (Lord C.P. Snow's "Two Cultures"). If modernism sought to annex the humanities to the domain of natural science, postmodernism, in a sense, is a move to assimilate the rigorous discipline of natural science to the "soft" and "fuzzy" regime of the humanities. Neither of these moves can really work. There is simply an irreducible difference between studying atoms and molecules and studying human beings. "Fuzziness," that is, lack of rigorous experimental control and predictability is not a weakness in the humanities, but a tribute to their vastly greater complexity, indeed to their qualitative uniqueness and superior importance. Unlike water molecules, human beings have will, choice, imagination, conscience. *Of course* such diverse entities cannot be subject to the same methods of research! One of our century's greatest philosophers of science, the late Sir Karl Popper, crusaded against what he called "historicism," the notion that history was subject to ironclad scientific laws and predictability! This, he rightly saw, attacked and subverted human freedom and dignity at their root, and justified the brutalities of Nazi and communist totalitarianism.[7]

But if history-as-physics is an absurdity, so is physics-as-poetry. Wilhelm Dilthey (1833-1911) suggested, by way of methodological differentiation, that the natural sciences pursue "explanation," and the "cultural sciences" (*"Geisteswissenschaften"*) or the humanities aim at "understanding." The latter, in turn, depended on "hermeneutics"—that fateful word—which Dilthey imported into philosophy from theology. Ever since, natural scientists have been content to "explain" phenomena, while their "hermeneutical" colleagues are forever "explicating."

The last few decades, however, have seen the "two cultures," the scientific and the hermeneutical, converging to a surprising extent. It turns out that natural science, even the showcase discipline of physics itself, is not as totally objective as the logical positivists had fancied. Nor of course are the hermeneutical disciplines simply a quagmire of unbridled subjectivity. Logic and the appeal to inter-subjective phenomena, in short, rational argument and discourse, are the common features of both fields of scholarship—with due regard for the differences in subject matter. *"[ALL science, and all philosophy, are enlightened common sense"* [8] But even the new, chastened "rationality in science is far from the model of the poet and the painter." [9]

To illustrate how far natural science has fallen from its former self image of purveyor of pure, infallible truth about nature, let me cite only two voices, by no means the most radical, from within recent philosophy of science. First, there is the late Sir Karl Popper, already mentioned above. A self-described "falsificationist fallibilist," Popper wrote: "Science does not rest upon rock-bottom. The bold structure of its theories rises, as it were, above a swamp. It is like a building erected on piles. The piles are driven down from above into the swamp, but not down to any natural or 'given' base..." [10] Others have gone even farther in rejecting "foundationalism" in science, the view that the temple of empirical knowledge is soundly and solidly based on irreducible truth and fact.

Secondly, the distinguished Cambridge University philosopher of science, Mary Hesse, who makes no secret of her Christian profession, wrote that "at any given stage of science it is never possible to know *which* of the currently entrenched predicates and laws may have to give way in the future." Further:

> Every scientific system implies a conceptual classification of the world into an ontology of fundamental entities and properties — it is an attempt to answer the question "What is the world really made of?" But it is exactly these ontologies that are most subject to radical change throughout the history of science ... all universally quantified sentences ascribing basic ontology to the world have probability zero, that is, are almost certainly false.[11]

Not content with science's new humility — granted, that is often difficult to detect in pet projects like the evolutionary fantasies about the origin of everything from nothing by itself!—post-modernism wants to reduce *all* cultural endeavors, including science, to an egalitarian porridge of whim and self-interest. This has led to the most absurd excesses, for example the zeal of some postmodernist feminists in professing to detect male, patriarchal oppression in the very achievements of physics, including the $E=mc^2$ equation itself![12]

The pretentious twaddle written by post-modernists about science inspired one enterprising physicist, Alan Sokal, to write up a "well-documented" spoof of the genre, titled "Transgressing the Boundaries: Toward a Transformative Hermeneutics of Quantum Gravity." The editors of *Social Text,* "an influential academic journal of cultural studies," took the parody at face value, and published it in their special spring/summer 1996 issue (46/47), which was "devoted to rebutting the criticisms levelled against postmodernism and social constructivism by several distinguished scientists!" Thereupon the author revealed the hoax![13] *Fashionable Nonsense* by Sokal and fellow-physicist Jean Bricmont is a romp through the muddle-headed fallacies that abound in the solemn pontifications of prominent post-modernists—including "Reader Response" ideologist Julia Kristeva (who, incidentally, receives repeated and well-deserved critical attention in Anthony Thiselton's splendid *New Horizons in Hermeneutics* 11992]). Another significant contribution is Noretta Koertke, ed., A House *Built on Sand: Exposing Postmodernist Myths About Science.* Oxford University Press, 1998.

When it comes to the conflict between modernism and postmodernism, then, one can only wish "a pox on both [their] houses." Both are sworn enemies of revealed, divine truth. One must remember that the opposite of a heresy is usually not the truth but the opposite heresy. (In our own circles we have a textbook example in the fracas about church and ministry, where pop-democratic misreading of Luther and Walther often clash with an equally wrongheaded romantic wistfulness for medieval priest craft!)

To conclude this excursus on a lighter note, let me cite a picturesque description of postmodernists as "a band of vainglorious contemporary artists following the circus elephants of Modernism with snow shovels."[14]

The "Foundationalism" of Faith and Theology

It may well be that today's postmodernists are only now catching up with the maudlin muddleheadedness that has long been taken for granted in "religion." Over a hundred years ago a much-reprinted editorial gushed: "Yes, Virginia, there is a Santa Claus!" It continued:

> He exists as certainly as love and generosity and devotion exist... Only faith, fancy, poetry, love, romance, can push aside that curtain and view and picture the supernal beauty and glory beyond. Is it all real? Ah, Virginia, in all this world there is nothing else real and abiding. No Santa Claus! Thank GOD! he lives, and he lives forever.[15]

So then theologians invented postmodernism, as they apparently invented "instrumentalism," the notion that science is not about truth but about measurements and calculations only.[16] Mortimer Adler takes up the problem in his *Truth in Religion* (1990), but by his own admission he has only clarified, not solved it. Still, along with some scholastic "theology of glory," there are useful observations and correctives in the book. Adler takes note of the special status of revealed knowledge, but presses the university of truth: "The logic of science and of mathematics is, like science and mathematics, global, not Western" (p. 144). He concludes with a ringing appeal to an underlying human unity beneath all the rich cultural variety, such as will "at last overcome the illusion that there is a Western mind and an Eastern mind, a European mind and an African mind, or a civilized mind and a primitive mind. There is only a human mind and it is one and the same in all human beings" (p. 156).

Empirical science can make do with conjectures and probabilities as foundation. The high-minded chatter of postmodernist "discourse" obviously needs no foundation. But faith requires—and has—the most certain and unyielding of foundations, against which the very gates of hell shall not prevail (St. Mt. 16:18). The foundation of faith is the same as that of the church: "For other foundation can no man lay than that is laid, which is Jesus Christ" (I Cor. 3:11). Again: "built upon the foundation of the apostles and prophets, Jesus Christ Himself being the chief cornerstone, in Whom all the building fitly framed together groweth unto an holy temple in the Lord" (Eph. 2:20-21).

This alone-saving Christ, the content and foundation of faith, is accessible through no "natural theology," reasonable apologetics, human wisdom, clever communication strategies, or free choice and self-determination, but **only** through the Holy Gospel (including the Sacraments) as means or channel of salvation (Rom. 10:13-17; I Cor. 1 & 2).

The Incarnate Word and the proclaimed, apostolic, inscripturated Word—these form an indissoluble unity as object and basis of faith: "I know *Whom* I have believed" (II Tim. 1:12). "The words that I speak unto you, they are spirit and they are life" (St. Jn. 6:63). "If ye continue in My word, then are ye my disciples indeed; and ye shall know the truth, and the truth shall make you free" (St. Jn. 8:31-32). "If they have kept My saying, they will keep yours also" (St. Jn. 15:20). "But these are written, that ye might believe that Jesus is the Christ, the Son of God; and that believing ye might have life through His name" (St. Jn. 20:31). "... believing all things which are written in the law and in the prophets" (Acts 24:14).

"Scripture alone" *(sola Scriptura)* is thus a necessary corollary, indeed an implementation, of "Christ alone." Just as "by faith alone" *(sola fide)* excludes works not absolutely, but only from **justification,** so "Scripture alone" excludes not **tradition** as such or **reason** as such, but only false, unapostolic tradition, and a false, "magisterial" use of reason. "Scripture alone" is in fact the necessary guarantee that our faith and doctrine are really "handed down" (see I Cor. 11:23; 15:3) to us by Christ through His apostles, and are not the pseudo-traditions of men (St. Mt. 15:6; St. Mk.

7:8).

If modernism subverted all this by denying biblical inspiration, authority, and inerrancy, postmodernism makes a mockery of the clarity and sufficiency of Holy Writ. Thus arises the **hermeneutical crisis,** in its radical contemporary form, which in principle renders all interpretation moot if not incoherent. There is no point whatever to any titles or praises we may heap on Holy Scripture as Word of God, inspired, inerrant, and the like, if in the end it turns out that it is impossible to decide what this inspired Word really means! What is the use of a well or source, if it is not possible to draw water from it? But obviously Holy Scripture was given us that we might know and rejoice in its true meaning and message, not that we might puzzle endlessly over its "undecidable" interpretation!

It is the great merit of Dr. James Voelz's book, *What Does This Mean?*, to have raised this issue with urgency. We needed to be shaken out of our conventional hermeneutical slumbers in order to confront what is really going on today. As a "first approximation," as it were, it is not of course to be expected that such a book would really settle the complex issues. It suffices for now to have them raised. It will require a great deal of collegial collaboration to get hold of all that is involved here in a way that will be useful and satisfactory to the church. It is in this spirit that I offer the following observations, which are to be taken not as attacks, but as probing and thoughts suggested and stimulated by the book. I shall not attempt to exhaust the challenge implied in our student publication's heading, "What Does 'What Does This Mean' Mean?" (a sparkling "sight-bite" reminiscent of the only witty headline I recall reading in the dreary old pro-"Seminex" publication, announcing the new St. Louis Faculty: "Klug, Klotz, Klann").

In the first place, biblical hermeneutics is first and foremost a matter of doctrine or dogma, not of technical detail. The fundamental approach to biblical interpretation must be settled *a priori* from the unique nature of Holy Scripture as God's Word. It is difficult to see how an *a posteriori* approach via details and techniques to do with language generally, can in principle rise above the tactical level, to the necessary strategic decisions. For example, Anthony Thiselton does me the honor of noting my little contribution to the Lutheran Council in the USA hermeneutics symposium. *Studies in Lutheran Hermeneutics* (1979). He takes me to advocate a view, however, "which would preclude methods associated with modern historical criticism" (*New Horizons,* p. 190). Actually, I had specifically conceded that "most of the techniques (e.g., literary criticism, redaction criticism) can be used up to a point also by anti-critical scholars" (my p. 314). The objection, in other words, was not to details of scholarly techniques, but to the historical-critical approach or ideology as such, and to techniques only insofar as they necessarily involved the violation of biblical authority.

If biblical hermeneutics is first of all a matter of doctrine, located in theological *prolegomena,*[17] its decisive features need to be defined *a priori,* from Holy Scripture itself. So for instance, it is certain from the outset that God intends His inspired words to convey precise and definite meanings, which express exactly what He wishes to express, and do not depend on synergistic "merging of horizons" with muddle-headed readers. The preacher's job then, is not to illuminate obscure texts with his clever scholarship, but to illumine his and his hearers' darkness with the bright light of the divine Word. The chief obstacles to the right understanding of Holy Scripture are not intellectual or academic, but spiritual — e.g., worldly wisdom, such as the persistent *"opinio legis"* (inclination to law-dominated views) of unregenerate human nature. The antidote is the Spirit of God working through the Gospel.

Secondly, one cannot so easily appropriate or adapt ideology-laden writers like Gadamer. Hans Ineichen's penetrating analysis points out, for instance, "that the development of hermeneutics is marked by the loss of the critical dimension. This development finds its high point in the work of Heidegger and Gadamer, particularly in the retreat from the predicative concept of truth to an undifferentiated truth event."[18] Gadamer follows Heidegger, whose professorial prose is notorious for its dense opacity. The real trouble is that just in what "is lost in Heidegger's talk about the unveiling *[Entdeckendsein]* of truth, lies however the indication of the measuring stick, the standard of prepositional truth, which alone enables one to divide true from false sentences" (p. 169).

Thirdly, the clarity of Scripture is indispensable to its sufficiency. Scripture might hypothetically be clear without being sufficient; but it cannot be sufficient without being clear. How basic all this was to Luther's Reformation has recently again been pointed out by Mark D. Thompson, Director of Studies at the (Evangelical Anglican) Moore College in Sydney, in *"Claritas Scripturae* in the Eucharistic Writings of Martin Luther."[19] It was not tradition, habit, "the Church," or "the Fathers," or his "community," but the clear biblical text that held Luther's conscience captive to the Sacramental Presence. Against his Roman opponents he would say: "Let them shout themselves into a frenzy, crying 'Church, Church.' Without the Word of God it is nothing." The Smalcald Articles teach the same: "We do not concede to the papists that they are the church, for they are not. Nor shall we pay any attention to what they command or forbid in the name of the church. . ."[20]

Fourthly, here lies the difference between the Roman Catholic and the Eastern Orthodox tradition principle, and the Lutheran understanding of the creeds and confessions as part of the "Rule and Norm" (Formula of Concord). The latter are simply the Scriptures rightly understood. Thus the Augsburg Confession is authoritative "not because this confession was prepared by our theologians but because it is taken from the Word of God and solidly and well-grounded therein" (Tappert, p. 504). By contrast, the Ecumenical Councils and/or the infallible papacy are claimed to have intrinsic authority, so that they are to be believed and accepted in their own right, and not because they can be shown to be in agreement with Holy Writ. It is into this territory that disoriented ("evangelical catholic") Lutherans stray when, having sacrificed the authority, clarity, and sufficiency of Holy Scripture, they wander about looking for a

"Lutheran magisterium."

Sasse comments in his discussion of the new Scripture-and-tradition configuration of Vatican II: "But in the very moment in which we *de facto* subordinate the Scriptures to the authority of the Church, the Church becomes not only the judge, but also the source of doctrine."[21]

Here, too, one must reject certain "liturgical" pretensions to the effect that *"lex orandi* [the rule of prayer] precedes (normatively) the *lex credendi* of the community and the individual."[22] Theology is then divided up into "primary" and "secondary," such that "there exists a theology which liturgists in assembly do in a primary way, under ritual logistics." Aidan Kavanagh is quoted in support: "The language of the primary theologian ... more often consists in symbolic, metaphorical, sacramental words and actions which throw flashes of light upon chasms of rich ambiguity." Theology in the normal sense, as doctrine, is then regarded as "secondary" and derivative. All this is quite topsy-turvy. Not "ritual logistics" deployed upon "chasms of rich ambiguity," but God's Word and doctrine is "primary theology," e.g., St. Peter's confession: "You are the Christ, the Son of the living God!"

The flight from doctrine as primary and decisive contains more than a hint of postmodernist discomfort with the cognitive dimension of the Faith. Indeed, George Lindbeck's notion of doctrine as grammatical rules rather than concrete content is expressly cited (p. 299). Lindbeck summarizes his views in an essay published as part *of Postmodern Theology* (1989). An essay in the same volume by Sandra M. Schneiders brings to bear the full fury of postmodernism:

> It is not certain that the text can be saved; but it is certain that it cannot be saved as a simple container of revelation or literal transmitter of divine truth. Furthermore, feminist hermeneutics has made it clear that revelation cannot be equated with history in the sense of what actually happened, nor can the Bible be considered, without further ado, as a normative archetype for contemporary Christian life. In short, the questions that are being raised by liberation theology in general and feminist criticism in particular are not merely concerned with how the oppressed can relate to a patriarchal text but, more fundamentally, how the Christian community can appropriate its sacred literature in a postmodern world... Only a hermeneutics which effectively weds the best of the new forms of criticism with a genuinely liberating interpretation and praxis can allow the Bible to function as Word of *God* within a postmodern context (p. 71).

Perhaps the most deep-seated hermeneutical issue is the nature of the link between Holy Scripture and doctrine, or the doctrinal content of creeds and confessions. Reformed theology, and all pietistic Biblicism influenced by it, make *sola scriptura* into an abstract "timeless appeal to the open Bible and to the Spirit which from it speaks to our spirit," in Karl Barth's famous phrase. Lutherans by contrast insist that the Lord builds His church not through a simply "open Bible," but through the rightly understood and confessed Bible — that is through the concrete, purely preached Gospel and the rightly administered sacraments. Therefore there are authoritative symbolical books, confessing orthodox, biblical doctrine, and sharply differentiating that from all heterodox, unbiblical doctrine. Right confession then is the divine, biblical truth and doctrine itself, not a mere surrogate, pointer, approximation, interpretation, or anything of that sort. Theologically this is known as the "unity of the Word of God": the Word and truth of God remains that even when it is reformulated—correctly of course—as in preaching or translation. Indeed preaching is the primary form in which God's Word reaches us, as in the meaning of the Third Commandment, that we are not to "despise preaching and His Word."

To all genuine preaching and confession there applies what the Lord said to Peter: "flesh and blood have not revealed [this] to you, but My Father in the heavens." The "this" is even missing in the text, and has to be supplied. The "this" here is the content. What Peter confesses is exactly the same thing that God revealed to him—not some "secondary" attempt at "explicating" some "primary" but ineffable givens. When later the church confesses Christ to be homoousion with the Father, this adds or changes nothing, but only safeguards precisely the truth of Peter's confession of Christ as the "Son of the living God." The same is true of all the divine "mysteries" which the Lord has "given" His apostles "to know"—and to transmit to us (St. Mt. 13:11; compare Eph. 3:3-10, Col. 1:25-28, etc.). It is not as if, in false analogy to physics or botany. Scripture supplied us with mere "data," from which we would then have to derive the proper generalizations, hypotheses, conclusions, theories, and the like. No, Holy Scripture teaches us the actual divine truths and certainties themselves, which we are to confess and transmit without change, even in new and different languages and terminologies. Eeva Martikainen's important monograph, *DOCTRINA: Studien zu Luther's Begriff der Lehre* (Helsinki, 1992) reminds us again of the Reformation's joyful confidence in the identity of the pure doctrine with God's own Word and truth. That is why preaching it purely is "the greatest, holiest, most necessary, highest worship of God . . . for the office of preaching *[Predigtamt]* is the highest office in the church" (German of Ap. XV, 42). Here is "primary theology" at its best.

It is the office and function of all decent hermeneutics to support and further such preaching of the true faith, and to thwart and ward off everything that would hinder or undermine it. It is a matter of resisting the pseudo-hermeneutics of "the old devil and the old serpent who made enthusiasts of Adam and Eve," by leading them "from the external Word of God to spiritualizing and to their own imagination" (SA III/VIII, 5). Then we shall "hear" only Him Who being in the bosom of the Father "has declared— 'exegeted' — Him" (St. Jn. 1:18).

St. John Chrysostom—or at least a writing attributed to him already centuries before the Reformation — commends to us this antidote for bad hermeneutical times:

203

When you shall see the impious heresy, which is the army of Antichrist, standing in the holy places of the Church, then let those who are in Judaea flee to the hills, that is, let those who are in Christendom flee to the Scriptures. For the true Judaea is Christendom, and the mountains are the Scriptures of the Prophets and Apostles, as it is written: His foundations are in the holy mountains. But why must all Christians at that time flee to the Scriptures? Because at that time, when heresy shall have taken over the churches, there will be no other possible proof of true Christianity, no other possible refuge for the Christians, desiring to recognize the truth of the faith, except the divine Scriptures. Before it was shown in many ways, which was the true Church of Christ... But now those who want to know, recognize which is the true Church of Christ in no other manner than through the Scriptures alone. Why? Because heresy keeps everything similar. He therefore who wishes to recognize which is the true Church of Christ, where will he recognize it, in such a confusion of similarity, except solely and alone through the Scriptures? The Lord therefore, knowing that such a confusion of affairs would arise in the last days, commands that the Christians who are in Christendom, and who wish to attain to the firmness of true faith, should flee to nothing else except to the Scriptures. If they pay attention to anything else, they will be offended and perish, not understanding which is the true Church, and thereby falling into the abomination of desolations which stands in the holy places of the church (49th homily, on St. Mt. 24)

K. Marquart
20 January 1999

Footnotes

1 Formula of Concord, SD, VIII, 33, Tappert, p. 597.

2 Wilhelm M. Oesch, *An Unexpected Plea. Since 1977: Addenda to the Formula of Concord.* Translated by J. Valentinus Andreae, edited and with introduction by Eugene F. Klug. Ft. Wayne: CTS Press, 1983. 109 pp. Compare E. Klug, "A Call for Addenda to the Formula of Concord," *Concordia Theological Quarterly,* vol. 44, no. 4 (October 1980), pp. 234-237. For an overview of Oesch's work see his *Solus Christus, Sola Scriptura. Grundzuege Lutherischer Theologie,* ed. Dieter Oesch. Gr. Oesingen: Verlag der Lutherischen Buchhandlung Eichenring 18, 1996. 375 pp.

3 Thomas C. Oden, *Two Worlds: Notes on the Death of Modernity in America and Russia* (Downers Grove: Intervarsity Press, 1992), p. 43.

4 See Roger Scruton, *Modern Philosophy* (New York: Allen Lane, The Penguin Press, 1994), pp. 500-504.

5 Gene Edward Veith, Jr., *Postmodern Times* (Wheaton: Crossway Books, 1944); pp. 20, 42, 192-193.

6 James W. Voelz, *What Does This Mean?* (St. Louis: Concordia, 1995), p. 12.

7 See his *The Poverty of Historicism* (London: Routledge and Kegan Paul, 1957-1979) and *The Open Society and Its Enemies,* 2 vols.

8 Karl R. Popper, *Objective Knowledge* (Oxford: Clarendon Press, 1979), p. 34; italics in original.

9 W. H. Newton-Smith, "Rationality, Truth and the New Fuzzies," in Lawson and Appignanesi, *Dismantling Truth,* p. 37.

10 Paul Arthur Schilpp ed., *The Philosophy of Karl Popper* in *The Library of Living*

Philosophers (La Salle, Illinois: Open Court, 1974), 1:488.

11 Mary Hesse, *Revolutions and Reconstructions in the Philosophy of Science* (Bloomington and London: Indiana University Preas, 1080), pp. 76 and 147.

12 So apparently Luce Irigaray, quoted in Alan Sokal and Jean Bricmont, *fashionable Nonsense: Postmodern Intellectuals' Abuse of Science* (New York: Picador USA, 1998), p. 109.

13 *Fashionable Nonsense,* p. 2.

14 Charles Newman, cited in Floyd Merrell, *Semiosis in the Postmodern Age* (West Lafayette: Purdue University Press, 1995), p. 3.

15 Reprinted in the Ft. Wayne *News-Sentinel,* 25 December 1998.

16 With the unerring killer-instinct of a master-polemicist Popper names as the three godfathers of instrumentalism a Roman Catholic cardinal (Robert Bellarmine), an Anglican bishop (George Berkeley), and a Lutheran theologian (Andrew Osiander), *Conjectures and Refutations* (Harper & Row, 1968), p. 99.

17 Note the stress on explicit hermeneutical axioms in C.F.W. Walther's *The Evangelical Lutheran Church, The True Visible Church of God on Earth.*

18 Hans Ineichen, *Philosphische Hermeneutik* in Elisabeth Stroeker and Wolfgang Wieland, eds., *Handbuch Philosophic* (Muenchen: Alber, 1991), p. 20, my translation.

19 *Westminster Theological Journal* 60 (1998) 23-41.

20 SA III/XII/1, 2, Tappert, p. 315.

21 H. Sasse, *His Church or Holy Writ?* (Sydney: IVF Graduate Fellowship [Australia]: 1967), p. 22.

22 David W. Fagerberg, *What Is Luturgicul Theology?* (Collegeville: The Liturgical Press, 1992), p. 211.

1. The shape of faith is ____.
2. Faith is in every case the work of ____.
3. Revealed, divine truth does not ____.
4. The Four Gospel culminate in the ____.
5. None of the three confessions of the sixteenth century dreamt of questioning ____.
6. What was opened at the Second Vatican Council? ____
7. Why was the defeat of "Seminex" in the Missouri Synod only partial and a temporary measure? ____
8. Today we are involved in the nature and authority of ____ and very possibility of ____.
9. What is needed to clear the air of symbolical silence? ____
10. Marquart concurred with William Oesch about ____.
11. Postmodernists have cast out ____.
12. What absurd story do the Scientologists promote? ____
13. When it comes to the conflict between modernism and postmodernism then one can only wish ____.
14. There is only a ____mind and it is one and the same in all ____.
15. The alone saving Christ is only accessible through ____.
16. "Scripture alone" is in fact the necessary guarantee that our faith is in fact ____.
17. The decisive features of biblical hermeneutics need to be defined a priori from ____.
18. What held Luther's conscience captive? ____
19. Preaching is the primary form in which God's Word ____.

A WORD OF ENCOURAGEMENT
Christian News, May 19, 2003

Having been asked by friends to address the plight of those who are so deeply discouraged by the turn of events in our Missouri Synod that they are tempted simply to leave, I humbly offer a few thoughts:

It is quite natural to become discouraged when things go wrong. To see our Synod - once known throughout the world for its firm, unyielding, and united stand for the pure Gospel of Christ - now awash in confusion and contradiction, even about such dear and basic issues as joint services with official representatives of paganism, that is of course profoundly and painfully sad.

And while the Lord founded His Church so solidly on Himself that the very gates of hell shall not prevail against her (St. Mt. 16:18), it is true that no visible church of a particular town, region, nation, or continent has the guarantee of remaining faithful to the truth forever. Indeed, history teaches us that even great and strong churches can ultimately abandon the truth. Think only Jerusalem, Rome, Wittenberg!

But now is not the time to abandon our Synod. It is not a false, heterodox church, but an orthodox church with serious troubles. For confessionally sound pastors and people to leave the Synod now, is simply to hand it over to those who hate its strict confessional stand. Besides, we didn't get into this mess in a hurry, and we're not going to get out of it quickly either. But to put it colloquially, "the old girl is worth fighting for"! Think of all the generations of devout souls who prayed and sacrificed for this Synod — and of those many who still do! Our Dr. Walther himself wrote to a confessional student in Erlangen, who wanted to leave the Bavarian Lutheran state church:

"I can advise separation from a degenerated communion which formerly had taken the right stand, only when it is notorious that it has 'hardened' (verstockt) itself and that is notorious only when everything has been tried to lead it back, but in vain . . . Would to God that I had had this understanding thirty some years ago, then I would likely still be in America, yet not as one who had abandoned his office, but as an exile (Briefe von C.F.W. Walther, Concordia, 1916, pp. 196-197, my translation)."

And to another pastor in Germany he wrote:

"From a heretical or schismatic communion one must exit without consulting flesh and blood, also from a syncretistically constituted one; it is not so with a church which originally took the right stand, and in which false faith and unbelief still fight for the right to exist. Here it is a matter of leaving the sinking ship, not the one that has sprung a leak (p. 194)."

It seems that most of our troubles in doctrine began as loose practice: open communion, neo-Pentecostalism, joint services with official representatives of false doctrine, and so forth. Then there came the pragmatic urge to adjust our formerly strong theology to our weak practice. The basic problem, it seems to me, ban organizational, bureaucratic approach to theology and church life. People want to justify any status quo that has become customary, and habitual — "like petty public official [who] quietly approved the errors of their superiors, without understanding them." (Apology XII, 69, Tappert p. 192).

The problem is not new: The Commission on Constitutional Matters (CCM) "now has well-nigh total and absolute power to turn any issue involving the practical application of the Confession into a constitutional one," and then to issue a "binding" decision! "The real question is the wisdom of such total concentration of virtually unchallengeable power in a small body of administrative appointees. Should someone be thinking of theological, churchly remedies?" (*Church Polity and Politics*, John Fehrman and Daniel Preus, eds, Luther Academy and Association of Confessional Lutherans, 1997, pp. 199-200).

The cat is fully out of the bag in the new CCM ruling that one can't be charged for actions for which one had prior approval from one's ecclesiastical supervisor! The practical import is that bureaucratic standing may now override Holy Scripture and the Confessions! For details see the argument in the attached resolution. You are free to use the resolution or any part or aspect of it you find helpful, as you see fit.

Of course only God can help us. Relying on Him alone let us do what we can to encourage good outcomes at the 2004 Convention, and the one after that and the one after that etc.

That will mean sharing relevant factual and doctrinal information, also at District conventions, sending in appropriate resolutions, nominating and electing confessionally responsible people, and defeating the dishonest emotional propaganda which seeks to exploit the sacred urgencies of Mission to sweep inconvenient doctrinal issues under the carpet.

Finally, the battle for the sacred truth of the Gospel must be fought with kindness and love. We must not demonize human opponents, but realize, as St. Paul teaches us, that "our struggle is not against flesh and blood, but against the rulers, against the authorities, against the powers of the dark world and against the spiritual forces of evil in the heavenly realms." (Eph. 6:12, NIV). The Lord of the Church bless us with zeal and courage and joy in Him Whose mercies are new to us every morning!

Fraternally yours,
Kurt Marquart,
Ft. Wayne, IN, 8 May 2003

1. Did Marquart maintain in 2003 that now was the time to leave the LCMS? ____
2. What do you think Marquart would say 12 years later in view of what has happened in the LCMS since 2003 and what is now being tolerated in the LCMS? ____
3. The basic problem is an ____ approach to theology and church life.
4. The Commission on Constitutional Matters has well-nigh ____.
5. Only ____ can help us.

PUTTING MISSOURI BACK ON TRACK

By: Dr. Kurt Marquart
Fifth National Free Conference on C.F. W. Walther, Nov. 8, 2003
Christian News, November 17, 2003

Dear brothers and sisters of our Lord Jesus Christ: Thank you for the great honor of your invitation. In accepting the assigned topic, "Putting Missouri Back on Track," I wish to make it very clear that I have neither the wisdom nor the resources to cure all that ails our dear Synod. We are beyond human help-only God Himself can deliver us! The best we can do is to try to understand our needs in the light of God's revealed Word, and then to pray and work accordingly.

Some years ago, during one of the many attempts to "restructure" our long-suffering Synod, the "task force" in charge coined a phrase about the Synod being a "servant structure." That sounds attractively modest-until you recall that the very papacy calls itself ever so humbly "servant of the servants of Christ"! Well-intentioned as the task-force's phrase no doubt was, it betokened a deep misunderstanding of what the Synod is. To define the Synod as "servant structure" is to understand it basically as a bureaucratic organization, governed and held together by constitution and bylaws! No, dear friends, the Synod is not its bureaucracy. Rather, the Synod, in its essence, is simply its member-congregations, acting together in the Lord's mission! The Synod is all its local churches bound together by faith and love!

The bureaucratic organization is strictly secondary, and does not belong to or determine the nature and essence of the Synod. The outward structure is there to serve the Synod's confessional purposes, and must be changed or even abolished if it gets in the way of the confession of the evangelical truth. Joint confession of the divine truth is the purpose that shapes and defines the Synod-and all constitutions, bylaws, and structures must either serve and support that, or else get out of the way and make room for a genuine and faithful implementation of Synod's confession.

That has from the beginning been our Synod's self-understanding. According to the original constitution the very first obligation of the Synod was "To stand guard over the purity and unity of doctrine within the synodical circle, and to oppose false doctrine." The whole point was "that the confessing and teaching church might devote herself to the enabling and promoting of every particular churchly purpose. . . [the Confession must exercise] an ordering and shaping influence on the whole constitution and on the church's entire mode of action." [2] In other words, the Confession alone shapes, defines, and determines the constitution, not the other way round!

As Francis Pieper put it in his 1880 Iowa District theses on Law and Gospel:

"Our Lutheran Church has no special church constitution which might hold her together. Only Law and Gospel are her bond of unity. The external constitution of the church is after all not prescribed in Holy Scripture; therefore there exist in the Lutheran Church quite different constitutions in different countries. There are Lutherans under an episcopal polity [Verfassung, constitution], under a presbyteral polity, etc., that comes from the light which shines in the Lutheran Church. To true unity in the church there belong, as our Confession says, only the pure Word and the right administration of the sacraments. That the sects make so much of external forms is due to the fact that they do not maintain the difference between Law and Gospel.[3]"

Pieper appeals here to the famous Seventh Article of the Augsburg Confession. This incidentally was the first dogmatic definition of the church, and the Roman Catholic and the Calvinist confessions later defined their understandings or misunderstandings of the church in response to the clear definition of the Augsburg Confession. In the Middle Ages the church had come to be distorted into a sacred bureaucracy, a chain of command, with the laity at the bottom, the papacy at the top, and the bishops and clergy in-between! The Augsburg Confession rejected this caricature and returned to the biblical understanding of the church not as a bureaucratic command structure, but as the glorious Bride of Christ, consisting of all believers in Christ, the sacred royal priesthood!

And if the church is the believers, then the one thing that matters is the Gospel, for only by the Gospel can people become and remain believers! The purely preached Gospel and the rightly administered sacraments, these, says the Augsburg Confession, are enough for the true unity of the church. It is not necessary that human customs and ceremonies and traditions in rituals or church structure be everywhere the same. Rome and Eastern Orthodoxy, and of course Anglicanism, demand conformity to an episcopal so-called "apostolic succession," and so on. This also got into the Ecumenical Movement, in the form of "Faith and Order". And once these are linked together, the human order begins to trump the divine faith, as the "Baptism, Eucharist, Ministry" document of 1982 clearly shows.

Contrary to all traditionalism and insistence on human regulations, the Lutheran ecumenical principle is "the life-giving evangelical Truth alone"! Only one thing is needful in the church, and that is the liberating message of Him Whose words are spirit and life (St. John 6:63). The pure Gospel and sacraments, these and these alone are the true marks or signposts of the church, and absolutely everything in the church's life and structure must be subject to them and be judged by them!

Our tragedy is that this absolute priority of the divine truth has become displaced in our Synodical life. By what? By organizational, bureaucratic concerns. Our disease is, you might say, "bureaucratitis." When theology is done bureaucratically, it simply dies and turns into a caricature of itself. Please note that when I talk here about "bureaucracy" and "bureaucratic" attitudes, I have in mind not those dear people of God who labor in various capacities in our Synod and its Districts, but rather a certain pathological attitude of mind.

Let me begin with the clearest, crassest example of this bureaucratic malady. That surely is none other than that recent ruling of the Commission on Constitutional Matters, which held that the prior advice of one's "ecclesiastical supervisor" trumps any substantive arguments to the contrary. In this way the issue of truth posed by the syncretistic service in New York, was totally bypassed in favour of purely organizational, bureaucratic trivia. This was the most dramatic triumph in our Synod of what Hermann Sasse called "the institutional lie." He wrote:

Alongside the pious and dogmatic lies, there stands the institutional lie. By this we mean a lie which works itself out in the institutions of the church, in her government and her organization. It is so dangerous because it legalizes the other lies in the church and makes them impossible to remove.[4]*

All the argumentation from Holy Scripture and the Church's Confessions was simply set aside on the grounds that the relevant "ecclesiastical supervisor" had given his opinion, advice, and interpretation of a Synodical resolution! That is nothing but papal pretences all over again! The Lord says: "But in vain do they worship Me, teaching for doctrines the commandments of men" (St. Mt. 15:9)! Nothing should be more self-evident in the Church of "sola scriptura," Scripture alone! The Reformation threw out all shameful slavery to human opinions and regulations, and restored to us the liberty of the children of God under His alone-saving Word. As the Formula of Concord (X,21) quotes from the Treatise on the Power and Primacy of the Pope. "No one shall burden the church with traditions or allow the authority of any person to count for more than the Word"!

In this connection I cannot sufficiently thank God for the clear witness to this very point borne by the St. Louis Faculty Statement and especially by the detailed analysis of Professors David Berger and James Voelz in the October, 2003 issue of the *Concordia Journal*. That both theological faculties are on record against the public whitewash of a notorious case of syncretism surely bodes well for the future of our Synod. May the Lord of the Church richly bless that testimony!

Another piece of bureaucratic trickery is the pretence that certain public actions or pronouncements may not be discussed until the "proper authorities" have finished their sometimes longwinded consideration of the matter. At times the Eighth Commandment is enlisted to prevent public rebuke of public evil. But remember our official Lutheran Confession, Luther's *Large Catechism*:

But where the sin is so public that the judge and everyone else are aware of it, you can without sin shun and avoid those who have brought disgrace upon themselves, and you may also testify publicly against them. For when something is exposed to the light of day, there can be no question of slander or injustice or false witness. For example, we now censure the pope and his teaching, which is publicly set forth in books and shouted throughout the world. Where the sin is public, appropriate public punishment should follow so that everyone may know how to guard against it.[5]

Especially where the truth of the Gospel is at stake, there can be no diplomatic silence or false scruples about upsetting bureaucratic apple-carts. When St. Peter compromised the truth of the Gospel by withdrawing from the Gentile Christians, did St. Paul reproach him gingerly at night and in private? No, he at once "opposed him to his face, because he was in the wrong" (Gal. 2:11). When St. Paul "saw that they were not acting in line with the truth of the Gospel," he spoke to Peter "in front of them all" (v. 14).

It is shameful to hide behind human regulations and "proprieties" when the Gospel is being falsified. Nothing in the church may take precedence over the truth of the Gospel and the need to confess it faithfully. If our Synod cannot recover this absolute, overriding priority of truth and confession over all sorts of organizational considerations, it will cease to be a Lutheran church and become just another bureaucratic sect. And the trend from truth to bureaucracy is very much in the air. Here is how a perceptive Presbyterian summed up the tragic experience of his church:

Following the dominant patterns of American life, there was an increasing tendency to think of the Church as a kind of business corporation chartered to do the Lord's work. The subordination of questions of truth-though only of those regarded as "unessential"–to efficiency of operation carries a recognizable suggestion of pragmatism...

The problem of power and freedom has thus been solved to date by simultaneously increasing administrative centralization and decreasing theological centralization; . . .increasingly prominent. . . was a pragmatic conception of the Church which, in the interests of avoiding divisions that would injure the Church's work, has substituted broad church inclusion of opposing theological views for theological answers to them. To adapt Santayana's figure, the Church's theology has been living in a modest colonial house, more and more overshadowed by the skyscraper of the Church's active work.[6]

Can anyone honestly deny that this is the very plague that is now killing our beloved Synod? And while the disease is raging within our own church-body, it is also affecting those with whom we are in fellowship. I cannot but mention a specific example close to my heart: the Evangelical Lutheran Church of Haiti, with which we declared church fellowship at our last Synodical Convention.

Had I not previously committed myself to our Walther Conference here in St. Louis, I should today be in Indianapolis, where an urgent effort is underway to rebuild a network of support for our fast-growing sister church in Haiti. It was a bureaucratic preoccupation with the formalities of "protocol documents" and insistence on rigid details of channeling funds-instead of love and respect for a dear sister church in dire need-that led to the collapse of necessary support. Can you imagine the emergency created by the sudden cessation of the agreed support of $ 40,000 per month?

I thank God for courageous men like Pastors Kevin Kolander of California and John Fiene and David Mommens of Indiana, who are now taking energetic steps to secure continued support for our sister-church's vital work, in full cooperation, I understand, with our Synod's mission department. And I beg anyone here in a position to do so to direct any support for Haiti through those men and the new support-group being formed this very weekend.

Apart from the cases already mentioned, what then are the vital issues of truth that urgently require clear confession rather than bureaucratic evasion on the part of our Synod? It is my firm conviction that the chief issues of doctrine confronting our Synod are the following:

In the first place, it is essential to discontinue any joint church or chaplaincy work with the ELCA. I would of course warmly support cooperation with genuine Lutherans in the ELCA, who are in a public state of confession against their church's public departures from the Word of God. But we cannot practise any form of church-fellowship with the pseudo-Lutheran ELCA as such. Yet it appears that, in addition to joint chaplaincies, there are actually still parishes maintaining membership both in the ELCA and in the LC-MS. That cannot be harmonized with the truth of the Gospel.

Secondly, the Synod needs to reassert effective doctrinal discipline within its Concordia University System. It appears that the old Seminex theology has its defenders here and there- including open pro-evolutionism, together with a historical-critical debunking of Genesis! Such things cannot go unchallenged without risking a total loss of the Word of God, as has happened in other American churches.

Thirdly, the continued existence of neo-Pentecostalism in our Synod is an open scandal. The pro-Charismatic "Renewal In Missouri" should have been decisively dealt with long ago. As former President Robert Kuhn put it in his Presidential Report in 2001: "There are some who may hope to 'Lutheranise' charismatic theology, but finally it is not possible" (2001 LC-MS Proceedings, p. 69). The distressing news now is that the Commission on Theology and Church Relations has advised President Kieschnick that a few agreed statements with "Renewal in Missouri" have sufficiently settled the matter, and that there is no need for further official meetings! The fact remains, as President Kuhn clearly saw, that one cannot be both neoPentecostal/Charismatic and Lutheran! That issue cries out for honest resolution.

Fourthly, the Synod needs to regain the firm biblical, Reformation "middle ground" on the nature of the Gospel ministry. On the one hand there are those who, contrary to Augsburg Confession XIV, advocate, for instance, "lay ministry" of Word and Sacrament. And the Commission on Theology and Church Relations in its recent report on the Divine Call has abandoned the historic Lutheran opposition in principle to "temporary calls". On the other hand some prefer Loehe's exaggerated clericalism to the plain Reformation doctrine of Luther and Walther. The Synod needs to restore full confessional unanimity on this score. The public reaffirmation of Walther's theses on Church and Ministry at the 2001 Convention was a step in the right direction, but needs to be followed up.

Finally, Missouri's trumpets need to give a clear sound when it comes to global ecumenical relations. For example, it was unfortunate that a representative of the Missouri Synod told the Lutheran World Federation assembly in Winnipeg last summer, that we have "much in common," namely, the Lutheran name and the Confessions! That was profoundly misleading. As one of my students remarked, that's rather like saying that the police and the criminals have a lot in common, namely the law!

What must be clearly understood is that the so-called "Lutheran" World Federation is the chief engine for the destruction of the Lutheran Confession in today's world. In the shameful "Augsburg Concession" to the Vatican on Justification, and in the widespread acceptance of the Leuenberg Concord with Calvinist churches, the LWF has surrendered both major focal points of our Confession: Justification, and the Real Presence of the Lord's body and blood in the Holy Supper. In both cases the basis was the historical-critical destruction of biblical authority. And in its ecumenical recipe of "Reconciled Diversity" the LWF has expanded the Prussian Union by the inclusion of Rome and other confessions. That view advocates full church fellowship among the various Christian confessions, while the differences remain un**resolved**! That is a total surrender of the Lutheran confession.

Given the disarray of "world Lutheranism," it is important to provide for a joint global witness on the part of all the truly confessional Lutheran churches of the world. But that would mean giving up bureaucratic games with church fellowship, such that we can accept full church fellowship with churches which maintain fellowship with churches to which we must refuse fellowship! "Communion, or fellowship, is one," says a maxim of the ancient church. And that is certainly biblical. A church is either faithful to the apostolic doctrine (Acts 2:42) or it isn't.

We need to pray for the divine gift of a global Lutheran confession, which need not be long, and which would do for the Book of Concord what the Formula of Concord once did for the Augsburg Confession: settle its true meaning once and for all. Then there would be a clearly understood global difference between a nominal pseudo-"Lutheranism," paying lip-service to the Confessions, and the worldwide confessional Lutheran Church actually taking the Book of Concord seriously.

Some of our sister churches, e.g. the Lithuanian and the Belorussian, have indicated at least four points on which there must be clarity: they have stated that since fellowship must be based on doctrinal, confessional unity, they cannot accept church fellowship with churches which deny or compromise the authority of the Bible as the Word of God, or surrender of compromise the central article of Justification, or surrender or compromise the truth of the real presence of Christ's body and blood in the Sacrament, or yield on the twin issues of female clergy and approval of homosexual behavior.

If these doctrinal challenges are to be faced honestly, we need to return at every level of our Synodical life, to the overriding importance of the divinely revealed truth-including the God-pleasing separation from those who refuse to teach and practise in accord with the Word of God as rightly confessed in the Book of Concord. But that would mean the conscious rejection of bureaucratic thinking, according to which what is being said is less important than who says it.

Henry Jacoby, in his The Bureaucratization of the World (1976), wrote: "Because of the increasing number of individuals who 'build a career' in the bureaucratic system (or would like to do so), there must be a corresponding growth in the number of people who ought to keep silent" (p. 155). And Ralph Hummel, in The Bureaucratic Experience (1987), said: "Culturally, the basic values of bureaucracy tend to be those that can be reduced to numbers; quantity not quality rules" (p. 251).

It may be a salutary shock to our present organization-mindedness to look at actual examples of how confessional Lutherans used to think before the bureaucratic obsession with rules and regulations set in. Let me cite two examples. In 1874 the LC-MS Convention held that since "the entire churchly authority of the congregations is represented in the Synod when the latter holds its sessions," the Synodical assembly must therefore "be conceded the right in case of necessity to bypass the electoral procedure prescribed as the rule in the constitution," and to elect teachers for Synod's institutions directly (1874 Proceedings, p. 59, my translation)! The concern here is for churchly, confessional integrity-and the human regulations are strictly subsidiary!

Here is another example, from Francis Pieper's great *Christian Dogmatics*, vol. 3: The normal, agreed upon order of course prevails ordinarily. "Nevertheless," writes Pieper, "every Christian has the right to call a meeting of the congregation, synod, council, etc., if he is convinced that conditions demand a meeting and that the officials are lax in doing their duty" (p. 433)! This sounds positively quaint today--yet it represents the great truth that "love is empress in ceremonies" (Luther), and that emergencies take precedence over normal human regulations. It also upholds the priestly dignity of each Christian believer, in being able to hold "ecclesiastical supervisors" accountable for their stewardship! I doubt that the present Commission on Constitutional Matters would uphold Pieper at this point. Well, so much the worse for that Commission-but Pieper was right!

I tried to warn against the potential mischief of an infallible constitutional oracle already in the days of Dr. Barry's presidency: "That Commission now has well-nigh total and absolute power to turn any issue involving the practical application of the Confession into a constitutional one, and to decide it with unappealable finality."[7] And now we have seen just how that is done. I must say that I am deeply grateful that a number of District Conventions have understood the peril, and asked the next Synodical Convention to set aside the shameful ruling which let's the opinion and advice of an "ecclesiastical supervisor" trump all biblical and confessional arguments by mere ordinary people.

We have reached the point when coercion has replaced advice, and at that point Luther insisted: "We must tear the consistories to pieces, for we do not by any means want to have the pope and the lawyers in them." Walther often quotes that, for instance in his The Form of a Christian Congregation, p. 11. There is no room in an evangelical church for infallible oracles in the name of human constitutions. Let the opinions of the

214

Constitutions Commission be advisory, like those of the CTCR. Dr. Walther warned in his first presidential address:

Also our synodical body has the same prospects of salutary influence if it does not attempt to operate through any other means than through the power of the Word of God. Even then we must expect battles, but they will not be the mean, depressing battles for obedience to human laws, but the holy battles for God's Word, for God's honor and kingdom... [Otherwise] Our chief battle would soon center about the execution of manufactured, external human ordinances and institutions and would swallow up the true blessed battle for the real treasure of the church, for purity and unity of doctrine.[8]

Forgive the length of this diagnosis. But unless we see the depth of the malady, our proposed cures are likely to be superficial.

Even the world can, in its own sphere, see the destructiveness of the bureaucratic spirit. Among the finest spoofs of it are the British comedy series Yes, Minister, and Yes, Prime Minister. The latter has an episode called "bishop's gambit." A vacancy has occurred among the Anglican bishops, and the Prime Minister must recommend a suitable person to the Queen. Sir Humphrey Appelby, the Permanent Under-Secretary, comes up with a candidate, but the Prime Minister is disturbed by the man's liberal or nonexistent theology. "But Prime Minister," says Sir Humphrey, "don't you realize that theology is simply a device to enable unbelievers to remain in the church?" Even the people of this world can see the bankruptcy of that approach!

Yet that essential malady, putting organizational, statistical success ahead of truth, infects so much of our Synodical life. The impassioned pleas for "mission" apart from doctrine are like calls for harvesting without sowing or planting, or like invitations to eat without food! Akin to this is the low value placed on an adequate theological education for certain "ethnic ministries"-as though immediate action were more important than responsible pastoral preparation.

We Lutherans, who with Luther stress preaching the Gospel as the toughest and most important task of the Gospel minister, cannot skimp in the proper preparation of such preachers. There is none of that popular mission hysteria in the New Testament. Our Lord, upon first meeting Peter, Matthew, and the rest, did not send them out in haste with a few basic cliches, but He trained them for three intensive years before sending them out into the world. Can we do any less?

The September, 2003, issue of what, in deference to the Second Commandment, I shall call "Jerry First," has an article about a picture of Jesus knocking at the door of the United Nations Organization in New York. The picture is said to need a frame. Then this: "Doctrine in our Lutheran Church-Missouri Synod, our theology, is like that frame," etc. No, dear friends, the doctrine of the Gospel, that is, the articles of faith as distinct from the Commandments of the Law, are not simply a suitable frame: they convey Jesus Himself. He comes in His Gospel and Sacraments, and in no other way! And that is precisely our evangelical, confessional doctrine-it is not frame but content!

If the evangelical truth is to regain top priority again in our Synod, we shall need quite deliberately to combat the bureaucratic spirit, which can never put truth first. This will require some short-term and some long-term planning and action. In the short term two things are urgent: First, the Constitutions Committee needs to become advisory, rather than dictatorial.

Secondly, the Dispute Resolutions system needs to return to a proper adjudication and appeals system interested in pursuing and asserting the divine truth, rather than simply sorting out personal conflicts by means of mediation, arbitration, and compromise, important as that can be at times. But the chief aim of an adjudication system is to safeguard the pure doctrine of God's Word in teaching and practice. Our Book of Concord says:

Thus the pope exercises a double tyranny: he defends his errors with violence and murder, and he forbids judicial inquiry. The latter does more harm than any cruel act. For when the church has been deprived of valid judicial process, it is not possible to remove ungodly teachings an impious forms of worship, an they destroy countless souls generation upon generation.[9]

In the long term we need to reverse the unaffordable trend of growing Synodical and District bureaucracies. Already we have had to recall missionaries, and we can no longer afford Synodical support for our seminaries. If that trend is allowed to continue, we shall finally be able to afford only Synodical and District office buildings and staff. Supporting missionaries and training pastors, teachers, and deaconesses, were the prime activities for which local churches first banded together as a Synod.

It is not in the Synodical interest to force the seminaries to be, as they now are, basically self-supporting, without Synodical subsidy. Seminaries deprived of the institutional support of their churches, may in the end be tempted also to thumb their noses at their churches' doctrine, and to become independent theologically as well as institutionally. American higher education is full of prominent examples of this very secularizing trend, for instance, Harvard, Yale, and Princeton!

Also we need to consider the office of District president. According to the Lutheran understanding, there is only one kind of Gospel minister, although ministers may work in highly specialized areas, e.g. chaplains, seminary professors, foreign missionaries, etc. By divine right there is no difference between bishop or district president and pastor. A bishop is simply first among equals.

Until relatively recently our District presidents were also pastors of parishes, although of course they were given assistants for their increased work loads. Perhaps our Districts need to be reduced in size, and to be served by parish pastors once again. Ditto for the Synodical presidency. In that way the abuse of "temporary calls" is avoided, and a churchly mentality encouraged-contrary to the Gilbert and Sullivan advice in H. M. S. Pinafore: "Stay close to your desk and never go to sea, And you all may be rulers of the Queen's navy!"

It is not a question of spiting anyone, but of restoring the truth of the

Gospel to its rightful place in the church. It is my fervent hope and prayer that the Lord of the Church in His mercy will restore to our dear Synod once more the utterly undeserved gift of truth and unity in His holy and life-giving Gospel. May He have mercy on us all.

Footnotes:

1 Concordia Historical Institute Quarterly, vol. XVI, no. 1 (April, 1943), p. 5.

2 Die Veiftissung der deutschen evangelisch-lutherischen Synode von Missouri, Ohio, und anderen Staaten, nebst etner Einleitung und erlaeuternden Bemerkungen (St. Louis, 1846), pp. 3-4.

3 Thosen Vom Unterschied des Gesetzes und Evangeliums," Iowa District Proceedings, I 880, p. 44.

4 R.R.Feuerhahn, M. C. Harrison, and P. T. McCain, eds., Christ and His Church: Essays by Hermann Sasse, Vol. I:Union and Confession (St. Louis: Office of the President, LC-MS, 1997), p. 3.

5 R. Kolb and T. Wengert, eds., The Book of Concord (Minneapolis: Fortress Press, 2000), p. 424.

6 Lefferts A. Loetscher, The Broadening Church (Philadelphia: University of Pennsylvania Press, 1954), pp. 59, 93.

7 J.Fehrmann and D. Preus, eds., Church Polity and Politics: Papers presented at the Congress on the Lutheran Confessions, Itasca, Illinois, April 3-5, 1997 (Luther Academy and Association of Confessional Lutherans, 1997), p. 199.

8 Concordia Journal, vol. 2, no. 5 (September, 1976), p. 202.

9 Treatise on the Power and Primacy of the Pope, 51. Kolb & Wengert, Book of Concord.

1. We are beyond ____ help, only ____ can deliver us.
2. To define Synod as a "servant structure" is to understand it as basically ____.
3. Synod in its essence is simply ____.
4. According to the Missouri Synod's original constitution, the first obligation of Synod was to ____.
5. What belongs to the true unity of the Church? ____
6. The one thing that matters is ____.
7. What is necessary for the true unity of the Church? ____
8. Who demands conformity to "apostolic" succession? ____
9. The Lutheran ecumenical principle is ____.
10. Our disease is you might say ____.
11. What did Hermann Sasse call the "institutional lie?" ____
12. Where the sin is public, appropriate ____ should follow.
13. It is essential to discontinue any ____.
14. One cannot be both Pentecostal and ____.
15. What has the Lutheran World Federation surrendered in the shameful "Augsburg Concession?" ____
16. The basis was the ____ destruction of biblical authority.
17. Should an orthodox Lutheran Church remain in fellowship with churches in the LWF? ____
18. "We need to pray for a global Lutheran ____ which would do for the Book of Concord what the Formula of Concord once did for the ____."
19. The Lithuanian and Belorussian churches have said that they cannot

be in fellowship with churches which surrender on the central article of ____ and yield on the twin issues of ____.

20. God pleasing separation from those who refuse to teach and practice in accord with God's World would mean rejection of ____ thinking.

21. Would the present Commission on Constitutional Matters uphold Pieper on human regulations and calling a meeting of the synod? ____

22. Should the opinion and advice of an "ecclesiastical supervisor" trump all biblical and confessional arguments by mere ordinary people?____

23. Luther said "we must tear the consistories ____."

24. What infects so much of synodical life? ____

25. Lutherans cannot skimp on the proper preparation of ____.

26. Our evangelical, confessional doctrine is not ____ but ____.

27. The Dispute Resolution system need to return to ____.

28. We need to reverse the unaffordable trend of growing ____.

* Editor's Note: Marquart first met Hermann Sasse in 1959 in San Francisco, California. He had contact with Sasse during his years in Australia. See the book Hermann Sasse and Christian News.

"BUREAUCRATITIS" BASHED

Marquart Receives Rising Ovation From "Grassroots Conservatives" at Walther Conference, Concordia Seminary, St. Louis.

Christian News, November 17, 2003

"Our tragedy is that this absolute priority of the divine truth has become displaced in our Synodical life. By what? By Organizational, bureaucratic concerns. Our disease is, you might say, 'bureaucratitis'" Dr. Kurt Marquart, a professor at Concordia Theological Seminary, Ft. Wayne, Indiana told the National Walther Conference meeting at Concordia Seminary, St. Louis on November 8.

Marquart, whom "grassroots" conservatives are supporting for LCMS president in a drive to defeat LCMS President Jerry Kieschnick, continued: "When theology is done bureaucratically, it simply dies and turns into a caricature of itself. Please note that when I talk here about 'bureaucracy' and 'bureaucratic' attitudes, I have in mind not those dear people of God who labor in various capacities in our Synod and its Districts, but rather a certain pathological attitude of mind."

Kieschnick has been sharply critical of Christian New for opposing the growing "bureaucracy" in the LCMS today.

Prior to Marquart's speech on "Putting Missouri Back On Track" (published in this issue of *CN*), the conference saw on a large screen in the seminary's Werner Auditorium the key segments of the prayer service which took place in Yankee Stadium on September 23, 2001. The LCMS's Atlantic District had urged that the conference not proceed with its plan of showing the video of what actually took place and allowing a speaker opportunity to oppose Dr. David Benke's participation in the prayer service. Benke is the president of the Atlantic District. He maintains that Muslims and other non-Christians are not lost in Hell if they do not trust in Jesus Christ, as their only savior and believe, in the Holy Trinity.

One of the conference speakers noted that the director of the Anti-Defamation League of B'nai B'rith said after speaking to and with many Atlantic District pastors that many of them agree with Benke's position.

The opening worship service at the conference began with a confession of The Athanasian Creed. "Grassroots" conservatives confessed this ancient ecumenical Creed which all true Christians accept: "Whosoever will be saved, before all things it is necessary that he hold the catholic (i.e., universal, Christian) faith.

"Which faith except everyone do keep while and undefiled, without doubt he shall perishe everlastingly.

"And the catholic faith is this, that we worship one God in Trinity and Trinity in Unity."

Although LCMS President Jerry Kieschnick says he accepts the Athanasian Creed, he has refused to state that his close friend David

Benke, whom he encouraged to pray with non-Christians, is in error when he says that Muslims also worship the true God. Benke's statement on Muslims worship the true God and Kieschnick's refusal to ask Benke to retract are in *Luther Today*, a book many of the more than 200 registered delegates purchased at the conference. The first fifty students and faculty members who attended were given free copies of *Luther Today*. 100 copies of volume V of the *Christian News Encyclopedia* were also distributed to faculty and students.

Marquart told the conference that "the synod in its essence, is simply its member-congregations, acting together in the Lord's mission! The synod is all its local churches bound together by faith and love! The bureaucratic organization is strictly secondary, and does not belong to or determine the nature and essence of the Synod."

Marquart noted: "In the Middle Ages the church had come to be distorted into a sacred bureaucracy, a chain of command, with the laity at the bottom, the papacy at the top, and the bishops and clergy in-between! The Augsburg Confession rejected this caricature and returned to the biblical understanding of the church not as a bureaucratic command structure, but as the glorious Bride of Christ, consisting of all believers in Christ, the sacred royal priesthood!"

"Let me begin with the clearest, crassest example of this bureaucratic malady. That surely is none other than that recent ruling of the Commission on Constitutional Matters, which held that the prior advice of one's 'ecclesiastical supervisor' trumps any substantive arguments to the contrary. In this way the issue of truth posed by the syncretistic service in New York, was totally bypassed in favor of purely organizational, bureaucratic trivia."

"All the argumentation from Holy Scripture and the Church's Confessions was simply set aside on the grounds that the relevant 'ecclesiastical supervisor' had given his opinion, advice, and interpretation of a Synodical resolution! That is nothing but papal pretenses all over again!"

"In this connection I cannot sufficiently thank God for the clear witness to this very point borne by the St. Louis Faculty Statement and especially by the detailed analysis of Professors David Berger and James Voelz in the October, 2003 issue of the *Concordia Journal*. That both theological faculties are on record against the public whitewash of a notorious case of syncretism surely bodes well for the future of our Synod. May the Lord of the Church richly bless that testimony!" The November 3, 2003 *Christian News* published the St. Louis faculty statement and the Berger-Voelz statement which was also signed by Norman Nagel, Louis Brighton, Thomas Manteufal, Ronald Feuerhahn, and David Adams of the St. Louis faculty.

Marquart went on: "Another piece of bureaucratic trickery is the pretense that certain public actions or pronouncements may not be discussed until the 'proper authorities' have finished their sometimes long winded consideration of the matter."

"Especially where the truth of the Gospel is at stake, there can be no diplomatic silence or false scruples about upsetting bureaucratic apple-carts."

"If our Synod cannot recover this absolute, overriding priority of truth and confession over all sorts of organizational considerations, it will cease to be a Lutheran church and become just another bureaucratic sect."

Doctrinal Discipline

"Secondly, the Synod needs to reassert effective doctrinal discipline within its Concordia University System. It appears that the old Seminex theology has its defenders here and there- including open pro-evolutionism, together with a historical-critical debunking of Genesis! Such things cannot go unchallenged without risking a total loss of the Word of God, as has happened in other American churches.

"Thirdly, the continued existence of neo-Pentecostalism in our Synod is an open scandal. The pro-Charismatic 'Renewal In Missouri' should have been decisively dealt with long ago."

"Fourthly, the Synod needs to regain the firm biblical, Reformation 'middle ground' on the nature of the Gospel ministry. On the one hand there are those who, contrary to Augsburg Confession XIV, advocate, for instance, 'lay ministry' of Word and Sacrament. And the Commission on Theology and Church Relations in its recent report on the Divine Call has abandoned the historic Lutheran opposition in principle to 'temporary calls'. On the other hand some prefer Loehe's exaggerated clericalism to the plain Reformation doctrine of Luther and Walther. The Synod needs to restore full confessional unanimity on this score. The public reaffirmation of Walther's theses on Church and Ministry at the 2001 Convention was a step in the right direction, but needs to be followed up.

"Finally, Missouri's trumpets need to give a clear sound when it comes to global ecumenical relations. For example, it was unfortunate that a representative of the Missouri Synod told the Lutheran World Federation assembly in Winnipeg last summer, that we have 'much in common,' namely, the Lutheran name and the Confessions! That was profoundly misleading. As one of my students remarked, that's rather like saying that the police and the criminals have a lot in common, namely the law!

"What must be clearly understood is that the so-called 'Lutheran' World Federation is the chief engine for the destruction of the Lutheran Confession in today's world."

Statistics Before Truth

"Yet that essential malady, putting organizational, statistical success ahead of truth, infects so much of our Synodical life. The impassioned pleas for 'mission' apart from doctrine are like calls for harvesting without sowing or planting, or like invitations to eat without food!"

"The September, 2003, issue of what, in deference to the Second Commandment, I shall call 'Jerry First,' has an article about a picture of Jesus knocking at the door of the United Nations Organization in New York. The picture is said to need a frame. Then this: 'Doctrine in our Lutheran Church-Missouri Synod, our theology, is like that frame,' etc. No, dear friends, the doctrine of the Gospel, that is, the articles of faith as distinct from the Commandments of the Law, are not simply a suitable frame: they convey Jesus Himself. He comes in His Gospel and Sacraments, and in no other way! And that is precisely our evangelical, confessional doctrine-it is not frame but content!

"If the evangelical truth is to regain top priority again in our Synod, we shall need quite deliberately to combat the bureaucratic spirit, which can never put truth first."

"In the long term we need to reverse the unaffordable trend of growing Synodical and District bureaucracies. Already we have had to recall missionaries, and we can no longer afford Synodical support for our seminaries. If that trend is allowed to continue, we shall finally be able to afford only Synodical and District office buildings and staff. Supporting missionaries and training pastors, teachers, and deaconesses, were the prime activities for which local churches first banded together as a Synod. It is not in the Synodical interest to force the seminaries to be, as they now are, basically self-supporting, without Synodical subsidy. Seminaries deprived of the institutional support of their churches, may in the end be tempted also to thumb their noses at their churches' doctrine, and to become independent theologically as well as institutionally. American higher education is full of prominent examples of this very secularizing trend, for instance, Harvard, Yale, and Princeton!"

"Perhaps our Districts need to be reduced in size, and to be served by parish pastors once again. Ditto for the Synodical presidency."

"Two Decades of Change," a table in the 2003 Lutheran Annual, which formerly was labeled "Two Decades of Growth," says that in 1981 there were 242 LCMS pastors serving "Synod Districts, and others" rather than congregations and that in 2001 there were 835 LCMS pastors serving "Synod Districts and others." It says in 1981 the LCMS had 2,721,883 baptized members and in 2001 the LCMS had 2,540,045 members. While the LCMS has less members than it had in 1981 it has 600 more pastors "serving Synod, Districts, and others."

1. Marquart said that our disease is ____.
2. LCMS President Jerry Kieschnick refused to says that his close friend, Atlantic District President David Benke, is in ____.
3. The bureaucratic office is strictly ____.
4. What did Marquart say about a ruling of the LCMS's Commission on Constitutional Matters? ____
5. The Synod will cease to be a Lutheran church if it cannot ____.
6. What is being promoted in the LCMS's Concordia University System? ____
7. The continued existence of neo-Pentecostalism should have been ____.
8. What did the CTCR abandon in its report on the Divine Call ____.
9. Some in the LCMS prefer ____ exaggerated clericalism.
10. The public reaffirmation of Walther's theses on Church and Ministry was a ____.
11. The chief engine for the destruction of Lutheranism in today's world is ____.

12. Pleas for "mission" without doctrine are like____.
13. Our evangelical doctrine is not framed but ____.
14. We need to reverse the trend of growing ____.
15. Seminaries deprived of institutional support from their churches may in the end ____.
16. District need to be reduced in size and one again be served by ____.
17. While the LCMS has fewer members than it had in 1981 it has ____ pastors "serving Synod, districts, and others."

MARQUART DEFENDS
THE RIGHTS OF LAYMEN
Censoring Showing of "Crisis at the Crossroads
- Summer 2004"
Christian News, February 9, 2004

"The Atlantic District Leadership calls upon you to cancel the presentation and eliminate the proposed video distribution for the sake of the Church," the leaders of the Atlantic District ordered just prior to the 2003 Walther Conference at Concordia Seminary, St. Louis, November 7 and 8. The video of what actually happened at Yankee Stadium on September 23, 2001 was nevertheless shown. *Christian News* paid no attention to the orders of Benke and his chief supporters. *CN* sent the video "Crises at the Crossroads - Summer 2004" to all the congregations of The Lutheran Church - Missouri Synod.

No insurance company, foundation, or millionaire considered this video worthy of their support. Organized conservatives did not finance or publicize the effort to give all congregations of the LCMS an opportunity to see for themselves exactly what happened at the Yankee Stadium Prayer Service on September 23, 2001. It was the grassroots conservatives who have a high regard for Dr. Kurt Marquart who made the $30,000 project possible. The February 2, 2004 *CN* includes a letter which LCMS President Jerry Kieschnick sent to the entire LCMS. A copy was sent by first class to all LCMS congregations. It was marked "important" and "'A Matter of Concern' For The LCMS." (Above)

The February 2 *CN* published a letter which *CN* sent to Dr. Kieschnick on December 22, 2004 when *CN* sent him a copy of the video and *Luther Today*. *CN* told him that the video would be going to all LCMS churches and convention delegates. *CN* will also be sending each convention delegate a copy of *Luther Today*. *CN* invited Kieschnick to respond.

LCMS pastors should present both Dr. Kieschnick's letter and the "Crisis At The Crossroads - Summer 2004" to their congregation.

It is not surprising that liberals do not want their congregations to see the video Benke and the Atlantic District wanted banned.

However, it is discouraging that many of the organized conservatives, particularly the "high churchmen," who have referred to themselves as hyper-euros, are not showing "Crisis at the Crossroads - Summer 2004" to their congregations. While some of their many publications and websites publicize and promote all kinds of meetings, conferences, and publications, *CN* has yet to see any mention of the video and *Luther Today* in any of the conservative media except Reclaim News, the website of Pastor Jack Cascione. Some say that anything *CN* publishes, including An American Translation of the Bible, the first English translations of Walther's *American Pastoral Theology*, John Gerhard's *Manual of Comfort*, and *Islam In The Crucible* by Riccoldo Montecroce and Martin Luther and the *Christian News Encyclopedia* will never be mentioned by most conservative publications and web-sites. One major reason is that the editor of *CN* has never been certified by Concordia Seminary. It is not considered scholarly, particularly among the hyper-euros to quote anything published by someone who does not have the approval of an LCMS seminary and the officials of the LCMS. Many conservatives ask *CN* to promote their publications but they will not mention *CN* or any of *CN*'s publications. *CN* has freely advertised for decades the publications and books of many conservatives and also liberals. The fact that Dr. Marquart takes a strong stand for the rights of laymen and opposes the hierarchicalism and anti-congregationalism promoted by Wilhelm Loehe, whom he names on the video, has highly displeased the Loehe-Grabau-Stephan conservatives who have even produced a button for their hyper-euro society of Loehe-Grabau-Stephan and Walther.

Dr. Marquart for years has generally been the most popular speaker at the annual symposia of Concordia Seminary, Ft. Wayne. Dr. Robert Preus, who had been president of the Seminary, told this editor that students think "Kurt walks on water." When Dr. Wallace Schulz was on the Board of Regents of this seminary, he said that Marquart appears to be the favorite professor of most of the students.

Many of the Ft. Wayne students who graduated during the Robert Preus years subscribed to *CN* after graduation. This is no longer the case, even though *CN* has not changed.

This year some have asked why Dr. Marquart was "shipped off" to teach in Kenya just at the time of the annual symposia. Years ago when the conservative Dr. Alfred Rehwinkel, a great champion of the laymen, was "out of step" with some of the professors and administrators at Concordia Seminary, St. Louis, they were only too happy to have him teaching at Concordia, Selma, in Brazil, Australia and elsewhere.

Much good would have been accomplished if during this year's annual symposia the video "Crisis at the Crossroads - Summer 2004," which features Dr. Marquart, had been shown at the symposia. The lectures presented at the symposia are available on the Seminary's website. Compare them with Dr. Marquart's "The Church in the Twenty-First Century: will There Be a Lutheran One?" a speech which Dr. Marquart presented at the 1998 symposia (p. 1). Also see Dr. Marquart's review of some of Dr. Francis Schaeffer's books in this issue.

Dr. Marquart is out of step with those at the seminary who are working on a curriculum change which some claim will minimize the Walther-Pieper- and Preus tradition at the seminary which Marquart says should not change. Some appear to place the patristic fathers in higher regard than the scripture based theology of Walther, Pieper and Preus. The curriculum change should be stopped by the seminary's Board of Regents and major donors.

1. What did the leaders of the LCMS's Atlantic District order just prior to the 2003 Walther Conference at Concordia Seminary? ____
2. *Christian News* sent the video "Crisis at the Crossroads" to ____.

3. Who paid for this project to show the LCMS what happened in Yankee Stadium on September 23, 2001? ____
4. Who refused to show "Crisis at the Crossroads" to their congregations? ____
5. The conservative media in the LCMS generally avoids publicizing ____.
6. What displeased the Loehe-Graubau-Stephan conservative about Marquart? ____
7. Robert Preus said that students think "Kurt walks ____."
8. Wallace Schulz reported that Marquart was the favorite professor of ____.
9. Marquart was out of step with those at the Ft. Wayne seminary working on a ____.

OVERTURES FOR LCMS CONGREGATIONS TO ADOPT

Christian News, January 19, 2004

Do Not Let Status and Privilege Override Truth in the Church

Whereas, Dr. Kurt Marquart of Concordia Seminary, Ft. Wayne, a member of the Lutheran Church-Missouri Synod's Commission on Theology and Church Relations, has suggested that Lutheran Church-Missouri Synod's congregations submit the following overture to the Lutheran Church-Missouri Synod's 2004 convention:

Whereas, the Commission on Constitutional Matters (CCM) has ruled that the "Constitution and Bylaws of the Synod do not allow or contemplate the expulsion of a member of the Synod on the basis of an action taken with the full knowledge and approval of the appropriate ecclesiastical supervisor" (02-2296, *Reporter*, March 2003, p. 10); and

Whereas, this ruling flatly contradicts Holy Scripture, which repeatedly warns against "respect[ing] persons in judgment" (Deut 1:17; see also Eph. 6:9, Col. 3:25, James 2:1,9), "making the word of God of none effect through [human] traditions" (St. Mk. 7:13), or "teaching for doctrines the commandments of men" (St. Mk. 7:7), and insists that "we must obey God rather that men" (Acts 5:29); and

Whereas, the CCM ruling is incompatible with the Lutheran Confessions, which teach that "it is not lawful for a human being to repeal an obligation that is plainly a matter of divine right" (Augsburg Confession XXVII, 24; Kolb-Wengert, p. 85): Make the 'mark' of the church all-decisive, namely "the pure teaching of the gospel and the administration of the sacraments in harmony with the gospel of Christ" – not the whim or discretion of "supreme external monarchy" of ecclesiastical supervisors (Apology VII/VIII, 3; p. 174-184); warn against those who "demand that their traditions be observed more carefully than the gospel" (Apology XXVIII, 3, p. 289); deny that texts like St. Lk. 10:16 and Heb. 13:17 grant ecclesiastical supervisors any authority beyond the Gospel itself (Apology XXVIII, 17-21, pp. 291-292); reject as "also purely religious raving [enthusiasm]" the claims of the chief of all ecclesiastical supervisors, "in that the pope boasts that 'all laws are in the shrine of his heart' and that what he decides and commands in his churches is supposed to be Spirit and law – even when it is above or contrary to the Scriptures of the spoken Word. This is all the old devil and old snake, who also turned Adam and Eve into enthusiasts and led them from the external Word of God to 'spirituality' and their own presumption... It is the source, power, and might of all the heresies, even that of the papacy and Mohammad" (Smalcald Articles III/8/4,5,9; pp. 322,323); treat as a "mark of the Antichrist" the fact that a notorious ecclesiastical supervisor "is not willing to be judged by the church or by anyone else and places his authority above the judgment of counsels and of the whole church. To refuse to be judged by the church or by anyone is to make himself God." Further: [Forbidding judicial inquiry] "does more harm than any cruel act. For when the church has been deprived of valid judicial process, it is not possible to remove ungodly teachings and impious forms of worship, and they destroy countless souls generation upon generation ...since, however, judgments of the councils are judgments of the church, not of the pontiffs, it is wholly appropriate that rulers restrain the wantonness of the pontiffs and ensure that the power to examine and to make judgments according to the Word of God is not snatched away from the church" (Treatise on the Power and Primacy of the Pope, 40,51,56; pp. 337, 339); recognize no privileged "official" zone of immunity from the normal demands of truth; quite on the contrary: "we also believe, teach , and confess true teaching and everything that pertains to the whole of religions freely and publicly. They are to do so not only with words but also in actions and deeds' (Formula of Concord, S.D., X, 10; p. 637); and

Whereas, the CCM ruling makes a mockery of the Synodical constitution by, in effect, amending Article VI, Condition of Membership, as follows: "2. Renunciation of unionism and syncretism of every description, such as: a. Serving congregations of mixed confession, as such, by ministers of the Church —UNLESS AUTHORIZED BY THE APPROPRIATE ECCLESIASTICAL SUPERVISOR; b. Taking part in the services and sacramental rites of heterodox congregation or of congregations of mixed confession – UNLESS AUTHORIZED BY THE APPROPRIATE ECCLESIASTICAL SUPERVISOR; c. Participating in heterodox tract and missionary activities – UNLESS AUTHORIZED BY THE APPROPRIATE ECCLESIASTICAL SUPERVISOR; etc." and

Whereas, since "Christians can be ruled by no other means than by God's Word alone" (Luther, cited in C.F.W. Walther, Church and Ministry, p. 316), the Missouri Synod was intended to rely on God's Word alone, not on human authority and regulations:

Also our synodical body has the same prospects of salutary influence if it does not attempt to operate through any other means than through the power of the Word of God. Even then we must expect battles, but they will not be the mean, depressing battles for obedience to human laws, but the holy battles for God's Word, for God's honor and kingdom ... [Otherwise] our chief battle would soon center about the execution of manufactured, external human ordinances and institutions and would swallow up the true blessed battle for the real treasure of the church, for the purity and unity of doctrine (C.F.W. Walther, First Presidential Address, *Concordia Journal*, vol. 2, no. 5 [Sept. 1976] p. 202);

All government of the Church which does not bind the consciences of Christians to Christ's Word, but to the word of men, is pseudo-government (Pieper, *Dogmatics* II:399);

Resolved, that the LCMS in convention assembled in 2004 rejects and overturns the CCM ruling in questions, and declares it null and void and of no further effect.

Whereas, Trinity Lutheran Church of New Haven, along with many other congregations support Dr. Kurt Marquart's concerns; therefore be it

Resolved, That Trinity Lutheran Church ask the 2004 convention of The Lutheran Church-Missouri Synod to reject and overturn the CCM ruling in questions, and declare it null and void and of no further effect.

Trinity Lutheran Church,
New Haven, Missouri

1. What did the LCMS's CCM rule? ____
2. The ruling contradicts ____.
3. The CCM ruling makes a mockery of ____.
4. Christians can be ruled by no other means than by ____ alone.

AVERSION TO SANCTIFICATION?
Christian News, October 24, 2005

I'm growing increasingly concerned that with the necessary distinction between faith and works that we must always maintain, we Lutherans are tempted to speak of good works and the life of sanctification in such a way as to either minimize it, or worse yet, neglect it. I read sermons and hear comments that give me the impression that some Lutherans think that good works are something that "just happen" on some sort of a spiritual auto-pilot. Concern over a person believing their works are meritorious has led to what borders on paranoia to the point that good works are simply not taught or discussed as they should be. It seems some have forgotten that in fact we do confess three uses of the law, not just a first or second use. Luther says it beautifully in our Small Catechism. When considering and confessing all the blessings given by our good and gracious God, Luther concludes, "All for which it is my duty to thank and praise, serve and obey him." A life of good works is...a life devoted to doing good according to God's Holy Word.

The Apostle, St. Paul, never ceases to urge good works on his listeners and readers. I recall a conversation once with a person who should know better telling me that the exhortations to good works and lengthy discussions of sanctification we find in the New Testament is not a model at all for preaching, since Paul is not "preaching" but rather writing a letter. This is not a good thing.

Two years ago an article appeared that put matters well and sounded a very important word of warning and caution. It is by Professor Kurt E. Marquart of Concordia Theological Seminary in Fort Wayne, Indiana. I strongly encourage you to give it your most serious attention.

Antinomian Aversion to Sanctification?

An emerited brother writes that he is disturbed by a kind of preaching that avoids sanctification and "seemingly questions the Formula of Concord . . . about the Third Use of the Law." The odd thing is that this attitude, he writes, is found among would-be confessional pastors, even though it is really akin to the antinomianism of "Seminex"! He asks, "How can one read the Scriptures over and over and not see how much and how often our Lord (in the Gospels) and the Apostles (in the Epistles) call for Christian sanctification, crucifying the flesh, putting down the old man and putting on the new man, abounding in the work of the Lord, provoking to love and good works, being fruitful . . . ?"

I really have no idea where the anti-sanctification bias comes from. Perhaps it is a knee-jerk over-reaction to "Evangelicalism": since they stress practical guidance for daily living, we should not! Should we not rather give even more and better practical guidance, just because we distinguish clearly between Law and Gospel? Especially given our anti-sacramental environment, it is of course highly necessary to stress the holy means of grace in our preaching. But we must beware of creating a kind of clericalist caricature that gives the impression that the whole

230

point of the Christian life is to be constantly taking in preaching, absolution and Holy Communion-while ordinary daily life and callings are just humdrum time-fillers in between! That would be like saying that we live to eat, rather than eating to live. The real point of our constant feeding by faith, on the Bread of Life, is that we might gain an ever-firmer hold of Heaven-and meanwhile become ever more useful on earth! We have, after all, been "created in Christ Jesus unto good works, which God hath before ordained that we should walk in them" (Eph. 2:10). Cars, too, are not made to be fueled and oiled forever at service-stations. Rather, they are serviced in order that they might yield useful mileage in getting us where we need to go. Real good works before God are not showy, sanctimonious pomp and circumstance, or liturgical falderal in church, but, for example, "when a poor servant girl takes care of a little child or faithfully does what she is told" (*Large Catechism*, Ten Commandments, par. 314, Kolb-Wengert, pg. 428).

The royal priesthood of believers needs to recover their sense of joy and high privilege in their daily service to God (1 Pet. 2:9). The "living sacrifice" of bodies, according to their various callings, is the Christian's "reasonable service" or God-pleasing worship, to which St. Paul exhorts the Romans "by the mercies of God" (Rom. 12:1), which he had set out so forcefully in the preceding eleven chapters! Or, as St. James puts it: "Pure religion and undefiled before God and the Father is this, to visit the fatherless and widows in their affliction, and to keep himself unspotted from the world" (1:27). Liberal churches tend to stress the one, and conservatives one the other, but the Lord would have us do both!

Antinomianism appeals particularly to the Lutheran flesh. But it cannot claim the great Reformer as patron. On the contrary, he writes:

"That is what my Antinomians, too, are doing today, who are preaching beautifully and (as I cannot but think) with real sincerity about Christ's grace, about the forgiveness of sin and whatever else can be said about the doctrine of redemption. But they flee as if it were the very devil the consequence that they should tell the people about the third article, of sanctification, that is, of new life in Christ. They think one should not frighten or trouble the people, but rather always preach comfortingly about grace and the forgiveness of sins in Christ, and under no circumstance use these or similar words, "Listen! You want to be a Christian and at the same time remain an adulterer, a whoremonger, a drunken swine, arrogant, covetous, a usurer, envious, vindictive, malicious, etc.!" Instead they say, "Listen! Though you are an adulterer, a whoremonger, a miser, or other kind of sinner, if you but believe, you are saved, and you need not fear the law. Christ has fulfilled it all! . . . They may be fine Easter preachers, but they are very poor Pentecost preachers, for they do not preach... "about the sanctification by the Holy Spirit," but solely about the redemption of Jesus Christ, although Christ (whom they extol so highly, and rightly so) is Christ, that is, He has purchased redemption from sin and death so that the Holy Spirit might transform us out of the old Adam into new men . . . Christ did not earn only gratia, grace, for us, but also donum, "the gift of the Holy Spirit," so that we might have not

231

only forgiveness of, but also cessation of, sin. Now he who does not abstain from sin, but persists in his evil life, must have a different Christ, that of the Antinomians; the real Christ is not there, even if all the angels would cry, "Christ! Christ!" He must be damned with this, his new Christ (On the Council and the Church, *Luther's Works*, 41:113-114).

Where are the "practical and clear sermons," which according to the Apology "hold an audience" (XXIV, 50, p. 267). Apology XV, 42-44 (p. 229) explains:

"The chief worship of God is to preach the Gospel...in our churches all the sermons deal with topics like these: repentance, fear of God, faith in Christ, the righteousness of faith, prayer . . . the cross, respect for the magistrates and all civil orders, the distinction between the kingdom of Christ (the spiritual kingdom) and political affairs, marriage, the education and instruction of children, chastity, and all the works of love."

"Grant, we beseech Thee, Almighty God, unto Thy Church Thy Holy Spirit, and the wisdom which cometh down from above, that Thy Word, as becometh it, may not be bound, but have free course and be preached to the joy and edifying of Christ's holy people, that I steadfast faith we may serve Thee, and in the confession of Thy Name abide unto the end: through Jesus Christ, Thy Son, our Lord. Amen."

Kurt Marquart
Concordia Theological Quarterly
July/October 2003
Pages 379-381

1. ___ are simply not taught or discussed as they should be.
2. We have been created in Christ Jesus unto ____.
3. What is pure religion? ____
4. He who does not abstain from sin but persists in an evil life must have

   ____.

PLACING HUMAN REGULATIONS ABOVE GOD'S WORD
Lutheran Church-Missouri Synod May Cease To Be A True Evangelical Church
Christian News, 2005

"Unless these tragic lapses into medieval legalism are corrected and reversed, our Synod (The Lutheran Church-Missouri Synod ed.) will cease to be an evangelical church," writes Dr. Kurt Marquart, a professor at the LCMS's Concordia Theological Seminary, Ft. Wayne, Indiana, in the June, 2005 *Reporter*.

Marquart and other conservatives in the LCMS have been complaining that the LCMS is beginning to follow the liberal Evangelical Lutheran Church in America and other denominations who have long placed human regulations above God's Word. Most LCMS pastors, like the pastors of other denominations, have not been informing laymen about what has been going on theologically within their denominations.

Dr. Wallace Schulz, who was removed by liberals from his position as Lutheran Hour speaker and Second Vice President of the LCMS, has similarly deplored the placing of man's word above God's Word in the LCMS. He wrote in an official report:

"Through the erroneous dependence on man made documents, some leaders of the LCMS have now forced our beloved Synod into the greatest crisis in its history." Schulz's entire report is in *Crisis in Christendom - Seminex Ablaze*, a 510 page book published by *Christian News*, $16.95. Schulz says that LCMS President Jerry Kieschnick, who has been defending liberals in the LCMS, is responsible for much of the divisiveness in the LCMS.

Marquart writes in the June *Reporter*:

A new pattern?

The LCMS Commission on Theology and Church Relations "guide to district presidents dealing with 'state of confession' protests" (May '05) regrettably follows a new pattern in our Synod that puts human regulations ahead of God's Word. God forbids giving the Holy Supper to an impenitent public errorist. Yet someone who obeys this prohibition faithfully is to be treated in the same way as one who, contrary to God's Word, practices "open communion"!

Then there is the notion of "ecclesiastical supervisor" invented by the Synod's Commission on Constitutional Matters (CCM). A pastor cannot be disciplined for participating in a joint service with official representatives of pagan religions if his "ecclesiastical supervisor" pretends that it is not a joint service! Further, the 2004 synodical Handbook attributes papal infallibility to the CCM and the CTCR by stating that dispute-resolution panels "must follow" their opinions.

The Reformation understood that only God's Word can bind Christian consciences. Accordingly, the founders of our Synod refused to mix

233

human regulations with God's Word, but made only that Word binding and decisive. The Lord Himself said, "They worship me in vain; their teachings are but rules taught by men" (Matt. 15:9). Unless these tragic lapses into medieval legalism are corrected and reversed, our Synod will cease to be an evangelical church.

Rev. Kurt E. Marquart
Associate Professor of Systematic Theology
Concordia Theological Seminary
Fort Wayne, Ind.

1. ELCA and other denominations have long placed ____ above ____.
2. Most pastors have not been informing laymen about ____.
3. What did Wallace Schulz complain about? ____
4. The CCM ruled that a pastor may participate in a joint serve with representatives of pagan religion if he has the permission of his ____.
5. The Reformation understood that only God's Word can bind ____.
6. The LCMS will cease to be an evangelical church unless____.

INDEX

A Lively Legacy - 147
A Statement of 1945 – 154
A Statement of Scriptural and Confessional Principles – 69
Adam – 94
Adam and Eve – 61,70,132
Adams, David – 220
Adiaphora – 181
Adjudication – 216
Adjudication-and-appeals – 139
Adler, Mortimer – 199
Affirm – 67,98
Africa – 73
African Strategy – 161
After the Purifying – 70
ALC – 62,70,97
Allen, Roland – 161
America – 64
American Lutheran – 28
American Lutheran Church (ALC) – 44,86
An American Translation – 224
Anatomy – 88
Anatomy of an Explosion – Missouri in Lutheran Perspective – 76
Anderson, J.N.D. – 82
Andrada – 107
Anglican Church – 31
Anglican-Lutheran – 100
Ann Arbor – 67
Anti-Defamation League of B'nai B'rith – 219
Antinomian – 230,231
Anti-Preus – 69
Appignanesi, Lisa – 196
Aquinas, Thomas – 134,180
Arch, Walther – 30
Arianism – 60,165
Arius – 15
Arnoldshain Theses – 81
Asmussen, Dr. Hans – 74,78
Athanasian Creed – 27,219
Atlantic District – 219,224
Augsburg Confession – 182,193, 213

Augustana – 175
Aulen, G. – 47,48,55
Australian Council of Churches – 73
Babylonian – 5
Bangkok Assembly – 73
Barclay – 47
Barry, Alvin – 139
Barth, Karl – 24,45,47,48,131, 133,182,202
Bartling, Prof. W. – 70,79
Behnken, John – 12,50
Bell, Dean – 153
Belorussian – 213
Benke, Dr. David – 110,219,224
Berger, David – 210,220
Berlin Congress – 135
Berlin Wall – 195
Bethany Lutheran College – 40
Bethany Lutheran Seminary – 128
Biblical criticism – 56
Biblical Inerrancy – 136
Black hole – 176
Black Rubric – 101
Blaumeiser, Hubertus – 180
Blue Book – 132
Board of Control – 1
Bodily resurrection – 70
Body – 243
Bohlmann, Dr. Ralph – 122, 139,148
Bonhoeffer, Dietrich – 47
Book of Concord – 19,59,77, 145,180,181,193,213
Book of Mormon – 14
Bosch, David J. – 161
Bouman, Herbert J.A. – 22,62,44
Bouman, Prof. W. – 79
Braaten, Carl – 100,102
Braaten/Jenson – 112,119
Brakemeier – 179
Brand, Dr. – 189
Brand, Eugene L. – 188
Brege, William – 148
Bretscher, Paul – 70,79

235

Bricmont, Jean – 198
Brief Statement – 2-4,7-10,13,14
Brighton, Louis – 220
Bruesewitz, Oskar – 84
Brux – 76
Budget – 35
Bultmann, Rudolf – 27,75,80,
96,109,112,183
Bunkoske, Eugene – 148
Bureaucracies – 137,216
Bureaucracy – 214
Bureaucratic – 206
Bureaucratic organization – 208
Bureaucratitis – 209,219
Bureaucratization of the World –
214
Burgdorf, Paul H. – 154
Burkee, James C. – 1
By-laws – 79
C.T.M. – 16
Caemmerer, Richard R. – 140
Calov, Abraham – 134,149
Calvinism – 182
Cascione, Jack – 224
Cassidy, Edward I. – 187
Ceremonial – 36
Chairman of the Council of Presidents – 65
Chalcedon – 47,55
Charisma – 236
Chemnitz, Martin – 107,121,
149,182
Cho, Pastor – 162
Christian Dogmatics – 112,119,
214
Christian music – 170
Christian News – 1,52,81,88,224
Christian News Encyclopedia –
220
Christology – 44,54
Christus Victor – 48
Church and ministry – 125
Church fellowship - 117
Church growth – 125,135,159,
164,178
Church in the Twenty-first Century – 170
Church Membership Initiative –

160
Church, Francis P. – 112
Civil courts – 139
Clark, Franklin – 174
Commission on Constitutional
Matters – 157,207,210,
220,227,233
Commission on Theology and
Church Relations – 25,153,
212,221,227,233
Commissioned ministries – 125
Common Confession – 4,9
Communion – 173
Communist – 74
Concordia – 135
Concordia Journal – 210,220
Concordia Publishing House –
79,180
Concordia Seminary (St. Louis) –
1,129,145
Concordia Seminary Board of
Control – 68
Concordia Seminary in Exile –
133
Concordia Theological Monthly –
76
Concordia Theological Quarterly –
89,93
Concordia University System –
212
Confession – 31,174,211
Confessional Lutheran Dogmatics
– 121,150
Confessions Congress – 145
Conflict-resolution – 139
Constitution – 209
Constitutions Committee – 216
Contextualization – 165,166
Conzelmann, Hans – 96
Council of Chalcedon – 45
Council of Presidents – 65,158,177
Council of Trent – 107,182,193
Cresset – 16,28,104
Crisis at the Crossroads – 225
Crossroads – 16
CTCR – 20,53,119,215
Cullmann, Oscar – 183
Curriculum – 225

236

Czechoslovakia – 73
D'Arcy, John M. – 187
Daly, Mary – 102
Danker, Frederick W. – 141
Davis, Wade – 196
De Chardin – 47
Dead orthodoxy -1
Delphic Oracle – 65
Détente – 64
Dialog – 100,104
dictatio – 131
Dilthey, Wilhelm – 197
Disneyland – 64
Dispute resolution – 158,216
District Presidents – 64,65,66
Doctor of Theology - 154
Doctrina – 203
Doctrinal certainty - 8
Doctrinal discipline –
    8,114,212,221
Doctrinal division – 68
Doctrine – 21,174,202
Document of Union – 72
Dodge, Fred – 7
Dogma – 189
Donatism – 165
Dorn, Paul – 3,6
East German – 74
Eastern District – 66
Eastern Orthodox – 201
Eastern Orthodox Church – 180
Ecclesiastical supervisor – 233
Ecumenical Movement – 41,43,
    101,209
Ecumenism – 187
ELCA – 212
Elert, Dr. Werner – 75,192
ELIM – 64,69
Elosser, Robert – 6,9
ELS – 63
Encouragement – 206
Engel, Frank – 73
English District – 66
Enlightenment – 194
Episcopal - 100
Episcopalians – 101
Etuk, Udo – 167
Eucharist – 251

Evangelical Catechism – 140
Evangelical Lutheran Church in
    America – 125,233
Evangelical Lutheran Synod – 129
Evangelical Lutherans in Mission
    – 67
Evangelicalism – 230
Evangelism – 191
Evolution – 2
Excommunicated – 8
Existentialism – 13
Fackler, John – 174,175
Faith – 35
Faith and Order – 209
Farley, Edward – 146
Federation – 72
Fehrman, John – 207
Female pastors – 121
Feuerhahn, Ronald – 220
Fiene, John – 211
Flacius, Matthias – 126
Ford, President Henry – 64
Forde, Gerhard O. – 100,103
Foreign Missions – 161
Formal principles – 149
Formula of Concord –
    58,83,103,132,194
Forum Letter – 69,93
Fourth of July – 64
Franzmann, Martin H. – 42,44,
    47,116
Free speech – 157
Freemasonry – 42,90
French Revolution – 195
From Out of the Desert – 81
Fuerbringer, O. – 44,47
Full Gospel – 245
Fuller Seminary – 133
Fund-raising – 37
Futurology – 171
Gadamer – 201
Genesis – 2,41,94
Geneva – 170
George, Carl F. – 161,178
Gerhard, Johann – 134,149
Gerken, O. – 68
German Evangelical Church – 176
Germany – 67

Gifts – 235
Gilson, Etienne – 134
God's Needs – 33
Good works – 230
Graebner, Dr. Theodore – 76
Graham, Billy – 127
Gratitude – 33
Habel, Norman – 168
Haggadah – 31
Hägglund, Bengt – 133
Haiti – 135,211
Hallgren, Richard – 152
Hamann Dr. Henry – 73
Handbook of Evangelical Theologians – 127
Hanson, James – 105
Harms, Dr. Oliver – 18,53,62,63
Harrison, Matthew – 190
Head covering – 123
Healing – 241
Hefner, Philip – 96,104
Heidegger – 201
Heinecken, Martin – 44,45
Helsinki Assembly – 73
Hendry, George S. – 46
Heresy-hunting – 9
Hermeneutics – 197
Hesse, Mary – 197
Hick, John – 108,109
High churchmen – 224
Historical-critical – 13,69,79-82,
    87,95,114,115,131,132,145,146,
    194,212,213
Historicism – 197
Hitler, Adolph – 176
Hoekema, Anthony A. - 241
Holland – 42
Holy Scripture – 194
Holy Supper – 183,233
Homoousion – 203
Hoyer, Horst – 7
Hulxey, Julian – 57
Humanity – 33
Humility – 22
Hummel, Prof. H. – 102
Hummel, Ralph – 214
Hunter, Ken – 178
Hyper-euros – 224

Ineichen, Hans – 201
Inerrancy – 12,13,25,30,31,40,
    70,83,87,89,90,99,104,105,200
Inerrant – 61
Infallibility – 101
Inspiration – 1,6
Institutional lie – 210
Instrumentalism – 199
Integrity – 90
Intellectualism – 22
Inter-Connections - 167
International Council – 136
International Council on Biblical
    Inerrancy – 146
International Foundation for
    Lutheran Confessional Research – 138
Ivory tower – 150
Jacobsen, William – 3,4
Jacoby, Henry – 214
Jenson, Robert – 103
Jerry First – 215
Jersild, Paul – 112
Jesse, Albert – 16
Jesus – 57
Jonah – 61
Jordahl, Leigh - 80
Judisch, Douglas – 76
Justification – 73,75,149,149,182-
    184
Justification and Rome – 180
Kant, Immanuel – 133
Kavanagh, Aidan – 202
Khrushchev – 64
Kieschnick, Jerry – 157,219
King, Robert – 148
Knox, Ronald – 252
Koenig, Richard – 104
Kolander, Kevin – 211
Krentz, Edgar – 87
Kretzmann, Dr. Martin Luther –
    179
Kretzmann, O. P. – 50
Kristeva, Julia – 198
Kuhn, Robert – 191,212
Langstaff, John Brett – 101
Lapp, Paul – 6,7,9
Last Supper – 97

Latin – 31
Laughing gas – 160
Lausanne – 146
Lausanne Congress – 135
Law and Gospel – 167,209,230
Law/Gospel – 164,192
Lawson, Hilary – 196
Lay worker – 125
LCA – 104
LCUSA – 42,44,49,52,63,93
LCUSA Report – 60
Lehman, Lillian – 67
Lehre Und Wehre – 15
Lenin – 171
Leuenberg Agreement – 73
Leuenberg Concord – 103,176,213
Levels of fellowship – 116
Lewis, C.S. – 84
Lex orandi – 202
Liberal theology – 112
Liberation – 73
Liermann, Hans – 176
Lindbeck, George – 202
Lindsell, Harold – 133
Linkletter, Art – 67
Literary criticism – 200
Lithuanian – 213
Liturgical – 202
Living Bible – 77
Loehe, Wilhelm – 212,225
Loehe-Grabau-Stephan – 225
Lohrengel, Ralph – 57
Love – 8
Ludwig, Theodore M. – 108
Luther Academy – 138,207
Luther Today – 220
Luther Tower – 30
Luther's Works – 40,129
Lutheran Church in America – 86
Lutheran Church of Australia – 67
Lutheran Confessions – 62
Lutheran Council in the USA – 77,86,138
Lutheran Heritage Foundation – 152,158,180
Lutheran Missiology – 159
Lutheran Orthodoxy – 146

Lutheran Quarterly – 46,78
Lutheran scholasticism – 131
Lutheran School of Theology at Chicago – 133
Lutheran Synod Quarterly – 40
Lutheran Witness – 16,18,52,104
Lutheran World – 74
Lutheran World Federation (LWF) – 27,28,42,49,63,72-74, 77,78,86,163,167,176,179,188, 213
Lutherans Alert-National – 70
Lutherans Concerned – 160
Magisterial – 134,199
Mahayana Lutherans – 110
Maier, Walter – 148
Manicheism – 60
Manns, Peter – 180
Manteufal, Thomas – 220
Mariolatry – 22
Marquart, Kurt – 2,3,5,44,98, 110,148,188,230
Martens, Barbara – 152
Martikainen, Eeva – 203
Marty, Martin – 16
Marxism – 195
Mary – 45
Mass – 183
Material principles – 149
McCain, Paul – 110
McCarthyism – 7,9
McGavran, Donald – 135,162,178
Means – 245
Meany, George – 64
Melanchthon, Philip – 121
Menchu, Rigoberta – 196
Mennicke, August – 148
Merkens – 3
Millennialist – 127
Ministerial – 134
Minneapolis Theses – 90,116
Mission – 191,215
Mission Affirmations – 179
Missions – 135
Missouri In Perspective – 86
Missouri Synod – 18,91,177
Moderates – 69
Modern Critical Studies – 8

Modernism – 198
Mommens, David – 211
Money – 33,37,38
Monophytism – 165
Montana District – 171
Montgomery, John Warwick –
30,130,140
Mosaic Code – 5
Mother of God – 45
Muggeridge, Malcolm – 31,84,195
Muller, Lyle D. – 160
Muslims – 220
Mutual Responsibility – 4
Nagel, Norman – 220
National Lutheran Council – 116
Nazirites – 36
NCC – 42
Nelson, W. Clifford – 27,89,90,
114,130
Neo-Orthodox – 21
Neo-Pentecostalism – 76,191,212,
235
Nestorianism – 165
Neuchterlein, James – 120
Neuhaus, Richard – 93,100,110
New China – 74
New Haven, Missouri – 52,229
New Lutheran Church – 98,105,
113
New Orleans – 68,91
New Testament – 56
New Theology – 30
*News and View*s – 12
Nicene Creed – 19
Nickel, Dr. Theodore – 52
Niebuhr, Reinhold – 96
NLC – 98
No Other Gospel – 78
*No Room in the Brotherhood: The
Preus-Otten Purge of Missouri -*
141
Noack, Pres. F.W. – 44,53
Noack-Marquart 57
North American Synodical Con-
ference – 173
North Vietnam – 73
Norway – 128
Nuechterlein, Anne Marie – 160

Oden, Thomas C. – 195
Oesch, Dr. William – 154,194
Old Testament – 5,21
Old Testament prophecies – 57
Opinion legis – 201
Ordination of women – 122
Organization – 171
Organized conservatives – 224
Original languages – 167
Orthodox – 175
Orthodox Lutheran Church – 144
Orthodoxy – 146
Otten, H. – iii,5
Out of the Desert – 79
Overtures – 156
Patriotic Observance – 64
Pelagianism – 165
Pelikan, Jaroslav – 16,40
Pentecostalism – 77
Persecution – 74
Philosophy – 134
Pieper, Francis – 20,21,25,46,82,
121,122,208,209,214
Piepkorn, Arthur Carl – 30,31,40
Plastic Ruler – 24
Playing Dues – 35
Pledge Card – 36
Poellot, Luther – 144
Pontifical Council of Promoting
Christian Unity – 187
Pope – 38
Pope John Paul II – 187
Popper, Sir Karl – 197
Porvoo Declaration – 177,184
Post-modernism –
196,198,199,202
Praeceptor of the Missouri Synod
– 52
Praesidium – 139
Pragmatism – 211
Preaching – 203
Prenter – 47
Prepositional truth – 201
Presbyterian – 211
Presbyterian Outlook – 25
Preus of Missouri – 141
Preus, Christian – 128
Preus, Daniel – 207,153

Preus, Dr. Robert D. – 76,88, 91,121,127,144,149,150,180,225
Preus, Governor Jacob – 128
Preus, Herman – 128
Preus, J.A.O. – 64,65,67,144
Preus, Jacob – 81,131
Preus, Mrs. J. – 68
Preus' Statement – 70
Pro-communist – 73
Prolegomena – 193
Promise Keepers – 178
Prophecy – 242
Proprieties – 211
Pro-Seminex – 69
Protestant Principle – 189
Prussia – 171
Psychology – 58
Public – 210
Quanbeck, Warren – 102
Quinelly, J. – 68
Rahn, Robert – 153,158
Rahner, Karl – 176
Rathmann, Hermann – 131
Real presence – 70
Reclaim News – 224
Redaction criticism – 200
Redal, Dr. R.H. – 70
Reformation – 193,210
Reformed-Lutheran union -176
Relativism – 196
Relativity – 101
Renewal In Missouri – 212
Report – 57
Reporter – 233
Resolutions – 207
Restructure – 208
Resurrection – 79,183
Retirement – 139
Reumann, John – 96,99,102,104
Revival – 235
Richardson – 47
River Forest – 31
Roegner, Robert M – 161
Rogness, Alvin N. – 44
Roman Catholic – 180
Routley, Erik – 47,48,55
Ruperti, Dr. – 15
Russell, Bertrand – 57

Saarinen, Eero – 135
Sacraments – 38
Saffen, Wayne – 53,54,60
Sanctification – 230
Santa Claus – 112,198
Sasse, Dr. Hermann – 117,131, 157,170,173,177,192,210
Sauer, Robert – 148
Scaer, David P. – 76
Schaeffer, Dr. Francis – 225
Schaller, Lyle – 178
Scharlemann Case Settled – 16
Scharlemann, Dr. Martin – 12,16,25,133
Scharlemann, Dr. Robert – 79
Scherer – 74
Scherer, Dr. James – 72,74
Schiotz, Dr. Frederik – 89,90, 62,104,114
Schmidt, Herb – 7
Schneiders, Sandra M. – 202
Schoedel, W. – 2,3,5
Schulz, Dr. Wallace – 225,233
Science – 20,197
Scientology – 195
Scripture alone – 199
Second Vatican Council – 194
Selective fellowship – 117,174
Seminarian – 3,4,7,16,110,130
Seminex – 64,67,69,131,136,138, 194,212,230
Senior College – 67
Sense and Nonsense in Religion – 80
Separation – 16,206
Shelby Spong, Dr. John – 101,109
Sittler, Joseph – 46,47,54
Smalcald Articles – 83,175
Snow, Lord C. P. – 196
Social Gospel – 73
Sokal, Alan – 198
Sola Scriptura – 70,83,210
Solzhenitsyn, Alexander – 64,77,84
Southern Africa – 73
Southern Baptist Convention – 137
Speaking in tongues – 167

Spiritual – 33
Spiritual gifts – 236
Spitz, Paul – 3,6
Springfield Seminary – 67
St. Augustine – 60
St. Gregory of Nyssa – 58
St. Louis University – 133
Stalin – 57
Statement of Scriptural and Confessional Principles – 132
Statement of the 44 – 178,179
Stenson, Sten H. – 80
Stoll, David – 196
Stube, John – 148
Syncretism – 220
Synergism – 144
Synod – 6,208
Temporary calls – 212,221
Texas District – 16
Texas District Convention – 12
Textual criticism – 56
Thatcher, Margaret – 154
Thatcher, Mark – 154
The Christian Century – 101
The Confessional Lutheran – 154
The Crucible – 154
The Lutheran Quarterly – 19
The Word That Can Never Die – 47
Theology – 20,21,68,100,146,149
Theology and Church Relations – 19
Theology of Glory – 107
Theology of the Cross – 107
Thiel – 16
Third Use of the Law – 230
Thiselton, Anthony – 200
Thompson, Mark D. – 201
Tietjen, Dr. John – 68,77,86,131
Tillich, Paul – 80
Tithe – 36
Togetherness in Mission – 72
Toolbox - 160
Toronto – 160
Transubstantiation – 42
Trinity – 119,192
Trong Lieu, Nguyen – 68
Truth – 189,194,207

Una Sancta – 16
Unitarian – 4,55
United Church of Christ – 177
United Testimony – 90
Universalism – 108
Universalist – 110
Untied Testimony – 91
Uppsala Report – 136
Valen-Sendstad, Olav – 47,55
Valparaiso – 108
Valparaiso University – 3
Valparaiso's *Cresset* - 107
Van Buren – 47
Vatican II – 41,107
Veith, Gene – 195
Venn, Henry – 162
Verbal Inspiration – 8,130
Verfassung – 209
Vicarious satisfaction – 56
Virgin birth – 70
Virginia – 198
Vocable – 31
Voelz, Dr. James – 196,200,210,220
Wagner, C. Peter – 162,178
Walther Conference – 211
Walther, C.F.W. – iii,44,49,68, 144,174,206
WCC – 63,73
WELS - 125
Wenthe, Dr. Dean O. – 187,190
White, Larry – ii
Who Can This Be? - 53
Wilken, Robert – 110
Wilkerson, David – 243
Wingren – 48
Wisconsin Synod – 63
Wittenberg Reformation – 182
Wollenburg, Dr. George – 66,171
Women's ordination – 191
Word – 12
Word of God – 201
World Congress on Evangelization – 146
World Council – 136
World Council of Churches – 42,73,90
Wuerffel, Dean – 4

Wurmbrand, Richard – 90
Wurst, Shirley – 168
Yoido Full Gospel – 178
Zwingli – 107

Printed in the USA
CPSIA information can be obtained
at www.ICGtesting.com
LVHW012120041023
760082LV00003B/138